Illinois
Bird Watching

A Year-Round Guide

D0874315

Published by Cool Springs Press, a Division of Thomas Nelson, Inc., P. O. Box 141000, Nashville, Tennessee, 37214.

Thompson, Bill, 1962-
    Illinois bird watching : a year-round guide / Bill Thompson III and the staff of Bird watcher's digest.
        p. cm.
    Includes bibliographical references (p.   ) and index.
    ISBN 1-59186-170-5
    1. Bird watching--Illinois. 2. Birds--Illinois. I. Bird watcher's digest. II. Title.
QL684.I3T49 2005
598'.07'234773--dc22

                                2004029755

First Printing 2005
Printed in the United States of America
10 9 8 7 6 5 4 3 2 1

Managing Editor: Billie Brownell
Interior Designer: Bill Kersey, Kersey Graphics
Production Artist: S.E. Anderson
Map and Icon Illustrator: Heather Lynch
Sighting Notes Illustrator: Julie Zickefoose

Cool Springs Press books may be purchased in bulk for educational, business, fundraising, or sales promotional use. For information, please email SpecialMarkets@ThomasNelson.com.

Visit the Thomas Nelson website at **www.thomasnelson.com**

Photography Credits

Arthur Morris/Birds as Art: Front cover top photo (northern cardinal); intro photo page 6 (northern cardinal); Pages 8; 14; 18; 19; 22 (American white pelican); 26 (prothonotary warbler)
Charles Melton: Front cover featured photo (greater prairie-chicken); Pages 23 (greater prairie-chicken)
Barth Schorre: Back cover top photo (scarlet tanager); Pages 17; 20; 22 (Blackburnian warbler)
Tom Vezo: Front cover middle photo (saw-whet owl); front cover bottom photo (monk parakeet); Pages 16; 24 (monk parakeet); 25 (northern saw-whet owl); 25 (pileated woodpecker)
Ron Austing: Page 21
Brian Henry: Back cover bottom photo (Eastern bluebird)
Robert McCaw: Page 23 (bobolink)
R. Mellon: Page 26 (Smith's longspur)
B. K. Wheeler: Page 24 (Mississippi kite)

Illinois
Bird Watching

A Year-Round Guide

Bill Thompson, III
and the staff of
BirdWatcher's Digest

COOL SPRINGS PRESS
A Division of Thomas Nelson Publishers
Since 1798

www.thomasnelson.com

Dedication and Acknowledgements

Dedication

To my parents, Bill and Elsa Thompson, who were bird watching *way* before it was cool and who had the courage and optimism to launch *Bird Watcher's Digest* in the living room of our home back in 1978. Thank you, Mom and Dad, for opening the door to my lifelong passion for birds and bird watching.

To Julie, Phoebe, and Liam (my own little family) who make each day sweeter than the last.

And to my siblings, Andy and Laura, for always being there for me.

Acknowledgements

There's no such thing as "too many cooks spoiling the broth" when creating a book. From the outset I leaned on and drew upon the talents of publishing professionals and birding experts in creating this book. At *Bird Watcher's Digest*: Deborah Griffith (special editorial blue ribbon), Heather Lynch (map design kudos), Andy Thompson, Ann Kerenyi, Linda Brejwo, Bob Carlsen, Elsa "Catbird" Thompson, Helen Neuberger, Susan Hill, Joyce Abicht, Laura Kammermeier, and Katherine Koch deserve my never-ending thanks for covering for me at *BWD* so I could stay home and write.

Andy Thompson, Charles Kirkwood, and Russell Galen made early and important contributions to the launching of this book.

My deep gratitude to the folks at Cool Springs Press—especially Billie Brownell, Hank McBride, David Dunham, and Roger Waynick—for their enthusiasm, guidance, and support. Thanks also to the many people who helped in the development of this book "behind the scenes"—to Jamie Chavez for her copyediting expertise, to Bill Kersey for his art direction, and to S.E. Anderson for pulling it all together.

Helping me with the content creation were Norma Siebenheller, Howard Youth, and Julie Zickefoose, three peerless bird authors. Without them I'd still be laboring over a smoking-hot laptop.

There may be no more prolific writer about Illinois' birds than Sheryl DeVore, who wrote the "Welcome to Bird Watching in Illinois" chapter of this book. It was a pleasure tapping into her knowledge and enthusiasm for Illinois birds and birding.

Sheryl De Vore, a longtime birder in Illinois, is the chief and founding editor of *Meadowlark: A Journal of Illinois Birds*, published by the Illinois Ornithological Society. An award winning environmental and nature writer, Sheryl has written three books, *Birding Illinois*, *Birds of Illinois*, and *Northern Flights: Tracking the Birds and Birders of Michigan's Upper Peninsula*. She also leads workshops and classes on birds and bird song at the Chicago Botanic Garden and other nature centers. Her affinity for bird song relates to her training as a flutist and pianist.

Sheryl would like to acknowledge Steven D. Bailey, an ornithologist with the Illinois Natural History Survey, for sharing his expertise and knowledge over the years.

Creating a book requires a lot of "cooks" and I am grateful for everyone's contributions. Any errors or omissions contained herein are the responsibility of the author (me).

Finally, thank *YOU* for reading this book. I hope our paths cross someday in a beautiful natural place where there are lots and lots of birds. What could be better?

—*Bill Thompson, III*

Table of Contents

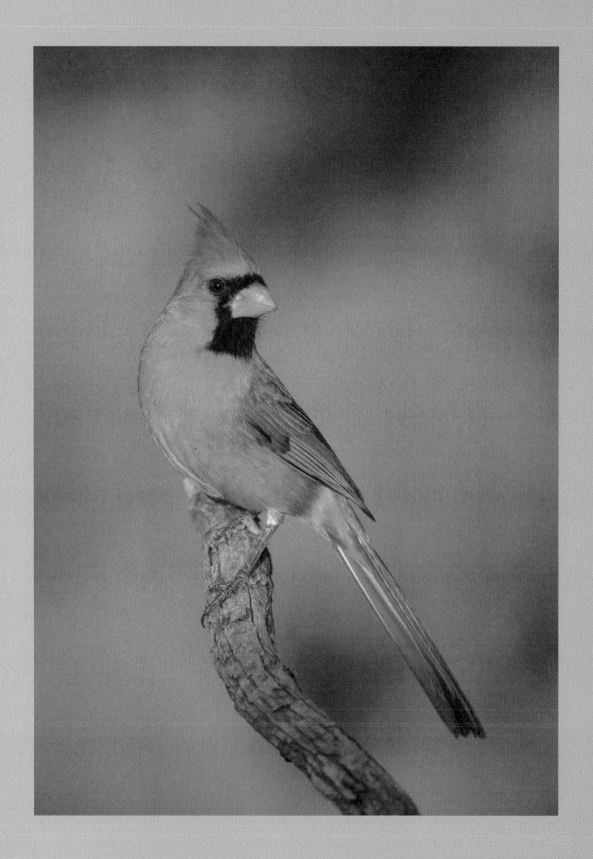

Welcome to Bird Watching

in Illinois . . . Sheryl DeVore

When John James Audubon passed through Illinois in the early 1800s, he likely witnessed waterways teeming with ducks and skies filled with passenger pigeons. Back then, greater prairie-chickens gathered on grasslands in early spring throughout the state to woo females in wild courtship dances. The ivory-billed woodpecker lived deep within southern Illinois swamplands, giving its toy-horn-like call and drumming on hollow trees. Prairie potholes in central Illinois offered breeding habitat for sandhill cranes, and even a few pairs of whooping cranes, as well as myriad ducks such as mallards and blue-winged teal. Wild turkeys and ruffed grouse roamed in upland woods statewide; the turkeys gobbling and the grouse drumming on logs to attract mates. Carolina parakeets nested in hollow trees or cavities along waterways, flashing their brilliant green colors as they took to the sky.

Today, the passenger pigeon, ivory-billed woodpecker, and Carolina parakeet are extinct—no longer to be found alive anywhere, but only as stuffed specimens in museums. Whooping cranes are listed as endangered on federal lists, and no longer breed in Illinois. The ruffed grouse is probably gone from the state as well, and numbers of shorebirds, ducks, songbirds, waterfowl and grassland birds have greatly diminished. The greater prairie-chicken hangs on tenuously to one grassland site in southern Illinois, and only about twenty pairs of sandhill cranes nest here, confined mostly to the northeastern part of the state.

Overhunting, habitat destruction, unchecked development, and the introduction of nonnative species such as the European starling have led to the demise of many birds that once were part of Illinois' native avifauna.

But Illinoisans and the early settlers before them have always enjoyed watching and studying birds—and where there is joy in beholding a wild creature, there is hope for its preservation. So Illinois' story of bird watching includes not only the loss of species and numbers, but also the great gains made in the twentieth and twenty-first centuries to restore habitats for birds and, hence, for bird watchers too.

Bird watching in Illinois can be a thrilling, heady adventure filled with color and song. And you can enjoy it out in the field or from your own backyard. Year-round, black-capped and Carolina chickadees add spirit to the day, giving their *dee-dee-dee* calls as they snatch seeds from a feeder or build nests in a tree hole right in your backyard. Year-round, too, woodpeckers, nuthatches, cardinals, and blue jays will all come to your yard if you provide them with food, water, and habitat. And during spring and fall migration, Baltimore orioles will eat orange halves provided for them, while scarlet tanagers may enjoy the suet that you put out for the woodpeckers and nuthatches. Some birds readily nest in human-supplied bird boxes—these include the house wren, eastern bluebird, tree swallow, chickadees and others.

When you're ready to leave your yard and visit some local forest preserves you can enjoy many more bird species, those that require larger tracts of land and certain types of habitat for breeding and feeding. Venture out to the woods anywhere on a spring day and you'll be greeted with a riot of song and color. Perhaps you'll hear and see the black-throated green warbler, which indeed has a black throat and a green back with

Blue-winged teal (male)

lots of yellow on the belly, or the yellow-rumped warbler, which, indeed, has a yellow rump, along with yellow shoulders and a yellow crown patch. Rose-breasted grosbeaks sing melancholy songs in the trees, while wood thrushes sound like Pan playing his flute. Walk the prairies in summer to listen for the rollicking calls of bobolinks and the buzzy insect-like trills of Savannah sparrows—or take a walk in winter through the snowy landscape to enjoy the birds such as dark-eyed juncos that come to Illinois for their winter vacation!

Any day, any season, you can experience Illinois birds in their habitat, showing their unique plumages and giving you a glimpse into another world.

It began, perhaps, with Robert Ridgway, a well-known ornithologist of the nineteenth century. In the late 1800s, Ridgway, who later became the secretary of the Smithsonian Institution, wrote *The Ornithology of Illinois*. Because of Ridgway, we have data on the population, distribution, and natural history of birds dating back more than a century. In the early twentieth century, Steven A. Forbes of the Illinois Natural History Survey and other ornithologists visited various habitats statewide to get a systematic picture of the population and distribution of birds. In the 1950s, Richard and Jean Graber repeated many of those studies to observe the changes in avian life in Illinois.

Everyday, nature lovers have also been studying and enjoying birds for more than a century in Illinois. Incorporated in 1897, the Illinois

Audubon Society has worked to promote the perpetuation and appreciation of native flora and fauna of Illinois and the habitats that support them. Over the years, this society has purchased hundreds of acres of land in the state to provide permanent habitats for birds and other animals and plants.

In 1992, the Illinois Ornithological Society was founded, in part to publish a quarterly journal which includes population, arrival, and departure data of bird species in Illinois for all four seasons. Many citizen or amateur scientists gather that data, which can be used to help land managers and ornithologists understand what is happening to the native species and how they can be preserved. The Bird Conservation Network, founded in 1998, consists of volunteers who conduct bird surveys at particular sites year after year to document trends in populations of certain key species.

Many state and federal agencies, including the Illinois Department of Natural Resources and the U.S. Fish & Wildlife Service, have also worked to protect and restore the habitat birds need in Illinois. These agencies manage hundreds of parks and wildlife refuges for various recreational uses including hiking, fishing, hunting, boating, and bird watching.

Thanks to all of these scientists and organizations, as well as myriad bird clubs that have existed for years, a beginning birder can easily find interesting birds to watch in the state as well as someone willing to take them out to see and learn about Illinois' avian creatures.

Because it is on a major flyway—the Central Flyway followed for millennia by migratory waterfowl, shorebirds, hawks, and songbirds—Illinois is an exciting place for bird watching. Illinois spans 378 miles from the southern tip, where the habitat is reminiscent of a Louisiana bayou, to the northern edge where winters can feel as if you are near the Arctic tundra. And that means many different habitats for many different bird species. In fact, more than 425 species of birds have been documented in the state.

Bordered on the east by Lake Michigan and on the west by major rivers and their associated river valleys, Illinois funnels migrants as they fly south for winter or north to breed. Each spring and fall, the migration begins. First in spring come the ducks, loons, and hawks; then the songbirds and shorebirds arrive. In fall, the pattern is reversed, with ducks passing through last.

Ducks, both ornate and plain, feed in deep or shallow waters, depending on whether they are equipped to dive deep or to dip their bills at the water's surface. A shallow feeder, the wood duck is almost garish with its bright orange bill and green-crested head with red eye, white chin, and black cheek, while the blue-winged teal is more subtle, displaying powder-blue wing patches when it flies. Impressive numbers of waterfowl migrate along major river valleys such as the Illinois, where thousands of canvasback and other diving ducks can often be found in spring and fall. Because of their appeal to hunters, ducks probably have had more protection than other species in Illinois. Many human-made reservoirs offer respite and food for ducks—and the Illinois Department of Natural Resources and U.S. Fish & Wildlife Service manage public lands for the ducks. Some of these sites include Carlyle Lake, Clinton Lake, and Rend Lake.

Raptors offer impressive shows in Illinois as well. In September, hundreds to thousands of broad-winged hawks in groups called "kettles" fly upon the rising thermals from the heated ground—and a good place to watch them is at Illinois Beach State Park in Zion. Birders started a hawk watch there in 1999 and have learned that merlins and peregrine falcons use the Lake Michigan shoreline in northern Illinois for migration much more than was previously thought. Beginning birders can sit on their lawn chairs and listen to the experts point out the various characteristics of the raptors in the sky. The Illinois Ornithological Society is also organizing a winter raptor survey to learn more about the habits of these birds of prey.

Raptors are beguiling, but sometimes difficult for birders to identify when the birds are just pinpoints in the sky. Perhaps that's why songbirds offer such an attraction. In one season, Illinois birders see at least thirty-six different species of warblers—from the gorgeous, black-and-orange-hued Blackburnian warbler to the common black-throated green that sings *zoo-zee, zoo-zoo-zee* from atop trees, to the fairly ubiquitous palm warbler that often hops about the ground, constantly pumping its tail. These and other songbirds such as thrushes, tanagers, and orioles migrate along the Des Plaines River Valley and along the Lake Michigan shoreline in northern Illinois, and along the Cache River and its valleys in southern Illinois. Central Illinois, mostly soybean and cornfields, has protected river valleys and woodlands where hungry migrants also stop to refuel. Recent Doppler radar studies show that every piece of vegetation in the state is important to migratory birds—and that large swaths of songbirds fly over Lake Michigan at night during migration. These birds face many perils, including tall lighted buildings that mesmerize them and bring them to their doom. Throughout the migration season, volunteers gather birds that have hit these buildings and take them to rehabilitation centers. In addition, volunteers are educating the public about these hazards, and many building owners have agreed to turn off the lights at night during migration.

Shorebirds, though more difficult to identify than some of the woodland songbirds, offer the chance to explore different habitats. In mudflats, sod farms, and wetland edges, birders search for the more than forty species of shorebirds in Illinois. These include the lesser yellowlegs with its long legs and *tu tu* call, and the killdeer that calls its name in flight and feigns a broken wing when intruders get too close to its nest. Shorebirds, some of which fly from one end of the Earth to the other each year, to breed and winter, require many stopover sites for resting and refueling; now birders and scientists are documenting their numbers and species to get a better picture of the habitat required. It's been learned that Illinois harbors a significant percentage of the world's population of yellowlegs on migration—specifically, 100,000 greater yellowlegs and 500,000 lesser yellowlegs migrate through the state each season. Those numbers represent more than 10 and 20 percent (respectively) of the world's population of these species. Federal and state wildlife managers are taking note as they plan management programs, but conservation efforts for shorebirds in Illinois have only just begun. However, Lake Chautauqua in southern Illinois is acclaimed as an important international shorebird reserve.

Grassland and wetland birds need help, too. Since settlement, Illinois, often called the Prairie State, has lost nearly all of its grassland and wetland habitats—indeed less than one percent of the historical acreage of these native ecosystems remains today. Researchers, volunteers, and land managers are working to protect and restore those remaining acres, and purchase land to expand the acreage. These groups are restoring such areas as the Bartel and Orland Grasslands south of Chicago where bobolinks and Henslow's sparrows breed. Scientists are working at the Prairie Ridge State Natural Area to protect the last viable remaining population of greater prairie-chickens, and the Midewin National Tallgrass Prairie (the former Joliet Arsenal) is now serving as a model for managing a large site to attract grassland and shrubland birds. State and federal organizations are managing more than 19,000 acres of this mosaic of wetlands, shrubs, and various types of grasslands to provide places for breeding upland sandpiper, loggerhead shrike, bobolink, Henslow's sparrow, and other rare breeders in the state. We have learned that large, contiguous sites provide a better place for birds to raise young successfully. It is also known that isolated islands of habitat—whether they be woodlands, wetlands, or grasslands—do not provide the same level of breeding success as do large chunks of habitat.

Providing habitat for wetland birds is another twenty-first century conservation priority in Illinois. Wetlands have been drained for more than a century; and those that remain are becoming degraded as nonnative plant species encroach and the water is interrupted from its natural flow. Some of the state's best wetlands for viewing birds dependent on these habitats between land and water include the Cache River Wetlands in southern Illinois and a series of wetlands in northeastern Illinois that host the state endangered yellow-headed blackbird, as well as more common species including pied-billed grebe and sora.

Luckily for birders, many state and local bird clubs organize trips, most of them free and open to the public, to see ducks, warblers, shorebirds, wading species, grassland birds, and raptors. Leaders go into the wetlands at dusk and play tapes to coax rails and grebes to respond with their interesting vocalizations or they plan a trip to observe greater prairie-chickens perform their fascinating courtship display. They lead local trips to migratory hotspots, helping birders find their favorite warblers. Veteran bird watchers abound at these trips, eager to help beginners with identification tips.

New bird watchers can also join one of the many statewide clubs conducting Christmas Bird Counts and the Spring Bird Counts. Wherever you live in Illinois, you can find a Christmas Bird Count sometime between mid-December and early January during which you can help count chickadees, jays, cardinals, nuthatches, geese, and other common year-round species. It's a perfect opportunity to learn about Illinois birds, because the number of species in winter is so much smaller than in summer or during migration. That gives beginners a chance to focus in on identifying just a few species. The Spring Bird Count occurs at the height of songbird migration and it's a thrill to go out and count all the warblers, thrushes, tanagers, and orioles descending into the greenery.

Never before in Illinois' history have there been more bird watchers willing to help beginners or more conservationists working to help birds. Seek out a local resource and start watching and enjoying birds in Illinois.

Ecoregions of Illinois

Illinois contains at least fourteen distinct bioregions, according to the Illinois Natural History Survey. These include the driftless region and Rock River Hill country in the northwest; the woods and ravines in the northeastern part of the state; the bottomlands of the upper Mississippi and Illinois rivers in the west-central part of the state; a grand prairie in north-central and central Illinois; the western forest prairie and the Shawnee Hills; and coastal plain in the far south. These regions have distinct characteristics, such as soil composition, plant life—and in some cases, bird life—which define them. But even within these regions are subregions, smaller ecosystems that can harbor a distinct group of plants and animals.

Other scientific entities divide Illinois into different ecoregions; for example, the U.S. Environmental Protection Agency names five basic regions. For birding purposes, I have divided Illinois into four main regions—the Driftless Region, the Central Plains, the River Lowlands, and the Shawnee National Forest, with its associated highlands and cypress swamps.

What's important to remember about ecoregions is that no true or clear lines divide them and that various transitional zones exist between them. Knowing this helps with watching and appreciating birds, because even a small piece of prairie in your backyard or a wooded lot might be a little ecosystem just right for some birds.

The Driftless Region
The Driftless Region, consisting of parts of southern Minnesota and Wisconsin, northwestern Illinois, and northeastern Iowa, gets its name from having escaped the glaciers that covered neighboring areas. These glaciers leveled or smoothed out the surrounding landscapes. Meanwhile, erosion weathered the Driftless Region's old bedrock until a series of deep valleys and rock formations were formed. Nearby glaciers deposited silt, sand, and gravel into the Mississippi River Valley.

Today, this rugged, scenic region is dominated by the Mississippi River, its accompanying backwaters, and large rock formations. The landscape consists mostly of oaks and maples, along with various ferns on north-facing slopes of wooded limestone bluffs, and extensive stands of spring wildflowers such as Virginia bluebell and great white trillium. Sandy soils harbor prairie and savanna plants. Included within this region is the Mississippi Palisades State Park and the recently designated Lost Mound National Wildlife Refuge, much of which is a sandy substrate.

This unique habitat attracts some breeding bird species not normally found in northern Illinois, including the blue grosbeak, which uses sandy grassland habitat, along with yellow-throated warbler, Acadian flycatcher, Kentucky warbler, and pileated woodpecker, which use large, old trees in river bottom areas.

The natural dune system at Lost Mound, about 4,000 acres, provides habitat for myriad grassland species including grasshopper sparrow, lark sparrow, dickcissel, and eastern and western meadowlarks. Smaller numbers of common nighthawk and upland sandpiper also breed in these grasslands.

The Mississippi River and its backwaters attract dozens of waterfowl, including many ducks and breeding herons as well as wintering bald eagles. Migrating ducks include northern pintail, gadwall, canvasback, common goldeneye, and lesser scaup. Countless songbirds also use the river valley, which lies in the Mississippi Flyway, for migration.

The Driftless Region represents a small portion of Illinois, and is the smallest region by far of the three listed here. But the bird diversity is great and the protection being afforded it by the creation of Lost Mound National Refuge suggests it will continue to be a great natural area, and to be even more accessible to birders in the future.

The Central Plains

The Central Plains, encompassing much of the northern two-thirds of Illinois except for the western river lowlands, represent a transitional zone between the continent's eastern woods and the tallgrass prairies. Glaciers once inundated much of this region and helped create not only Lake Michigan but also bogs, wetlands, and prairie potholes. Glacier deposits turned into moraines, which are wooded hills. The glaciers also scoured the land and the elements they left behind created one of the richest soils in the world. These soils harbored thousands of acres of tallgrass prairie and oak savanna, which teemed with bluestem, side oats grama, and other native plants and wildflowers. Native Americans as well as natural lightning helped create fires in this region, sustaining renewal of the prairies and adding nutrients to the soils. River valleys carved by glaciers, such as the Des Plaines, were natural firebreaks and allowed mature woodlands to grow.

Most of the native grasslands have been tilled for agriculture or destroyed for development. But Illinois still has some representative grasslands that contain most of the historical native bird species, and restoration and protection will continue to provide habitat for birds. One shining example of the native grasslands of yesterday is the Midewin National Tallgrass Prairie. This 19,000-acre composite of wetlands, grasslands and shrublands holds habitat for breeding birds that were once much more abundant in Illinois: the upland sandpiper, bobolink, loggerhead shrike (northernmost breeding location for this species in Illinois), and northern harrier. Plenty of smaller grasslands in this region attract meadowlarks, Savannah sparrows, and other more common birds to breed. In winter, larger grasslands offer hunting habitat for the short-eared owl and northern harrier.

One of the nation's most endangered ecosystems, the oak savannas, grows in the Central Plains. A savanna contains roughly 20 to 30 percent forestation and is filled with grassland vegetation such as bottlebrush grass. The bur oak is the dominant tree species in a savanna, as they are able to withstand prairie fires. Some bird species that frequent savannas include the rapidly declining red-headed woodpecker and the great crested flycatcher. Conservationists are working to restore savannas, many of which are degraded or have disappeared from the Central Plains landscape.

Probably 90 percent of the state's wetlands have been drained to make way for development. These included central Illinois prairie potholes that provided tremendous breeding opportunities for mallards, blue-winged teal, and other ducks, as well as marshes that attracted breeding ruddy ducks, yellow-headed blackbirds, pied-billed grebes, cranes, various rails. The wetlands that remain can primarily be found in northeastern Illinois; those that are being protected as high-quality marshes provide habitat for some of these birds. Glacial lakes also dot the northeastern portion of this region. Though many are surrounded by development now, these deep lakes provide an excellent place for migrating ducks and loons to feed and rest.

The west-central part of this region also contains various wetlands that have been manipulated to attract ducks and are now being managed to help migrating shorebirds, such as the Lake Chautauqua and the Emiquon National Wildlife Refuges.

Today, numerous migratory birds use the river valleys and Lake Michigan shoreline to make their way to wintering and breeding grounds. Many warbler species as well as grosbeaks, thrushes, flycatchers, and orioles flood through these areas in May and September. Others remain to nest in summer, including the wood thrush, eastern wood-pewee, rose-breasted grosbeak, red-eyed vireo, and scarlet tanager. The woods in the southern parts of the Central Plains region contain a diverse list of breeding birds including summer tanager as well as scarlet tanager, yellow-throated vireo, red-eyed vireo, blue-gray gnatcatcher, and tufted titmouse.

The River Lowlands

The river lowlands follow the Mississippi River along the western part of the United States from about the northern top third of the state southward and into southern Illinois, north of the Shawnee National Forest. This region has glacial till plains as well as bottomland valleys and forests. Much of the glacial plains have been turned into agriculture, but where there still are some grasslands, western meadowlarks and other prairie birds breed. The river backwaters and accompanying forests attract breeding pileated woodpeckers, wood ducks, and American redstarts, which prefer these riverine areas for breeding. In the northern part of this region, tundra swans, American white pelicans, and canvasbacks, sometimes thousands of them, migrate along the river. In the southern part of the river lowlands, you'll find more southerly river bottomland nesters, including Kentucky warbler and Louisiana waterthrush.

The Shawnee National Forest

Glaciers never reached far southern Illinois, but other geologic action created the Shawnee Highlands and cypress swamps that dominate this region. Activity beneath the earth created the Shawnee National Forest and its highlands, while water running down these forest slopes created the canyons and steep hillsides. The varied topography includes bluffs as well as the lowlands and the flood plains of the Mississippi and Ohio Rivers. The flood plains are about 325 feet above sea level, while some nearby bluffs are more than 1,000 feet above sea level.

Heavy timbering threatened this region, but the Great Depression of 1929 halted the destruction and allowed tens of thousands of acres to be saved as the Shawnee National Forest. Today the forest is again under threat for timber purposes; however various groups are working to maintain the region's high-quality woods and swampland habitat.

There are five different types of regions within the Shawnee National Forest that lies at the edge of the glaciated area. These ecosystems provide for a huge diversity of plants and animals. Here you'll find oak/hickory uplands as well as buttonbush and bald cypress/black tupelo swamps meandering along the lengthy Cache River. Many of the cypress are more than 200 years old. Tulip poplar and sweetgum as well as shortleaf pine also grow in this region.

Nearly twenty species of warblers, including ovenbird, prothonotary warbler, and yellow-breasted chat, breed in this region. Summer tanager, orchard oriole, barred owl, wood thrush, Carolina wren, Acadian flycatcher, and indigo bunting breed in the right habitat throughout the region. Whip-poor-wills and chuck-will's-widow, which need large woods in which to breed, find the Shawnee National Forest a perfect place to do so. Black vultures and turkey vultures roost in the cypresses at night during summer. After the breeding season, the river backwaters and swamps abound with herons and egrets.

Visitors to southern Illinois may enjoy moments when they feel they have been transported back in time, as they hear green tree frogs calling from the swamps and pileated woodpeckers giving their jungle-like screams as they scan the wood of dying trees for their favorite food, carpenter ants.

The Shawnee National Forest encompasses seven designated wilderness areas including Bald Knob, Bay Creek, Burden Falls, Clear Springs, Garden of the Gods, Lusk Creek, and Panther Den Wildernesses. Here the adventurous hiker and birder can get some solitude among the amazing rock formations and scenic views.

Though much of Illinois' modern landscape has been altered since it was created, you can still get a glimpse of what the state looked like a thousand years ago. In the Driftless Region you can wander up and down bluffs and look to the Mississippi River for ducks and herons that have used this corridor for eons. Or you can watch the sky for eagles and hawks that are passing through. In the prairies, you can walk among big bluestem and copious wildflowers during breeding season to listen for the songs of grassland birds whose voices have echoed across the central plains of Illinois for centuries. And you can traverse the river valleys interspersed among the prairies to observe the long and amazing tradition of songbird migration. In the southern cypress swamps, you step back into history walking among the cypress and black tupelo, so tall and so crowded, where the bird songs resonate as they always have, long before humans entered the picture.

Illinois Bird Watching by Season

Spring

Spring comes to southern Illinois nearly a full month earlier than in northern Illinois. While Louisiana waterthrushes are returning to breed in the southern Illinois swamplands in late March, a snowy owl may still be lingering along the northern Lake Michigan shoreline in Waukegan before it returns to the tundra. And while the flowering dogwoods are unfolding white blooms in the south, native shrubs in the north such as redbuds are still bare of leaves and are a month and a half away from blooming. Still, no matter where you are in the state, spring migration typically begins in early March—but be aware that the migrants come through southern Illinois first, and the species you see there may not arrive in the northern part of the state until two weeks (or more) later.

In March, waterfowl are heading north to their breeding grounds and you can observe dozens of species of ducks on large downstate reservoirs, along the Illinois and Mississippi Rivers in northeastern Illinois wetlands, and from the Lake Michigan shoreline.

Dabbling ducks—those that tip their bills into shallow waters to search for aquatic vegetation, seeds, and invertebrates—include northern pintail, mallard, northern shoveler, green-winged teal, gadwall, blue-winged teal, and American wigeon. These ducks tend to have large, white wing patches. Look for them in thawed ponds, wetlands, and lakes with shallow edges. The diving ducks, such as common, red-breasted and hooded mergansers as well as canvasbacks and redheads, can be found on larger, deeper lakes and rivers. They dive deep to search for fish, mollusks, and aquatic plants. To become airborne, they must skitter on the water first to gain enough speed.

Migrating sandhill cranes and raptors also begin flying over Illinois in March. Listen for the high rattling call of the cranes overhead on a sunny day.

Meanwhile, American woodcocks are courting, finding a short patch of grass next to a wooded area in which to perform a most incredible show: at twilight, the males utter *peent* several times, fly high into the air out of sight, and then tumble back down, twittering back to where they started. Bluebirds, robins, and blackbirds are heading north; some of them will stay to breed in Illinois, while others will keep going. And spring is the best time to see greater prairie-chickens on their booming grounds at Prairie Ridge State Natural Area, as the males choose females and chase away competitors.

In April, the waterfowl continue to migrate, and the loons join them. A host of glacial lakes in northeastern Illinois attract migrating loons, which need deep, large bodies of water for feeding and for becoming airborne. Loons once nested in Illinois, but disturbance around lakes now keeps them moving northward to quieter lakes for breeding. You'll find them statewide on large reservoirs or lakes, but a great place to observe them and perhaps hear their mysterious yodeling is the aptly named group of Loon Lakes near Antioch, Illinois.

Sandhill crane

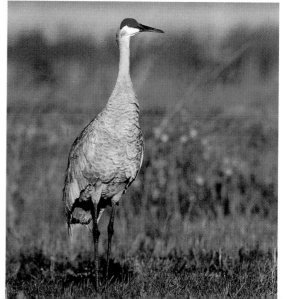

The rails, grebes, and many early shorebirds such as least and semipalmated sandpipers are also starting to pass through in April. Visit a medium-to-large, undisturbed wetland at dusk and you may hear the maniacal call of the pied-billed grebe or the horse-whinny song of the sora.

Sparrows of many kinds migrate through Illinois in March, April, and May—the song and fox sparrows arrive first, followed by swamp and vesper sparrows. Song sparrows are the most common and can be heard singing their *put on the tea kettle-ettle-ettle* songs in backyards and suburban parks as well as natural areas.

The swallows are returning too. Tree swallows snatch insects off lakes and wetlands and purple martins search for human-made nesting boxes. March and April also bring eastern phoebes, yellow-bellied sapsuckers, golden-crowned kinglets, brown creepers, and hermit thrushes.

Breeding herons and egrets return to Illinois in April. Great blue herons and double-crested cormorants are already starting to build or enhance large, bulky stick nests in their traditional nest-colony sites. Look for these groups of stick nests in the treetops near lakes and rivers.

If you're interested in combing the many cornfields in central Illinois, you might encounter the beautiful and rare Smith's longspur and its more common cousin, the Lapland longspur, as they pause to rest and feed before heading north to the tundra to breed.

If you want variety and excitement, the best time to bird Illinois is in May, when hoards of neotropical migrants including warblers, vireos, orioles, and tanagers pass through the state, some remaining to breed. Just about anywhere you go in May, you're bound to find some kind of warbler in the trees, even in your backyard. The yellow-rumped warblers show up first—and many are already in southern Illinois by March. Next come the palm, black-and-white, yellow, and black-throated green warblers, fol-lowed by magnolia, Nashville, Blackburnian, and then the latest migrant warblers, the bay-breasted, mourning, and Connecticut warblers. Birders covet the Connecticut warbler and often find this species at Chicago's Magic Hedge at Montrose Point along Lake Michigan in mid- to late May. On Spring Bird Count day, the first Saturday in May, southern Illinois birders often record thirty-two or more species of warblers. Often they record them by song as well as sight. Each warbler has its own song, which often is buzzy rather than "warbling" (for example, the blue-winged warbler sings *bee, bzzzzzzz*).

They also record summer and scarlet tanagers—two migrants that return from their winter habitats in South America. Summer tanagers are much more numerous in southern Illinois, while scarlets are found statewide. In May the rose-breasted grosbeak has returned and is giving a melancholy robinlike song that fills the woods on an early morning. He is often joined by the wood thrush, which gives lilting flutelike trills, often at dusk as well as in the morning. Various vireos including the red-eyed and the warbling vireo also add to the morning chorus. And the difficult-to-identify flycatchers are back too, including alder, willow, and least. Mid-May is also the height of shorebird migration, with many different species feasting in wetlands and along lakeshores, including greater and lesser yellowlegs, stilt sandpiper, and the rarer Hudsonian godwit and whimbrel.

The grasslands come alive with song in May, too—grasshopper sparrows and Henslow's sparrows give their insectlike songs while bobolinks offer rollicking, bubbling songs and the eastern meadowlark sings *spring of the year*.

As May comes to an end, most of the migrants are gone, though some linger into June. But by then many breeders are on nests, while others are starting their courtship rituals. Spring has ended, but each year, some Illinois birders remember the glow of seeing one hundred or more species of birds in a single day.

Summer

While the excitement of spring migration has passed, summer holds a more subtle form of wonder. The birds stay in one place now, raising a family and giving birders a chance to hear them sing and observe them feeding their young.

By June the familiar backyard birds such as northern cardinal, black-capped chickadee, and downy woodpecker are feeding young and if you have bird feeders or bird houses you may get to watch the youngsters begging for tasty morsels from their parents. House wrens will use nest boxes, and you can hear them singing their warbling melodies all summer long in your backyard. When the young have hatched, you can enjoy watching the adults gathering food all day long, and maybe one day get a glimpse of the young taking their first flight out of the box.

A visit to one of the state's many preserves and refuges can bring you close to other breeding birds, which require more specific kinds of habitats in which to raise their young.

In southern Illinois, you'll hear prothonotary warblers seemingly everywhere in the swamps, along with less-frequent cries of the red-shouldered hawk. At Trail of Tears State Forest, worm-eating warblers nest on steep, leaf-covered slopes. The male often sits high atop a tree giving his high-pitched, rapid trill to lure possible intruders away from the female who is sitting tightly and quietly on the nest. Kentucky warblers breed on or close to the ground, hidden in low understory at the park and at other places in southern Illinois. They sing a loud, melodic, *churry, churry, churry* song.

Giant City State Park is a great place to enjoy the breeding birds of southern Illinois, including summer tanager in the woodlands, orchard orioles in the shrubby areas, and twelve species of warblers (including northern parula and yellow-throated warbler) in tall trees such as sycamores. At night, listen for the whip-poor-

will call its name repeatedly. The chuck-will's-widow is another southern Illinois breeding specialty, and the best place to hear it call, beginning at dusk and through the night, is along the road at Lake Murphysboro State Park.

Drive around some of the shrub-laden roads of the Shawnee National Forest and you may find another southern Illinois specialty, the blue grosbeak. Indigo buntings seem to be ubiquitous in southern Illinois; they like shrubby areas for breeding and are often perched atop a tree singing their bouncing two-part song. Dickcissels commonly breed in agricultural fields where there are tall stands of wildflowers or weeds.

Mississippi kites are breeding in June, too, and can be found only in extreme southern Illinois as well as a few spots father north and west along the large river valleys. Southern Illinois is also the land of the barred owl; this fascinating species gives a most unusual courtship song. *Who cooks for you, who cooks for you-all?* the male calls. The female responds in kind, but with a slightly higher pitch, and soon the two are singing a duet in a raucous fashion to reinforce their bonds.

In woodlands throughout the state, eastern wood-pewees sing their names, while great crested flycatchers issue *wheep* from deep woods and woodland edges. Both nest high in trees, while wood thrushes choose lower shrubs within woodlands in which to build their nests.

Also in wetlands throughout the state are breeding herons and egrets. By June in southern Illinois, they are feeding their young, some of

Kentucky warbler (male)

Summer tanager (male)

which may even be ready to fledge. Lake Renwick Heron Rookery and Nature Preserve near Joliet, in northern Illinois, holds an impressive number of breeding great blue herons, double-crested cormorants, and great egrets. These birds build stick nests in trees, but conservationists have helped them by erecting platforms atop the trees in which nests have previously been built. In June, you can see hundreds and hundreds of these large waders sitting on nests, flying to and fro to add sticks to their nests, and feeding squawky, noisy young.

Purple martins breed statewide, too. This large swallow once bred in natural cavities, but competition from starlings and lack of habitat have required humans to intervene. Today, purple martins only breed in human-supplied houses in Illinois. Griggsville, a small west-central town calls itself the purple martin capital of the nation. Some 600 purple martin high-rises attract the birds and visitors each summer.

Eastern bluebirds also are raising young, mostly in nest boxes; you'll find this species statewide near boxes erected in appropriate places: open, low grassy areas for feeding adjacent to trees with perches for males to sing. The North American Bluebird Society has information on how you can start your own bluebird trail. Visit the Resources section of this book for more information.

Illinois grasslands are alive with bird song and activity in June and early July. Eastern meadowlarks can be found in most any size of grassland statewide, but some other species require more specific habitat. The bobolink likes medium-height grasses and will also nest in hayfields, while the grasshopper sparrow likes short, dry grasslands and the Henslow's sparrow prefers wetter grassy areas; find a large grassland complex with all those components and you will find all these species. Midewin National Tallgrass Prairie features these breeding grassland birds as well as the state endangered upland sandpiper and loggerhead shrike. Many of the state's grasslands are gone, replaced by agriculture and development, which is why it's essential to protect places like Midewin to provide habitat for grassland breeders.

Besides the huge acreage of swamplands in southern Illinois, the only remaining high-quality wetlands left in the state are mostly in the northeast. Here's where you'll find the breeding yellow-headed blackbird, as well as black tern, pied-billed grebe, king rail, and other secretive wetland species. The yellow-headed blackbird is a state endangered bird that breeds here only in northeastern Illinois; it can be found at Black Tern Marsh at the McHenry Dam portion of Moraine Hills State Park, where it gives its raucous, rusty-hinge-like song. Roughly twenty to twenty-five pairs of sandhill cranes now breed in various northeastern and northwestern Illinois wetlands including the Chain O' Lakes State Park. The species was once a more common breeder in the state.

Migration is already beginning in July—at least for shorebirds, which are heading south from their northern breeding grounds. In early to mid-July, greater and lesser yellowlegs are coming through, followed by the semipalmated and least sandpipers. Many recently hatched young shorebirds are flying through Illinois in July and August, taking their first long migratory journey. They come through northern Illinois first, flying south and stopping to rest and feed along the way.

By mid-August, it's plain to see that breeding season is closing and migration is once again upon us. Some of the first migrating warblers appear in northern Illinois, our yellow warblers have already left, and fall is in the air.

Autumn

Fall migration is a much less hurried affair compared with spring, when various species are rushing to get to their breeding grounds and find the best places to nest. You can enjoy migrating songbirds afield or even in your own backyard, especially if you provide water, food, and shelter. In August and September a hummingbird feeder will attract migrating ruby-throated hummingbirds, and dripping water will attract various warbler species, especially the more common ones like Tennessee warbler and yellow-rumped warbler. Cedar waxwings, Swainson's thrushes, and robins all love elder-berry and winterberry, among other native plants bearing fruit in early fall. American goldfinches will feed on thistle you provide or on the seeds of many native prairie plants such as purple coneflower and blazing star.

In fall, birds born that summer (juveniles) as well as adults migrate through Illinois, often at different times. Many of the young warblers and shorebirds look different from their parents and many of the adult warblers have changed

Peregrine falcon

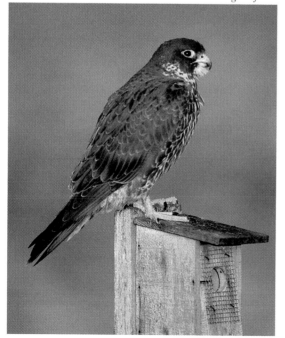

into nonbreeding plumage—so identifying all these species in fall can be a challenge.

September is the peak month for migrating song-birds such as warblers, grosbeaks, and tanagers—most of the bird species in these groups eat only insects and have to continue south as the weather turns cold and the population of their prey diminishes. In September, too, huge numbers of common nighthawks ply the skies, snatching the last of the season's insects on their way to Central and South America. On a warm September day at dusk, nighthawks can be seen, even right over your house, as they feed on the wing.

Lake Chautauqua National Wildlife Refuge is the place to go August through September to view thousands upon thousands of shorebirds. On a given day, 10,000 shorebirds representing dozens of species may be feeding and resting at this national wildlife refuge. The most common are pectoral sandpiper, lesser yellowlegs, and semipalmated sandpiper.

Meanwhile, buff-breasted sandpipers are visiting sod farms in northern Illinois. The short grassy fields mimic their favorite feeding grounds farther north where they breed. Sometimes during fall migration, a buff-breasted sandpiper will perform its courtship display, raising wings to show bright white underneath.

Also in August and September, young waders such as little blue herons and snowy egrets may wander north from their southern Illinois breeding grounds, searching for food. Herons, egrets, and other water birds often undertake a post-breeding dispersal, where breeding birds and recently fledged young spread out in all directions to find food. Some of these birds may head hundreds of miles north where they may spend a few days or weeks before heading south.

The end of September brings broad-winged hawks by the hundreds or even thousands. Hawk watchers look to the skies for a large group of these birds riding thermals in the sky. Thermals are wind updrafts created by the sun warming the earth—and they give hawks the boost they need to migrate.

Snow goose (dark or "blue" morph)

common as migrants in Illinois. This goose has a pinkish orange bill, white forehead, dark body, and bright orange feet.

Fall is a terrific time to search for rare birds. Young birds that have never migrated before may get off course, and hurricane season can also send birds out of their range—many of the state's rarities have occurred in October and November. Birders call state hotlines and check the state birding listserve to find out if any rare species have been spotted; and then they go chasing them. Some recent rarities seen in autumn in Illinois include western grebe, sharp-tailed sandpiper, vermilion flycatcher, and even brown pelican, a bird that typically lives along our ocean coasts.

In October, sparrows, ducks, scoters, and loons as well as different species of hawks migrate through Illinois. Sharp-shinned, Cooper's hawks, red-tailed hawks, peregrine falcons, and merlins fly over Illinois Beach State Park in northern Illinois and other hawk-watching spots in the state. Along Lake Michigan and on the downstate reservoirs you can see the mergansers, ruddy ducks, teal, and other ducks that migrate along the Mississippi Flyway.

Sandhill cranes are flying, too. In October and November on a clear, sunny day you can hear their rattling calls in the sky as they fly in formation to warmer climates. Many of them are headed to Jasper-Pulaski State Natural Area in Indiana, where they rest and feed until the cold weather drives them even farther south.

In Illinois impressive numbers of Canada geese fly overhead or feast in cornfields in October, November, and December—if you look among the crowd you may find some snow geese, a few greater white-fronted geese, and even an occasional Ross's goose.

Snow geese come in two color versions or morphs: the white morph, in which birds are all-white with black wing patches and the blue morph, in which birds are dark bodied with white heads. Greater white-fronted geese, which breed on the tundra, have recently become more

November can be a cold, rainy, blustery month, but if you dress warmly and visit the Lake Michigan shoreline or downstate reservoirs, you can glimpse flyby jaegers, kittiwakes, scoters, migrating tundra swans, and the arrival of wintering gulls such as Iceland and Thayer's gulls. November is also the month to search for the rare purple sandpiper—birders almost always find one or two purple sandpipers each November at Waukegan Harbor along Lake Michigan.

As November draws to a close, northern shrikes, pine siskins, crossbills, and other irruptive species have settled into Illinois for winter. An irruptive species is one that moves irregularly, and not every year, when its food source in its northern habitat is depleted. The northern shrike eats voles (as well as other mammals and small birds) in its breeding grounds in Canada and northern United States; but when the vole population crashes, the northern shrike moves farther south until it can find another source of food. This bird needs hundreds of acres of habitat in which to feed all winter long. It's the only songbird that hunts other songbirds and impales the carcasses of its prey on thorns of trees, barbed wires, and other places, storing the food for another day. In some years, shrikes are more plentiful than others, but there's no doubt that when a birder spots a shrike, it signals the end of fall and the beginning of winter birding.

Winter

The official start of an Illinois bird watcher's winter is during the Christmas Bird Count season. Throughout the state, beginning, intermediate, and advanced birders join forces to count every bird they see for one day. The counts occur beginning in mid-December and ending mid-January, with some nature lovers partaking in several counts throughout the season. In southern Illinois, birders count white-crowned sparrows, Carolina wrens, yellow-rumped warblers, and even an occasional lingering or wintering eastern phoebe, while in the north, birders are tallying scoters, wintering ducks, and wintering gulls resting in large flocks on Lake Michigan.

Gull and owl species that breed farther north come to Illinois for more food during the winter months. Ring-billed gulls live year-round in Illinois, but from December through March, the Iceland, Thayer's, and glaucous gulls join them. Identifying these species can be difficult, so several bird clubs created the annual gull frolic at Winthrop Harbor, Illinois. Here you can watch presentations about gull identification in the warmth of a club house, then venture outdoors to look through scopes set up by expert gull watchers who will help you learn the finer points of identification. Other good places to watch gulls in winter include Starved Rock Lock and Dam and Peoria Lock and Dam.

Locks and dams along the Mississippi and Illinois rivers also attract bald eagles in winter; Illinois may have one of the highest winter populations of bald eagles in the nation. Eagles visit dams where turbines stun shad and other fish, making them easy prey. Sometimes fifty or more bald eagles, juveniles and adults, can be counted at one point along the Mississippi River at such places as Mississippi Palisades State Park. The colder the winter and the more ice on our lakes and rivers, the more likely bald eagles are to concentrate along the locks where water remains open.

Where there's open water in winter, you'll also find geese as well as mergansers, scaup, goldeneyes, and other diving ducks. Thousands of snow geese winter along open rivers and lakes in central and southern Illinois, and Canada geese winter statewide, partaking of the leftover corn and other agricultural crops in fallow fields.

Winter finches and northern shrikes that came to Illinois at the end of fall remain throughout the winter where they can find food. Once a shrike establishes its territory, it remains there, allowing birders a chance to observe it if they are patient. The northern shrike is seen mostly in northern Illinois at places such as Glacial Park in McHenry County and the north unit of Illinois Beach State Park.

Finches such as red and white-winged crossbills visit pines and spruces—so the Sand Ridge State Forest, Morton Arboretum, and Illinois Beach State Park attract these birds in winter. You may also see white-winged crossbills as well as pine siskins and common redpolls at backyard feeders, where they are attracted to sunflower seed and thistle, or Niger, seed. Other small songbirds that spend summers farther north and winters in Illinois include snow buntings, Lapland long-

Carolina wren

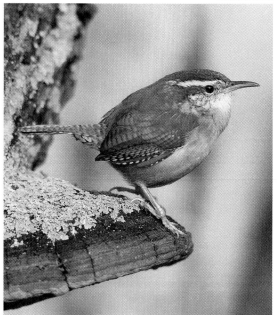

spurs, and American tree sparrows. The buntings and longspurs feed in fields and short grassy areas. When the snows fall, they move to roadsides searching for grains blown there by the wind. Tree sparrows prefer open areas dotted with shrubs, which mimic their northerly breeding grounds just south of the tree line.

If you love owls, you'll love winter birding in Illinois. Several owl species also come to Illinois from the North to spend the winters. These include the northern saw-whet, long-eared, short-eared, and snowy owls. While the saw-whet and long-eared owls roost by day and hunt actively by night, you may see the snowy and short-eared owls hunting by day, particularly when the skies are overcast with clouds. Signs of the owl's presence include pellets, regurgitated pieces of bone and fur the birds can't digest. If you see some whitewash (bird excrement) on a cedar tree and pellets at the base, look up—you might glimpse the 6-inch-tall northern saw-whet owl peering at you or asleep on a branch. Morton Arboretum in northern Illinois and Eldon Hazlet State Park farther south often have saw-whet owls in winter. In winter, long-eared owls roost in evergreens and willow stands, while short-eared owls roost in grasslands. The best chance to see the short-eared owl is at dusk when they come out to hunt, soaring low over large grasslands; this species' numbers continue to decline in Illinois both as a breeder and winter visitor due to loss of habitat.

The great horned owl actually nests in winter; already in November and December, the male courts the female with his deep hoots, which can be heard even in suburban neighborhoods. By January, the female is sitting on eggs in an old squirrel or hawk nest high in a tree. Young great horneds hatch while snow is still falling.

During years when food is scarce on its tundra breeding grounds, the snowy owl moves south to find food—rarely farther south than central Illinois and typically only to northern Illinois. In some years, seventy-five or more snowy owls will venture into Illinois; in other years birders are lucky if they find even one. Snowies typically choose cornfields or fields adjacent to Lake

Northern shrike

Michigan for hunting and roosting. Snowy owls eat voles up north, but will take wintering ducks and other birds for sustenance.

Several hawk species also live in Illinois year-round and can be seen in winter, but a few come from the North. Red-tailed hawks and American kestrels (a much smaller raptor than the red-tailed) hunt the open fields and sit atop telephone poles and other perches to watch for movement of prey below. Both of these hawks are widespread and common in Illinois year-round. Cooper's hawks visit neighborhoods to catch birds attracted to feeders. During lean food years, the rough-legged hawk winters to Illinois, too; this beautiful bird with a black belly can be seen hovering over a field before pouncing on its prey. There's always the chance for the rare prairie falcon or gyrfalcon to show up in Illinois on a cold winter day.

In middle to late February, the early red-winged blackbirds return to southern Illinois; a few may have even wintered there. For many birders, tired of the cold, the arrival of red-winged blackbirds, as well as the early singing of song sparrows, signals the beginning of spring and the promise of another spectacular migration to come.

Illinois' Ten Must-See Birds

American White Pelican
Pelecanus erythrorhynchos

A relatively new addition to Illinois avifauna, the American white pelican now migrates through the state along large rivers, sometimes stopping on lakes and other large reservoirs to rest and feed. Birders have observed as many as 4,500 pelicans at one time gathered along the Illinois River.

This mostly white bird with black wings has a long, large orange bill and throat pouch, which it uses to scoop up and swallow fish. It stands about 5 feet tall and has a 9-foot-long wingspan. In all plumages, the white pelican has a naked orange patch around its eye and bright orange-yellow legs and feet.

White pelicans don't dive to feed like brown pelicans do, but they have their own interesting way to search for a meal. They gather in lines to corral schools of small fish into groups by flapping their large wings onto the water's surface. A pelican gulps water and fish with its large pouch, then it squeezes the water out of the sides of its mouth as the fish head into its stomach.

Some white pelicans may linger in Illinois long after the rest of the spring migrants have left, and birders speculate that someday this species may begin breeding in the Prairie State. The best places to find large flocks of white pelicans include Lake Chautauqua and the Mark Twain National Wildlife Refuge, as well as along the Illinois River in southwestern Illinois. The best months to spot them are March, April, September, and October.

Blackburnian Warbler
Dendroica fusca

Birders never tire of seeing the Blackburnian warbler, and those seeing it for the first time can't help expressing amazement at the indescribable burnt-orange color of the male's throat.

This warbler breeds in the coniferous forests of northeastern United States, parts of Canada, and the Appalachian Mountains. Illinoisans get to see it during spring migration, usually throughout May. When it passes through Illinois in September heading for its South American wintering grounds, the male has lost much of his fiery brilliance and is more difficult to identify.

But in spring, you'll note not only this 5-inch-tall bird's brilliant throat but also the orange and black face markings. The male Blackburnian also has a dark back, large white wing patch, whitish underparts, and streaks on its sides. Females, immatures, and nonbreeding (fall) males typically have duller yellow-to-orange throats and breasts and streaks on the back, with two small white wing bars.

Look for this warbler (a fairly common migrant) in May anywhere you find migrating songbirds. Especially good spots are along Water Plant Road at Atwood Ridge and Hamburg Hill in southern Illinois, the Des Plaines River corridor in Lake and Cook Counties (Ryerson Woods, Wright Woods, and Half Day Road), and the Magic Hedge at Montrose Harbor.

Bobolink
Dolichonyx oryzivorus

Ask any Illinois birder and they'll probably tell you the bobolink is one of their favorite birds. They just can't resist the male's bubbly, energetic song combined with his "reverse-tuxedo" plumage.

About 7 inches tall, the male bobolink has a black belly, throat, and face, and a white back (the opposite of a man's white shirt and black jacket in a tuxedo). A lemon-yellow crown that extends to the nape finishes off the dapper look. Females, immatures, and nonbreeding males look like sparrows with a dark eye line and a light central crown stripe.

You'll find the males in spring and early summer flying over grasslands and hayfields, singing on the wing. The female, camouflaged by her grasslike colors, builds a cup nest in a shallow depression on the ground. When the young hatch in about two weeks, the female feeds them seeds and small insects. The males continue to defend territory with their songs until the young have fledged.

The bobolink may well be one of the fastest-declining songbirds in North America. Illinois volunteers and scientists have helped create better habitat for these birds. One of the best places in the state to see this species spring through fall is at the Orland Grasslands, a Cook County Forest Preserve holding near Orland Park. A major restoration project there has helped bobolinks and other rare grassland breeders. Midewin National Tallgrass Prairie near Joliet also offers habitat for these birds, which will accept nonnative hayfields in which to breed.

Greater Prairie-chicken
Tympanuchus cupido

One of Illinois' most endangered birds, the greater prairie-chicken exhibits an unusual and spectacular courtship. Beginning in March, male prairie-chickens gather on leks or booming grounds in short grasslands. Then they begin their dance to declare dominance over other males and attract nearby females. The males lift their tails, lower their wings, and inflate their yellow-orange air sacs, which produce a loud booming noise. They may also run around quickly and leap into the air.

Standing 18 inches tall, the adult male greater prairie-chicken has a heavily barred brown back with a rufous and buff belly on a plump body. The edge of its tail is black, and when in full courtship attire, the male has bright yellow eye combs. Long, pointy black ear tufts add to the almost comical appearance of this bird.

Once abundant statewide, the prairie-chicken can now only be found on about 3,000 acres of grassland in southeastern Illinois in or near the Prairie Ridge State Natural Area. A few bird clubs offer annual trips to watch the chickens from viewing blinds in March and April, when you can observe courtship displays from a safe distance.

The state Department of Natural Resources is working to save this species from extinction.

Mississippi Kite
Ictinia mississippiensis

Once more widespread in Illinois, the Mississippi kite now lives mostly in the southern part of the state and then only during breeding season. You can find this bird beginning in late April through early September, when it leaves to return to its South American wintering grounds.

This graceful raptor stands about 14 inches tall, and in flight its wingspan is 35 inches. The adult has a dark gray back with a long, dark tail. Its head and underparts are lighter gray. Look closely at a perched bird and you might see some chestnut color at the tips of the wings. Juveniles are darkish brown on the back and have streaks across the underparts.

In flight this kite displays long, pointed wings and a square tail as it dips and turns, catching its insect prey in midair. The kite prefers river bluffs and bottomland forests and often nests in large cottonwood trees overlooking water. Kites nest singly or in small colonies.

The Mississippi kite gracefully hawks insects in the air and occasionally takes bats in flight; sometimes it hunts lizards. A drive through Thebes, Illinois, along the river in May could reward you with the sight of dozens of Mississippi kites feeding in midair. Search for kites along river bluffs and bottomland forests at the Union County Conservation Area and the Fort Kaskaskia State Historic Site in spring, summer, and early fall.

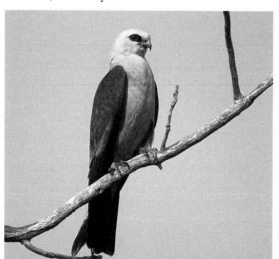

Monk Parakeet
Myiopsitta monachus

Parakeets in Illinois? Actually, yes. In fact, the native Carolina parakeet once plied the Prairie State's skies along with the passenger pigeon. Today both are extinct, but Illinoisans have a new parakeet, though not native, to observe. This South American species was introduced in the 1960s to North America by the exotic pet industry. Small colonies of escaped birds have survived in the wild and now even breed successfully in Illinois.

About 12 inches tall, the monk parakeet has green on its back, white on its throat, yellow-green on its belly, and blue on its wings. Its bright colors add pleasure to a dreary winter's day.

The monk parakeet survives the cold winters by feeding on ornamental berries and partaking of food from feeders. In addition, the species builds colonies of large nests made of sticks and grass, often atop transformers, where the birds huddle in winter to keep warm.

In summer, the parakeets raise six to eight young in their huge nests. Juveniles may help raise a second brood before autumn comes.

The best places to search for small flocks of parakeets are in the Hyde Park and Jackson Park regions of Chicago, at Addison and Armitage Roads in the town of Addison, and at the grain elevator in the town of Carlyle in southern Illinois. Small breeding colonies seem to be expanding south and north from Chicago.

Northern Saw-whet Owl
Aegolius acadicus

On a brisk winter day, several birders peer inside a group of cedars at Morton Arboretum in Lisle, Illinois, to view a seemingly tame and tiny owl, the northern saw-whet. The 7-inch-tall bird winks its yellow eyes at them, unaffected. This bird has found its daytime roosting place and there it will remain until dusk, when it swoops in a nearby field to catch a mouse or other small prey.

The northern saw-whet owl migrates through Illinois and some stay for winter, often remaining in the same roost for days or months if not disturbed. Its back is brown, spotted with white, its belly is streaked with rust, and a light facial disc frames its eyes.

Searching for this species in winter takes patience as well as knowledge about its mysterious ways. After eating, owls cough up pellets, a matted blend of bone and fur they cannot digest. Search at the base of evergreens—especially cedars, white pines, and yews—for the pellets as well as whitewash (bird excrement). If you find these clues, look up into the tree and you may see a saw-whet owl peering down at you.

Fairly reliable spots to find northern saw-whet owls in winter include the Morton Arboretum in northern Illinois, the Middlefork State Fish and Wildlife Areas in central Illinois, and Eldon Hazlet State Park in southern Illinois. Or join a local Audubon Society or birding club on one of their annual owl prowl trips.

Pileated Woodpecker
Dryocopus pileatus

The pileated woodpecker's loud junglelike call compels you to chase after it in the deep woods until you can find it. The largest of Illinois' woodpeckers, the 16-inch-tall, crow-sized pileated displays a bright red crest, yellow eyes, and a deep black body. The male sports a red moustache.

This woodpecker lives year-round in Illinois. It needs at least one hundred acres of mature woods with some dead or dying trees in which to breed. That kind of habitat is scarce in northeastern Illinois, so your best chance of seeing one is to hike the Illinois and Mississippi River valleys or the Shawnee National Forest in southern Illinois and listen for its call and deep, slow hammering on its favored sycamores, beeches, and tulip poplars.

The pileated hammers at the base of rotting trees to search for carpenter ants and beetle larvae. It has a long, sticky tongue that it uses to extract ants and grubs from deep inside its excavated feeding holes. After the hunt, the pileated leaves behind long, oval holes, which serve as telltale signs of its presence. Sometimes you can find pileateds on the ground pecking away at rotting logs to get to the ants within.

Pileated woodpeckers begin nesting in Illinois in April, excavating a hole up to 2 feet deep. The young fledge in about four weeks and spend the rest of the summer foraging for food with their parents.

Prothonotary Warbler

Protonotaria citrea

The prothonotary warbler symbolizes the swamp-lands of southern Illinois. Where there is stagnant water and trees, you'll often hear the loud *zweet zweet zweet zweet zweet* song of this brightly colored warbler throughout spring and summer.

The male has a plain, golden-yellow head set off by large black eyes, a greenish back, bluish wings and tail, and a yellow throat and belly. The female is a lighter version of the male.

The 6-inch-tall prothonotary is one of only two North American warblers that raises young in cavities. Tree holes will do, but so, too, will artificial cavities such as an old tin cup hanging in a barn located near water. The prothonotary won't choose nests sites near fast flowing bodies of water, but prefers the quieter, river backwaters and swamplands. Recent studies in southern Illinois show that the prothonotary readily nests in makeshift nest boxes made of milk cartons attached to trees in swamps.

In southern Illinois, the prothonotary can be ubiquitous in the proper habitat; but the farther north you go, the more difficult it is to find this species. One reliable northern Illinois spot during summer includes the McHenry Dam portion of Moraine Hills State Park, where officials have erected artificial nest boxes along the Fox River backwaters. In southern Illinois, you can search for these birds as early as late March at Cypress Creek National Wildlife Refuge and Pine Hills/LaRue Ecological Area. By September, the prothonotary has left for its Central and South American winter home.

Smith's Longspur

Calcarius pictus

Birders statewide and beyond covet a glimpse of the handsome and secretive Smith's longspur, most often seen in Illinois during March and April.

The sparrow-sized bird appears in various plumages as it migrates through the Prairie State in spring. About 7 inches tall, the breeding-plumaged Smith's longspur sports a black crown along with a golden-orange throat, breast, underparts, and collar. Its black-and-white facial pattern and its white wing spots are striking. Females and males still wearing winter plumage (shown in the photo below) show subtler colors with some faint streaking on the head and sides.

This longspur feeds on foxtail seeds among cornfields while migrating through Illinois in spring. Farmers who leave foxtail remnants in with their corn stubble over the winter instead of spraying their fields with pesticides offer feeding spots for this longspur as it travels north to breeding grounds along the Hudson Bay coast.

A ground feeder, the Smith's longspur often hides among rows of corn stubble. But sometimes a small group will take to the sky right in front of you, flashing their white outer tail feathers and giving a warbling spring song or a buzzy call.

The Illinois Ornithological Society leads a trip in April each year searching for the Smith's longspur and other migrants. Rarely if ever has a trip participant left without a good spotting-scope view of a male Smith's longspur in full breeding plumage.

Illinois' Top Ten Bird Watching Sites

Key Code

1. Illinois Beach State Park
2. Montrose Harbor and the Magic Hedge
3. Midewin National Tallgrass Prairie
4. Mississippi Palisades State Park
5. Starved Rock and Matthiessen State Parks
6. Lake Chautauqua National Wildlife Refuge
7. Carlyle Lake State Fish and Wildlife Area
8. Prairie Ridge State Natural Area and Newton Lake State Fish and Wildlife Area
9. Pine Hills/LaRue Ecological Area
10. Cypress Creek National Wildlife Refuge

Illinois Ecoregions

- DRIFTLESS AREA
- CENTRAL PLAINS
- RIVER LOWLANDS
- SHAWNEE NATIONAL FOREST

Carlyle Lake State Fish and Wildlife Area

RR 1, Box 233
Vandalia, IL 62471
(618) 425-3533

Carlyle Lake, the state's largest human-made lake, near St. Louis, Missouri, includes eighty miles of shoreline vegetation and mudflats that attract migratory shorebirds, songbirds, and waterfowl as well as winter gulls, owls, and finches. Bird here anytime for different groups of birds and the always-possible rarity.

In September, jaegers as well as Sabine's gull have been found on the lake nearly every year. Rent a boat and look for those and more common species, including ducks and geese.

In late fall and winter, hundreds of snow geese rest on the water, with fewer numbers of greater white-fronted geese and the occasional Ross's goose. For migratory songbirds, visit the Cherokee Nature Trail and Eldon Hazlet State Park, within the confines of the wildlife area.

In summer, thousands of double-crested cormorants feed and nest here; this site holds the state's largest breeding colony of these waterbirds. Eurasian collared-doves and monk parakeets hang around the Carlyle grain elevator year-round.

Cypress Creek National Wildlife Refuge

0137 Rustic Campus Drive
Ullin, IL 62992
(618) 634-2231

Designated as a wetland of international importance, this 14,000-acre site will eventually be expanded to include more than 35,000 acres of oak barrens, bottomland forests, and swamps containing large bald cypress trees that are hun-

dreds of years old. Situated between the Ohio and Mississippi rivers in southern Illinois, Cypress Creek offers a bit of a wilderness experience to bird watchers.

Those feeling less adventurous can check the Frank Bellrose Unit in spring and fall for migrating shorebirds and marsh birds and large numbers of wintering waterfowl, such as canvasback. Or you can just drive along Cache Chapel Road to look for breeding northern mockingbird, blue grosbeak, orchard oriole, and loggerhead shrike in summer.

The cypress/tupelo swamps attract prothonotary and yellow-throated warblers and northern parula to breed. Listen in spring and summer for the loud *kleeyur* call of the red-shouldered hawk at day and the chuck-will's-widow, a southern Illinois specialty, calling its name at night.

Interspersed throughout this huge refuge are grasslands that attract breeding Henslow's sparrow and bobolink as well as wintering northern harrier and short-eared owl.

Illinois Beach State Park

Lake Front Drive
Zion, IL 60099
(847) 662-4828

More than six miles of Lake Michigan shoreline and thousands of acres of oak woods, marshes, and pines comprise this state park off Sheridan Road near the Wisconsin border in Zion, Illinois. Each season presents a different scenic view and suite of birds.

The big show in fall is the raptor migration, when you can join volunteer hawk counters at the park's North Unit. The broad-winged hawks appear in September, followed by plentiful sharp-shinned hawks and fewer, but impressive numbers of merlins, peregrine falcons, and bald eagles as well as numerous red-tailed hawks.

In fall and spring, migratory songbirds including flycatchers, grosbeaks, tanagers, and dozens of species of warblers feast in the oaks and meadows. Shorebirds including sanderlings and the rarer red knot walk along Lake Michigan, searching for food.

Waterfowl such as grebes, scaup, goldeneyes, and scoters move along the shoreline in late fall, with some lingering in winter. Irruptive cold weather species such as red crossbills and red-breasted nuthatches visit the park in winter, especially in the pine stands.

More than 300 bird species have visited the park, including some real rarities such as the state's first red-cockaded woodpecker, a species listed on the federal endangered list.

Lake Chautauqua National Wildlife Refuge

19031 East County Road 2105N
Havana, IL 62644
(309) 535-2290

Lake Chautauqua National Wildlife Refuge, designated as a Western Hemisphere Shorebird Reserve, has attracted more than twenty-seven species of waterfowl and thirty species of shorebirds.

The 5,000 acres of floodplain woods, upland forest, open water, and mudflats in southwestern Illinois offer respite for tens of thousands of fall and spring migrants including pectoral sandpipers and lesser yellowlegs. Hundreds to several thousand American white pelicans also travel through the reserve. In late summer, many great egrets and fewer numbers of other heron species stop and rest at this waterbird mecca.

The best way to bird watch here is to join a group with a leader who can take you to the choice locations. The Illinois Ornithological Society offers an annual Lake Chautauqua trip at the end of

August, one of the most advantageous times to see huge concentrations of shorebirds.

Nearby Sand Ridge State Forest, just west of this refuge, is also worth checking. Oak hickory woods, pines, and sand prairie attract another suite of birds including wintering red crossbills and twenty-seven species of migratory warblers.

Midewin National Tallgrass Prairie

30071 South State Route 53
Wilmington, IL 60481
(815) 423-6370

Twenty-one native ecosystems, including oak savanna and sedge meadow, make up some 20,000 acres in the nation's first designated tallgrass prairie, located near Chicago's southernmost suburbs. The federal and state governments are working to open more and more of this former military arsenal to the public. Visitors can now camp here, as well as walk some trails.

Midewin provides habitat for 110 species of breeding birds, including some uncommon grassland species.

On an early June morning the site is alive with grassland bird song. Listen for the wolf-whistle call of the upland sandpiper, the rollicking song of the bobolink, and the insectlike song of the Henslow's sparrow.

Midewin offers good winter birding, too. Short-eared owls, rough-legged hawks, and northern harriers roost and feed here during the colder months.

Since much of this important ecosystem is still being renovated, officials schedule grassland and wetland bird tours during the breeding and migration seasons. You'll learn about the natural history and habitat needs of Midewin's birds while observing and photographing them.

Mississippi Palisades State Park
16237A Illinois Route 84
Savanna, IL 61074
(815) 273-2731

The Mississippi River and its backwater, along with mature, forested bluffs and wooded ravines, provide a scenic backdrop to the birding experience at this state park in northwestern Illinois. More than 200 species of birds migrate through this 2,500-acre park, and nearly one hundred of them remain to breed.

In winter a key attraction is the dozens of bald eagles observed flying above the bluffs or at nearby locks and dams. Also check pine stands in winter for crossbills, pine siskins, and red-breasted nuthatches. In March and April, as well as October and November, you can look for migrating waterfowl, including American white pelican, gadwall, common goldeneye, and common merganser. April, May, August, and September provide opportunities to observe migrating songbirds including thirty-four warbler species.

The north trail system offers habitat for breeding Carolina wren, yellow-billed cuckoo, wood thrush, veery, ovenbird, and scarlet tanager. Listen, and watch, too, for the boldly colored pileated woodpecker, a favorite at this park.

Montrose Harbor and the Magic Hedge
Chicago Park District
425 East McFetridge Drive
Chicago, IL 60605
(312) 747-1457

Arguably the state's best spot for migrants and rarities, Montrose Harbor and the Magic Hedge consist of a vegetated peninsula jutting into Lake Michigan. More than 325 species of birds, including some rarities such as Kirtland's warbler, have stopped here.

Some days can be quiet. But on other days when the winds are just right in spring (May) and fall (September), thousands of migrants land on the trees and shrubs to rest and forage, giving birders a spectacular show.

Volunteers and the City of Chicago have been working to restore this small but important migratory hotspot. For example, nonnative bluegrass has been replaced by taller native grasses, attracting migrating sparrows—seventeen sparrow species have been seen in one day in October.

You can reach this birding haven via Montrose Avenue. Follow Montrose east all the way to reach Lake Michigan. At the bait shop, turn right, drive about a block, park along the street, and join the other birders.

Pine Hills/LaRue Ecological Area
Shawnee National Fores
Route 45
South Harrisburg, IL 62946
(618) 253-7114

This 4,200-acre southern Illinois site proves again that the Prairie State is anything but flat. Here you'll find steep scenic bluffs overlooking the Big Muddy and Mississippi Rivers and the LaRue Swamp. Spring through early fall are ideal for birding. Spring brings an influx of migrants and early summer offers the best chance to hear and see some southern Illinois breeding specialties. Explore the steep ravines and forests to listen for the breeding worm-eating warbler, Kentucky warbler, Acadian flycatcher, wood thrush, yellow-billed cuckoo, and scarlet and summer tanagers, among many others. The campground area attracts breeding ruby-throated hummingbird, yellow-throated warbler, eastern wood-pewee, and red-eyed vireo. Also look for black vultures soaring overhead and listen for the *uh-uh* call of the fish crow, a species to be found only in extreme southern Illinois. In the LaRue Swamp bottomlands, you'll find abundant breeding wood ducks and prothonotary warblers. In late summer, look for large concentrations of herons and other wading birds.

---

⑧

Prairie Ridge State Natural Area and Newton Lake State Fish and Wildlife Area
4295 N. 100th Street
Newton, IL 62448
(618) 783-2685

This is the place to see the state-endangered greater prairie-chicken put on its fascinating courtship display. In March and April, nature lovers join guided tours to visit these state-owned lands in southeastern Illinois to watch the prairie-chickens from viewing blinds at dawn.

This 1,700-acre site of woodlands, grasslands, meadows, wetlands, and agricultural fields also attracts other rare species to breed, including loggerhead shrike, northern harrier, short-eared owl, and Henslow's sparrow.

Year-round look for northern mockingbirds, and in winter, watch for rough-legged hawks. In winter, you might also enjoy watching the "changing of the guard" at dusk as northern harriers finish feeding for the day while short-eared owls move in on their territory to begin the nighttime hunt.

In spring and summer you can find plenty of wading birds in the marshes, and at the large cooling lake, ducks and other migratory waterfowl abound.

At least 250 bird species have been documented here. Access is restricted in some places, so check with the office first to learn where you can go to get the best birding experience.

Starved Rock and Matthiessen State Parks
Box 509
Utica, IL 61373
(815) 667-4726

Starved Rock in northern Illinois proves the state is not all flat. Here you'll watch birds as you enjoy stream-fed canyons, waterfalls, and 125-foot-tall wooded bluffs. These habitats, as well as the restored grasslands nearby, have attracted more than 225 bird species.

Migratory waterfowl and songbirds visit the parks in spring and fall, especially in the woods around Lone Pine Shelter. American white pelicans stop along the Illinois River in spring and fall. In winter, bald eagles and unusual gull species feed at the nearby Army Corps Visitor Center and Lock and Dam. The Starved Rock Audubon Society sponsors a free Bald Eagle Days weekend every January.

In spring and summer, visit the bottomland woods to search for pileated woodpecker, prothonotary warbler, Louisiana waterthrush, Acadian flycatcher, barred owl, and Carolina wren, which breed in the park.

You can stay at the Starved Rock Lodge and Conference Center, but make reservations early—this is the state's most popular park.

Resources for Illinois Bird Watchers

The Illinois Ornithological Society
P.O. Box 931
Lake Forest, IL 60045
www.illinoisbirds.org

The Illinois Audubon Society
425B North Gilbert Street
Danville, IL 61832
www.illinoisaudubon.org

The Nature Conservancy in Illinois
http://nature.org/wherewework/north
america/states/illinois
The Conservancy has protected more than
760,000 acres of critical natural lands in Illinois.

Illinois and Chicago Net-Birding Website
http://home.xnet.com/~ugeiser/Birds/
Birding.html
This site contains many resources on local bird
clubs, bird sightings, Christmas Bird Count compilers, Spring Bird Count compilers, and more.

Illinois Department of Natural Resources
http://dnr.state.il.us/lands/education/
birding_in_illinois

Illinois Bureau of Tourism
www.enjoyillinois.com

National Wildlife Refuges
http://midwest.fws.gov/maps/illinois.htm

Statewide Birding List Serve
http://groups.yahoo.com/group/ILbirds/
Illinois Birders Exchanging Thoughts (IBET),
the Illinois birding listserve on the Web.

Regional Bird Clubs and Societies
Please note: Check Illinois Audubon Society
and Illinois Ornithological Society Websites for
a more inclusive list.

Bird Conservation Network
www.bcnbirds.org

Chicago Audubon Society
www.chicagoaudubon.org

Chicago Ornithological Society
www.chicagobirder.org

Du Page Birding Club
www.dupagebirding.org

Evanston North Shore Bird Club
www.ensbc.org

Illinois Audubon Society
www.illinoisaudubon.org

Webster Groves Nature Study Society
www.wgnss.org

Books
De Vore, S., Bailey, S. D., and Kennedy, G. 2004.
Birds of Illinois. Edmonton, AB, Canada: Lone
Pine Publishing.

De Vore, S. 2000. *Birding Illinois*. Guilford, CT:
Falcon Press.

Carpenter, L., and Greenberg, J. 1999. *A Birder's
Guide to the Chicago Region*. Dekalb, IL:
Northern Illinois University Press.

Newman, Debbie Scott. 2003. *Creating Habitats
and Homes for Illinois Wildlife*. Springfield, IL:
Illinois Department of Natural Resources
and University of Illinois. (Note: limited
availability; out of print.)

Getting Started in Bird Watching

Bird watching, or birding, is one of North America's fastest-growing and most popular hobbies. According to a recent survey by the U.S. Fish & Wildlife Service, there are as many as 44 million bird watchers in the United States. Back in 1978, when my family began publishing Bird Watcher's Digest in our living room, bird watching was still considered a bit odd. The image many people associated with bird watching was Miss Jane Hathaway of The Beverly Hillbillies. Fortunately, that stereotype is long gone now, and our culture has come to embrace bird watching as an enriching, exciting pursuit—one that can be done with little expense and enjoyed almost anywhere at any time.

Why Do We Watch Birds?

Birds have inspired humans for thousands of years. Birds can fly—something we humans have mastered only in the past 100 years. Birds have brilliant plumage, and some even change their colors seasonally. Birds are master musicians, singing beautiful and complex songs. They possess impressive physical abilities—hovering, flying at high speeds, and withstanding extreme weather conditions, as well as the rigors of long migration flights. Birds also have behav-

iors to which we can relate, such as intense courtship displays, devotion to their mates, and the enormous investment of effort spent in raising their young. Sound familiar? In short, birds are a vivid expression of life, and we admire them because they inspire us. This makes us want to know them better and to bring them closer to us. We accomplish this by attracting them to our backyards and gardens, and by using optics to see them more clearly in an "up close and personal" way.

Early Bird Study

Before the advent of modern optics that help us view birds more closely, humans used a shotgun approach to bird watching. Literally. Famed ornithologist and bird artist John James Audubon was the first European to document many of the North American bird species in the early 1800s. He did so by shooting every unfamiliar bird he encountered. Having a bird in the hand allowed him to study it closely and draw it accurately. This was an excellent method of learning a lot about birds quickly, but it was rather hard on the birds. This method of bird study continued largely unchecked until the

Millions of Americans enjoy bird watching.

early 1900s, when the effects of market hunting on birds became unhappily apparent. In 1934, a young bird enthusiast and artist named Roger Tory Peterson published *A Field Guide to the Birds*, with a system of arrows showing key field marks on the plumage of each species. This enabled a person to identify a bird from a distance, with or without the aid of magnifying optics. Modern bird watching was born, and it was no longer necessary to shoot birds in order to positively identify them. The era of shotgun ornithology was over.

Modern Bird Watching

Bird watching today is about seeing or hearing birds and then using these clues to identify them. To reach this identification, we use two important tools of the bird-watching trade: binoculars and a field guide. The binoculars (or perhaps a *spotting scope*, which is a telescope especially designed for nature watching) help you to get a closer, clearer look at the bird. The field guide helps you interpret what you see so that you can identify the bird species.

I like to say that we live in the golden era of bird watching. When I started birding more than 35 years ago, feeders, seed, birdhouses, and other supplies were hard to come by—we had to make our own. Now they are available in almost any store. We can buy a field guide or a book like the one you're holding in any bookstore. We can try out optics at camera stores, outdoor suppliers, and at birding festivals. We can learn about birds in special bird courses, on the Internet, in magazines, or from CD-ROMs, DVDs, and videos. We can join a local or state bird club and meet new bird-watching friends. We can take birding tours to far-off places.

Select binoculars that feel good in your hands and are easy to use.

There's never been a better time to become a bird watcher. So let's get started!

Basic Gear

If you're just starting out as a birder, you may need to acquire the basic tools—binoculars and a field guide.

Binoculars

You may be able to borrow optics from a friend or family member, but if your interest takes off, you'll certainly want to have your own binoculars to use anytime you wish. Fortunately, a decent pair of binoculars can be purchased for less than $100, and some really nice binoculars can be found used on the Internet or through a local bird club for just a bit more. The magnification powers that are commonly used for bird watching are 7x, 8x, and 10x. This is always the first number listed in the binoculars' description, as in 8x40. The second number refers to the size of the objective lens (the big end) of the binocular. The bigger the second number, the brighter the view presented to your eye. In general, for bird-watching binoculars the first number should be between 7x and 10x, and the second number should be between 30 and 45.

Try to find binoculars that are easy and comfortable to use. Make sure they focus easily, giving you a clear image, and that they are comfortable to hold (not too large or heavy) and fit your eye spacing. Every set of eyes is different, so don't settle for binoculars that just don't feel right. The perfect pair of binoculars for you should feel like a natural extension of your hands and eyes. Over time you will become adept at using your optics and, with a little practice, you'll be operating them like a pro.

Field Guide

When choosing a field guide, you'll need to decide what type of birding you'll be doing and where you plan to do it. If nearly all of your bird watching will be done at home, you might want to get a basic field guide to the backyard birds of your region, or at least a field guide that limits its scope to your half of the continent. Many field guides are offered in eastern (east of the Rocky Mountains) and western (from the

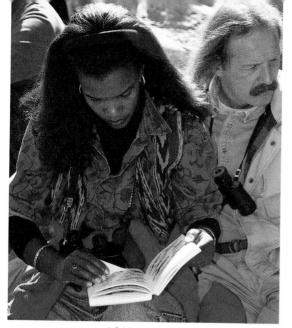
A field guide is one of birding's essential tools.

Rockies west) versions. These geographically limited formats include only those birds that are commonly found in that part of the continent, rather than continent-wide guides that include more than 800 North American bird species. Choose a field guide that is appropriate for you, and you'll save a lot of searching time—time that can be better spent looking at birds!

It Starts at Home

Most bird watchers like to start out at home, and this usually means getting to know the birds in your backyard. A great way to enhance the diversity of birds in your yard is to set up a simple feeding station. Even a single feeder with the proper food can bring half a dozen or more unfamiliar bird species into your yard. And it's these encounters with new and interesting birds that make bird watching so enjoyable.

Start your feeding station with a feeder geared to the birds that are already in your backyard or garden. For most of us this will mean a tube or hopper feeder filled with sunflower seeds. Place the feeder in a location that offers you a clear view of bird activity, but also offers the birds some nearby cover in the form of a hedge, shrubs, or brush pile into which the birds can fly when a predator approaches. I always set our feeding stations up opposite our kitchen or living room windows because these are the rooms in which we spend most of our daylight hours,

and because these rooms have the best windows for bird watching. We'll discuss bird feeding and attracting in greater detail in the next section.

Once you've got a basic feeder set up outside, you'll need to get yourself set up inside your house. You've probably already selected the best location for viewing your feeder. Next you should select a safe place to store your binoculars and field guide—somewhere that is easily accessible to you when you suddenly spot a new bird in your backyard. At our house we keep binoculars hanging on pegs right next to our kitchen windows. This keeps them handy for use in checking the feeders or for heading out for a walk around our farm.

Keeping Your Bird List

Most bird watchers enjoy keeping a list of their sightings. This can take the form of a written list, notations inside your field guide next to each species' account, or in a special journal meant for just such a purpose. There are even software programs available to help you keep your list on your computer. In birding, the most common list is the *life list*. A life list is a list of all the birds you've seen at least once in your life. Let's say you noticed a bright, black-and-orange bird in your backyard willow tree one morning, then keyed it out in your field guide to be a male Baltimore oriole. This is a species you'd never seen before, and now you can put it on your life list. List keeping can be done at any level of involvement, so keep the list or lists that you enjoy. I like to keep a property list of all the species we've seen at least once on our 80-acre farm. Currently, that list is at 181 species, but I'm always watching for something new to show up. I also update my North American life list a couple of times a year, after I've seen a new bird species.

Bird Watching Afield

Sooner or later you may want to expand your bird-watching horizons beyond your backyard bird feeders. Birding afield—away from your own home—can be a wonderfully exhilarating experience. Many beginning bird watchers are shy about venturing forth, afraid that their inexperience will prove embarrassing, but there's really no reason to feel this way. The best way to begin

Ten Tips for Beginning Bird Watchers

1. Get a decent pair of binoculars, ones that are easy for you to use and hold steady.

2. Find a field guide to the birds of your region (many guides are divided into eastern and western editions). Guides that cover all the birds of North America contain many birds species uncommon or entirely absent from your area. You can always upgrade to a continent-wide guide later.

3. Set up a basic feeding station in your yard or garden.

4. Start with your backyard birds. They are the easiest to see, and you can become familiar with them fairly quickly.

5. Practice your identification skills. Starting with a common bird species, note the most obvious visual features of the bird (color, size, shape, and patterns in the plumage). These features are known as field marks and will be helpful clues to the bird's identity.

6. Notice the bird's behavior. Many birds can be identified by their behavior—woodpeckers peck on wood, kingfishers dive for small fish, and swallows are known for their graceful flight.

7. Listen to the bird's sounds. Bird song is a vital component to birding. Learning bird songs and sounds takes a bit of practice, but many birds make it pretty easy for us. For example, chickadees and whip-poor-wills (among others) call out their names. The Resources section of this book contains a listing of tools to help you to learn bird songs.

8. Look at the bird, not at the book. When you see an unfamiliar bird, avoid the temptation to put down your binoculars and begin searching for the bird in your field guide. Instead, watch the bird carefully for as long as it is present—or until you feel certain that you have noted its most important field marks. Then look at your field guide. Birds have wings, and they tend to use them. Your field guide will still be with you long after the bird has gone, so take advantage of every moment to watch an unfamiliar bird while it is present.

9. Take notes. No one can be expected to remember every field mark and description of a bird. But you can help your memory and accelerate your learning by taking notes on the birds you see. These notes can be written in a small pocket notebook, in the margins of your field guide, or even in the back of this book.

10. Venture beyond the backyard and find other bird watchers in your area. The bird watching you'll experience beyond your backyard will be enriching, especially if it leads not only to new birds, but also to new birding friends. Ask a local nature center or wildlife refuge about bird clubs in your region. Your state ornithological organization or natural resources division may also be helpful. Bird watching with other birders can be the most enjoyable of all.

birding away from the backyard is to connect with other local bird watchers via your local bird club. Most parts of North America have local or regional bird clubs, and most of these clubs offer regular field trips. Bird watchers are among the friendliest people on the planet, and every bird club is happy to welcome new prospective members. If you don't know how to find a local bird club, ask your friends and neighbors if they know any bird watchers, check the telephone directory, search the Internet, or ask at your area parks, nature centers, and wild bird stores.

Getting out in the field with more experienced bird watchers is the fastest way to improve your skills. Don't be afraid to ask questions ("How did you know that was an indigo bunting?"). Don't worry if you begin to feel overwhelmed by the volume of new information—all new bird watchers experience this. When it happens, relax and take some time to simply watch. In time you'll be identifying birds and looking forward to new challenges and new birds.

Feeding and Housing

irds need four basic things to live: food, water for drinking and bathing, a safe place to roost, and a safe place to nest. These vital elements are actually quite easy for you to offer to birds, even if your backyard is small.

Food

Bird feeding is a good place to start your bird-attracting efforts. It's wise to begin with a single feeder, such as a hopper feeder or tube feeder filled with black-oil sunflower seeds. The black-oil sunflower seed is the most common type of sunflower seed available, because it's the seed type that most of our feeder birds can readily eat. Think of it as the hamburger of the bird world. The black-oil sunflower seed has a thin shell (easy for seed-eating birds to crack) and a large, meaty seed kernel inside. As you can see from the seed preference chart on page 147, many backyard bird species eat sunflower seeds.

Other excellent foods for birds include: mixed seed (a blend that normally includes millet,

milo, cracked corn, and other seeds), sunflower bits (shells removed), peanuts (best offered unsalted and without the shell), suet or suet cakes, cracked corn, thistle seed (also known as Niger or nyjer seed), safflower seed, nectar (for hummingbirds), mealworms, fruits, and berries. Bird feeding varies from region to region—don't be afraid to experiment with new feeders or food. Birds will vote with their bills and stomachs and will let you know their preferences

Eating the food at feeders is not the only way birds find sustenance. A backyard or garden that includes natural food sources for birds—such as seed-producing flowering plants and fruit-bearing trees and shrubs—will further enhance its attractiveness to birds. In fact, it's often the natural features of a backyard habitat that attract the birds' attention rather than the bird feeders. Read the Bird-Friendly Plants section on page 162 for more specific suggestions.

Feeder Types

It's important to match the foods and feeders to each other, as well as to the birds you wish to attract. Sunflower seed works in a wide variety of feeders, including tube, hopper, platform, and satellite or excluder feeders (that permit small birds to feed, but exclude larger birds), as well as for ground feeding. Mixed seed does not work as well in tube or hopper feeders for a couple of reasons. First of all, the birds that prefer mixed seed tend to be ground feeders, so it's less natural for them to go to an elevated feeder for food. Secondly, elevated feeder designs (such as tubes or hoppers) are built to dole out seed as it is eaten and the smaller size of most mixed seed kernels causes excess spillage. Mixed seed works best when offered on a platform feeder or when scattered on the ground.

Pictured from the top down:
Black-oil sunflower seed, peanuts, mixed seed, and cracked corn.

A fruit feeder will attract orioles, tanagers, and other fruit feeders.

When purchasing your feeders and foods, make sure they will work effectively with each other. Specialty foods such as suet, peanuts, thistle (Niger), mealworms, fruit, and nectar require specific feeders for the best results for you and the birds. The Food and Feeder Chart on page 147 is a great place to start.

Your Feeding Station

Place your feeding station in a spot that is useful and attractive to you and the birds. When we moved into our farmhouse, we looked out all the windows before choosing a spot for our feeding station. You may want to do the same thing. After all, the whole point of bird feeding is to be able to see and enjoy the birds. From the birds' perspective, your feeders should be placed adjacent to cover—a place they can leave from and retreat to safely and quickly if a predator appears. This cover can be a woodland edge, brushy area or brush pile, hedges or shrubs, or even a weedy fencerow. If your yard is mostly lawn, consider creating a small island of cover near your feeding station. This will greatly enhance the feeders' appeal to birds.

Be patient. You've spent the money and effort to put up feeders, but don't expect immediate dividends. Birds are creatures of habit, and it may take a few days or even a few weeks before they recognize your offering as a source of food. Sooner or later, a curious chickadee, finch, or sparrow will key into the food source, and the word will spread along the local bird "grapevine."

Housing for Birds

Almost every bird species builds or uses some type of nest to produce and rear its young. However, only a small fraction of our birds use nest boxes provided by humans. Birds that use next boxes or birdhouses are called *cavity nesters*, because they prefer to nest inside an enclosed space, such as hole excavated in a tree, as many woodpeckers do. Nest boxes simulate a natural cavity, but they have the added advantage (for humans) of our being able to place them in a convenient spot. To the birds' advantage, we can protect the nest box from predators, bad weather, and other problems.

Being a landlord to the birds is a thrilling experience. You are treated to an intimate peek inside the lives of your "tenants" and rewarded with the presence of their offspring, if nesting is successful. To help ensure the nesting success of your birds you need to provide the proper housing in an appropriate setting, and you should monitor the housing during the nesting season.

The Right Housing

Two factors are key to providing the right nest box for your birds: the size of the housing and

Male northern cardinals eat sunflower seed from a hopper-style feeder.

Exterior latex stain helps prolong the life of a birdhouse and protects the birds inside from the weather.

the size of the entry hole. Not all cavity nesters are picky about the interior dimensions of the cavity, except when it is excessively big or small. But the size of the entry hole is important because it can effectively limit the entrance of large, aggressive nest competitors, predators, and inclement weather. For example, an entry hole with a diameter of 1½ inches on a bluebird nest box will permit entry by bluebirds and many smaller birds, including chickadees, titmice, nuthatches, wrens, and tree swallows. But this same size keeps European starlings out and prevents them from usurping the box.

Use the Nest Box Chart (page 148) to help you determine the appropriate nest box details for your backyard birds. Whether you build your own birdhouses or buy them at your local wild bird products supplier, see page 40 for a few tips for "landlords" that you will want to consider.

An Appropriate Setting

Place your nest boxes where they will be most likely to be found and used by birds. Bluebirds and swallows prefer nest sites in the middle of large, open, grassy areas. Wrens, chickadees, nuthatches, flycatchers, woodpeckers, and other woodland birds prefer sites that are in or adjacent to woodlands. Robins, phoebes, Carolina wrens, barn swallows, and purple martins prefer to nest near human

dwellings, perhaps for the protection from predators that we provide.

Monitoring Your Nest Boxes

By taking a weekly peek inside your nest boxes, you will stay abreast of your tenants' activities, and you'll be able to help them raise their families successfully. During most of the year, your birdhouses will appear to be empty. This does not mean that the boxes are going unused. In fact, many birds use nest boxes during the win-

An example of a pole-mounted predator baffle below a bluebird nest box.

Nest Box Tips for Landlords

- Do build or buy sturdily constructed nest boxes that are built from untreated wood (or another weatherproof material) with walls that are at least 3/4 inch thick. See page 157 for a simple bird house plan.
- Do not stain or paint the interior of the box. Stain or paint on the box exterior will help the box last longer. Light colors reflect sunlight and keep box interiors from getting too hot.
- Perches by the entry hole are unnecessary and may actually encourage competitors and predators.
- The box roof should be slanted and extend out several inches over the entry hole to keep out the weather.
- Nest boxes should have an access door for monitoring. Access doors that swing upward to open on the side or front of the box are easiest to use and safest for birds.
- The box should have holes for ventilation at the top of the vertical walls. Drainage holes in the floor will permit excess moisture to escape.
- Mount boxes on poles away from nearby trees and structures.
- Place a pole-mounted predator baffle beneath the nest box to keep snakes and mammals from gaining access to the nest.

ter months as nighttime roosts. A loose feather, insect parts, berry seeds, or a few droppings are classic evidence of roosting activity.

During breeding season, your regular visits will help you know when nest building begins and when eggs are laid, and will give you an idea about how soon the eggs will hatch and the babies leave the nest. Bird nests are vulnerable

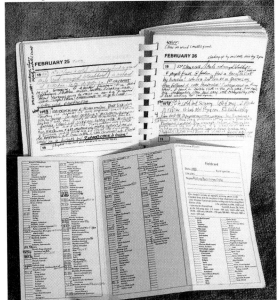

Top: A daily bird notes diary. Bottom: A checklist for sightings.

to a variety of dangers, including harsh weather and predators such as cats, raccoons, snakes, and even birds, as well as nest-site competitors. These dangers are greatly reduced when nest boxes are monitored because the birds' landlord (you) can take steps to protect the nest.

On my trips to check each of our 10 nest boxes, I keep a small notebook with me to record my observations. Each nest box has its own name and number in my notebook, along with the date of each visit and a note about what I've found. When nesting starts in a box I note the date, what materials are used to construct the nest, and the date that the first egg was laid. Once the clutch is complete and the female begins incubating the eggs, I can estimate the hatching date. This usually takes about 14 days. Another 14 to 21 days later, I know the young birds will be ready to leave the nest.

Peeking Inside
When checking a nest box, approach quietly. During the breeding season, you may scare the female off the nest temporarily when you open the box. Don't worry. If you keep your visit brief, she'll be back to the nest soon. I visit nest boxes

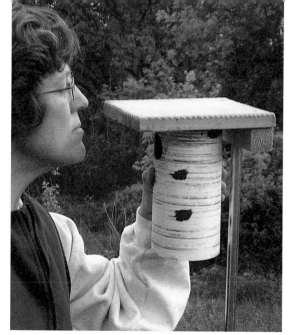
Checking the nest box.

in the late morning on sunny days, when the adult birds are likely to be away finding food. I open the box, quickly count the eggs or young, close the box and move away before pausing to record my notes. It's a myth that opening a nest box or checking the young will cause the adults to abandon the nest. In fact, over time many cavity-nesting birds that use nest boxes grow quite accustomed to regular visits.

One final note on nest monitoring. As fledging time approaches for the young birds—normally about two weeks after the eggs hatch—you should curtail your box visits to avoid causing a premature nest departure.

When Things Go Wrong

You open your nest box, and you find broken or missing eggs and the nest in disarray. What happened? The bad news is: A predator has raided your nest, and, in the natural order of things, the eggs or nestlings have been eaten. The good news: There are steps that you can take to avoid such an event in the future.

It's important to protect your nest boxes so predators cannot easily access them. For many landlords the best option is to mount the housing on galvanized metal poles with pole-mounted predator baffles installed beneath the boxes. An added advantage to pole-mounting (as opposed to mounting on a fencepost or tree) is

that the housing can be moved to a new location fairly easily.

Follow the steps outlined on page 148 for nest box placement, mounting, and baffling. You may also wish to consult one of the publications listed in the Resources section for specific strategies for dealing with nest box predators and pests.

Creating Bird Habitat

To make your backyard or garden a haven for birds, all you need to do is think like a bird. Look around your yard. Where is the food, the water? Where are the places to hide from predators or to shelter in bad weather? Is nesting habitat available?

An ideal bird habitat can be created in a tiny, urban garden just as it can be created in a large, rural setting. Birds love varied habitats; so when you are planning your yard, landscape, or gardens, resist the urge to plant matching plants in straight lines. Instead, let your imagination go wild—literally. Give the edges of beds or gardens natural curves. Scatter trees, shrubs, and vines in clumps or islands around the area you are designing. On the edges of your property, try to create natural transitions from the grass of your yard to the tops of your trees with short- and medium-height plants that provide food and shelter for birds.

Edible Habitat

Birds have evolved over millions of years right alongside the native plants with which they share the planet. These same native plants can work for you in your bird-friendly habitat plan. Your local nursery, nature center, or native plant society should be able to recommend plant species that are native to your region. Native plants not only provide food in the form of fruits and nuts, but birds may also eat the plants' buds, leaves, nectar, and sap, as well as the insects that live on the plants. When choosing your native plants, select a wide variety of species, sizes, shapes, and seasonality. Planting only one or two plant species will minimize the number of birds your habitat will attract. Consult the Bird-Friendly Plants chart on page 162 for suggested plant families.

Water

Birds need water all year long for drinking and bathing. The best way to offer water to birds is in a shallow birdbath with about 2 inches of water in it. I've always had good luck attracting birds to water in my yard when the bath was on or near the ground and when the water had some motion to it.

The sight and sound of moving water are highly attractive to birds. You can add motion to any birdbath or water feature with a mister, dripper, or a recirculating pump. Misters and drippers attach to your garden hose and let out a small amount of water that disturbs the surface of the bath; these ripples are eye-catchingly attractive to birds. Recirculating pumps, which require electricity, recycle the water from the main bath through a pump and filter, and then back to the bath. In winter, add a small, electric birdbath heater to keep the water open and available to birds.

If you already have a water garden or water feature, consider making part of it accessible to birds. This can be accomplished by placing a flat rock shelf on or near the water's surface, or by allowing recirculating water to trickle over an exposed flat rock. Our backyard water garden is ringed with American goldfinches almost every day all year-round. They use a large, flat piece of slate that gets splashed by our small waterfall as a place to grab a quick drink.

A male scarlet tanager bathes in a water feature.

Water is a universal attractant for birds—species that might otherwise never visit your yard, feeders, or birdhouses will visit a clean and alluring birdbath or water feature.

Shelter

When they need to rest, hide from danger, or get out of the weather, birds seek deep cover in the form of thick vegetation, vine tangles, dense evergreens, or brushy areas. These bits of habitat may not be first on a landscaper's list of backyard beautifying accents, but to a bird they are vital havens. Even a brush pile in a corner of your property can offer enough shelter during a storm to help sparrows, cardinals, and other backyard birds survive.

Look at your bird habitat, and observe where the birds go just before a storm or at dusk. These are the places in which they shelter themselves. Consider adding more such habitat, and your yard will be even more attractive to birds.

Places to Nest

The majority of North American birds do not use nest boxes. Most build their nests in places that are hidden from view—in trees, bushes, or in secluded spots on or near the ground. Birds—such as phoebes, barn swallows, and Carolina wrens—are bold enough to build nests on porch ledges, in garages, and in barns. House finches and mourning doves are known for building their nests in hanging flower baskets, but these sites won't satisfy most of our birds.

The places where birds choose to nest are similar to the places they choose to roost and shelter—in thick vegetation and deep cover out of view of passing predators. In providing a nesting habitat for birds, the key is diversity. As you read through the species profiles in this book, notice the habitat features that each species prefers. Then factor this information into your habitat plans.

Helping Other Nesting Birds

There are many things you can do to help non-cavity nesters—all those birds that build

Allow lawn edges to grow wild; bird species thrive in transition or edge habitat.

open-cup nests and will never use one of our nest boxes. The most important thing is to offer variety in your landscaping or backyard habitat. A backyard that is mostly lawn with a tree or two staked out in the middle will not be nearly as appealing as a yard featuring a variety of plant types, including grasses, perennial plants, shrubs, bushes, trees, and other natural elements. The more your landscape looks like nature, the more attractive it will be for birds.

Places for You

As you plan for your bird-friendly habitat, you'll also want to incorporate elements that you can use and enjoy, such as a water garden, benches, shady relaxation spots, and perhaps a location for your feeding station. Remember, the whole point of attracting birds to your property is so that you can enjoy them while they enjoy your offerings. Plan with your favorite viewing spots in mind, and you'll be rewarded with year-round free (and natural) entertainment.

Tips for Helping Nesting Birds

- Consider letting a portion of your yard grow up into a weedy patch for sparrows, finches, and towhees to enjoy.
- Offer a basket of nesting material, such as 2- to 3-inch pieces of natural fibers (yarn, pet or human hair, stiff dry grasses, and the like).
- Keep pets, especially cats, from roaming freely in your yard during nesting season.
- Try to limit or eliminate the use of lawn and garden chemicals in and around the parts of your property being used by nesting birds.
- Trim hedges, shrubs, and trees in early spring before nesting season, or in late fall, after nesting season. This way you'll avoid disturbing nesting birds, which are often so secretive that you are unaware of the nest until you stumble onto it.

How to Use This Book

Hello! *and welcome to the fun, friendly, and exciting word of bird watching. Birding is America's fastest-growing hobby and requires little more than some basic tools—binoculars and a field guide—and an interest in the fascinating world of birds. The primary purpose of this book is to start you down the path to a greater understanding and enjoyment of this engaging pastime. To that end, we've chosen the content carefully to provide you, the reader, with the ideal blend of information and detail on many of the most commonly encountered birds of your state. If we've done our job right, this will* not *be the last bird book you buy.*

At the heart of this book is a set of profiles of your state's 100 most commonly encountered birds. These are the birds that you're most likely to see and hear regularly. *But remember*—birds have wings and they tend to use them, so you'll certainly see and hear many other species as your bird-watching experience grows. For this reason we suggest that you augment this book with a good field guide to help you identify those unfamiliar species you encounter.

Each species profile features a beautiful photograph of the bird, typically an adult male in breeding plumage since this is the most identifiable version of many birds. Please note that adult females, winter-plumage adults, and young birds can look very different. We describe these plumage differences in the profile, but space constraints prevent us from showing images of all these variations. Once again, a good field guide (see the Resources section on page 166 for suggestions) will be useful in identifying any mystery birds you encounter.

We cover all the interesting and useful natural history information about each of the 100 birds—appearance, sounds, behavior, nesting, feeding, range, and migration—and we even tell you where to go and what to do in order to encounter a particular bird in the "Backyard and Beyond" section.

The profiles in the main body of the book are organized *taxonomically*—this means that related species are grouped by bird family using the same general order that ornithologists use to list and classify birds. See the facing page to find a convenient alphabetic listing. In the 100 species profiles, we've used a series of symbols to provide instant insight into the lives of these birds. Here is a key to what each of these icons represents:

 Will use a birdhouse for nesting or roosting.

 Can be attracted to bird feeders.

 Will visit birdbaths or water features for bathing and drinking.

 Has a song or call and can be identified by its vocalizations or sounds.

 A migrant species, seen primarily during spring or fall migration.

Also, turn to pages 7 through 32 to read more about the natural history and ecology of your state and its bird life. We focus on bird watching by season—the specific birds you're likely to encounter and how to attract them—by feeding and by offering the appropriate bird-friendly habitat. This section also describes the many migrants that pass through in spring and fall. As an extra bonus, we briefly describe the "Ten Must-See Birds" for your state. We also include a summary of the "Ten Best Bird-Watching Spots."

At the end of this book you will find a resources list for bird watching (feeding and planting charts, answers to frequently asked questions, birdhouse plans, bird books, field and audio guides, and more) to help you enjoy this hobby more.

Happy bird watching!

—*Bill Thompson, III*

100 Most Commonly Encountered Birds

Pied-billed Grebe

Podilymbus podiceps

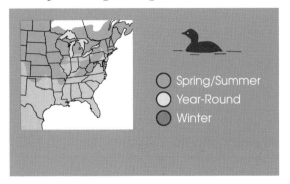

○ Spring/Summer
○ Year-Round
○ Winter

Most North American grebes either breed far to the north or in the West, but the stocky little pied-billed grebe also breeds through much of the eastern United States. You can find this frequent diver in varied wetlands, including ponds, lakes, and marshes that have a thick cover of cattails or other vegetation. Pied-billed grebes most often are seen singly or in twos or threes. They don't often vocalize, except during breeding season when they call out a series of penetrating, barking notes.

All About

In general, pied-billed grebes occur in sheltered, lush wetlands. This bird is smallish but has a big head, stocky neck, and a thick bill that differs from the more pointed bills of horned and eared grebes. During breeding season, the bill (which is pale in winter) becomes distinctively adorned with a thick, black band that wraps around an otherwise horn-colored bill. Breeding pied-billed grebes also have black throats, but at other times their soft-brown necks and bodies contrast with whitish throats and puffy, whitish undertails.

Habitat & Range

Pied-billed grebes nest in well-vegetated lakes, ponds, and pockets of marsh. You may find them in brackish water in winter, but they prefer freshwater habitats. The numbers of pied-billed grebes dwindle in the North and swell in the

South during winter and migration, when many northern nesters abandon their frigid habitats for warmer, more productive wintering areas.

Feeding

Pied-billed grebes are frequently seen diving for food or diving to evade predators or observers. Their wide-lobed feet push them beneath the water's surface in search of small fish, amphibians, and a wide variety of aquatic invertebrates, including crayfish and insects. They also eat some plant matter.

Nesting

Mates call to each other as part of their courtship. Together, they build a nest that is basically a mound of matted vegetation. This mound is fastened to nearby plants and may float or rise from the shallows. The female lays four to six eggs, with the pair sharing the three-week incubation period. Both parents feed the young, which can fly by two months of age.

Backyard & Beyond

Scan marsh edges and ponds to find pied-billed grebes; they are rarely spotted in flight. They have a tendency to appear as if by magic and to disappear just as fast, often leaving a ring of ripples on the water's surface as the only evidence of their presence.

Double-crested Cormorant

Phalacrocorax auritus

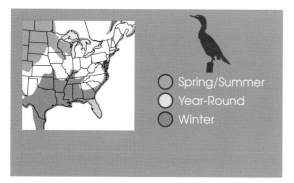

○ Spring/Summer
○ Year-Round
○ Winter

○ ften, the somewhat snakelike black neck and head is all that betrays the presence of a swimming double-crested cormorant. They are most numerous during the breeding season in spring and summer. In fall, long lines of cormorants can be seen migrating southward. A few may linger all winter in ice-free waters. Double-crested cormorants declined earlier in the twentieth century due to disturbance and hunting at nesting grounds, followed by DDT and other pesticide contamination. Protection, wetland conservation, and the DDT ban have helped these birds recover.

All About

With practice, birders can easily distinguish a distant, flying double-crested cormorant from a pelican, goose, heron, or other large bird by its all-dark form, thick and somewhat wavy neck, longish tail, and slow wingbeats. The cormorant's bright orange throat, bill, and lores stand out on its otherwise black body. Even its heavy webbed feet are blackish. Immatures are dull brown with whitish necks and chests. The double-crested cormorant is named for its pair of head crest plumes that are most visible during breeding season and rarely seen otherwise.

Habitat & Range

Most double-crested cormorant populations are migratory, and these birds turn up at rivers, marshes, swamps, large lakes, bays, and along the coast. Because they travel widely during the day, don't be surprised to see cormorants flying over inland habitats in loose formation. Double-crested cormorants breed in western Alaska, central Canada, and down both coasts of the United States; they winter along the coast and well inland throughout the eastern United States.

Feeding

Double-crested cormorants are very adaptable, seeking a wide variety of fish, and also crustaceans, amphibians, and other aquatic animals. Their webbed feet propel them under water after their aquatic prey, and much of their feeding is done not far beneath the surface.

Nesting

Double-crested cormorants nest in colonies in trees, on cliffs, and on islands. Females build much of the platform nest, while males provide the many sticks and other materials. Females usually lay three or four eggs, which both parents incubate for about a month. Young leave the nest 21 to 30 days after hatching, but are not fully on their own until after two months.

Backyard & Beyond

Watch for the "periscope" heads of partially submerged cormorants and try not to confuse them with those of the more dagger-billed loons, which have slimmer, straighter bills and at least some light coloration on the head. After long swims, cormorants often sun themselves on dead trees and shorelines, holding out their wings to dry.

Common Loop

Gavia immer

Spring/Summer
Year-Round
Winter

The common loon is one of the best-known North American water birds. Its high yodeling cry echoes across large, remote northern lakes evoking unspoiled wilderness to the listener. Once heard, the loon's wailing tremolo is hard to forget.

All About

The common loon is a large, long diving bird that rides low in the water. In profile the loon's massive head and bill help to separate it visually from other waterfowl. In breeding plumage it has a black head, bill, and neck band. Its throat and breast are white and its back is checkered in black and white; this nondescript plumage may render the loon unfamiliar to some bird watchers. In winter plumage the common loon is a dull gray-and-white. In flight the common loon appears dark above, white below.

Habitat & Range

Common loons breed on remote lakes as far north as the treeless tundra and as far south as New England and northern Michigan, Wisconsin, and Minnesota. In recent decades, the species has declined due to human disturbance, pollution, and habitat loss. Though most common loons spend winter on the ocean, some linger on large inland rivers, lakes, and reservoirs. They can be encountered on large bodies of water during spring or fall migration; huge concentrations occur on protected bays in the Great Lakes.

Feeding

A foraging common loon swims along with its head underwater scanning for schools of small fish, its primary food. It catches fish by diving in pursuit, powered by strong webbed feet. Once caught in the loon's bill a fish cannot escape. The loon's tongue and the roof of its mouth have small, inward-pointing barbules that enhance its grip. Fish are swallowed headfirst. Other foods include small crustaceans and aquatic plant matter.

Nesting

Common loons nest on remote lakes where both mates build a mound of aquatic plant matter for their one or two eggs on land but near the water. Both birds share the incubation duties, which can last a month. After hatching, young loons may leave the nest within a day and are able to swim and dive immediately, but they may hitch a ride on a parent's back. They are able to fly after about 10 weeks, at which point they become independent from the parents.

Backyard & Beyond

Loons are partial to large bodies of water because they need the "runway" space for take-off and landing. They are heavy-bodied birds that must run across the water's surface to build up speed for flight. Loons spend much of the non-breeding season alone, so scanning the surface of a lake or reservoir is a good way to spot a distant swimming loon.

Great Blue Heron

Ardea herodias

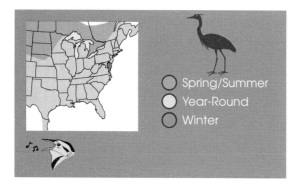

○ Spring/Summer
○ Year-Round
○ Winter

North America's largest and most widespread heron is found, at one time or another, virtually wherever water and small aquatic creatures are found. Although the best known of our dozen heron species, the great blue heron is not always called by its correct name. Many non-birders call it a crane or a stork, but the heron can be instantly distinguished from these other large, long-legged birds by its folded-back neck in flight and the S-shaped curvature of its neck at rest.

All About

Adult great blue herons have a black stripe running from the eye to the back of the neck; immature birds have a blackish cap. During the breeding season the heron's plumage is enhanced by long plume feathers on the head, neck, and back. The great blue heron's croaking *ccrraaaaaaaank* call is often heard as it takes flight.

Habitat & Range

Found across the United States, southern Canada, and up the Pacific coast to Alaska, the great blue heron ventures where few other herons dare. Many eastern birds migrate to the South or to the tropics—as far south as north-western South America—in winter. However, many great blues spend the winter in the Midwest, wherever there is ice-free water.

Feeding

Great blue herons seek a variety of prey in a range of wet habitats. Fish are a mainstay, but amphibians, reptiles, birds, small mammals, and invertebrates feature on the menu, as well. Feeding strategy varies: They may hunt alongside each other, wading slowly up to their bellies in water, or may stand alone for long periods, waiting to thrust their bills at unsuspecting prey. Great blue herons sometimes stalk rodents in dry fields or haunt beaches and docks in search of live or discarded sea life.

Nesting

Great blue herons nest in large colonies, often in tall trees away from human disturbance. They will nest in the company of other water birds, in areas with water beneath nesting trees, probably to thwart predators. Each year, great blue heron pairs form bonds through a series of posing displays, including stretching, preening, crest raising, circling in flight, and twig shaking. Males provide sticks, which females place in the large platform nest. Females usually lay three to five eggs, which they incubate for almost a month. Both parents feed the young, which take flight 2 to 2$\frac{1}{2}$ months after hatching.

Backyard & Beyond

Despite their large size, great blue herons sometimes turn up at small backyard ponds seeking fish and frogs. They are far more frequent in marshes, swamps, rivers, lakes, and reservoirs.

Green Heron

Butorides virescens

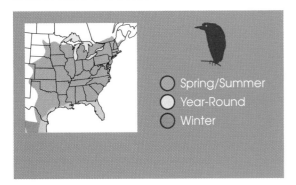

- ○ Spring/Summer
- ○ Year-Round
- ○ Winter

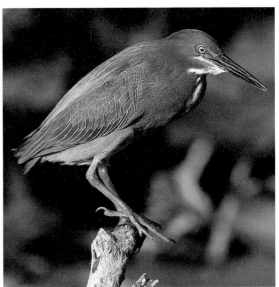

The green heron isn't exactly green, but it's the most greenish of the North American herons. Perhaps a better name would have been "squat heron" or "little heron" or "common pond heron." The bird was known until recently as the "green-backed heron," and this is an apt moniker since the adults have blackish green backs.

All About

The least bittern is our smallest heron, but the green heron is the smallest *easily seen* heron. While a green heron will sometimes stretch its neck out to peer at approaching birders or predators, its head is usually held close to the body, giving the bird a squat look. Identification of adults is straightforward: The back and crown are blackish with a green tinge, the neck and face are dark chestnut, and the belly is gray. Yellow legs flush to bright orange during breeding season. Young birds are brown streaked, and care should be taken not to mistake them for bitterns. Subadults are a mixture of brown and streaky and rusty necked. The piercing *KEEE-OWK* call will draw attention to birds flushed out to the open that might otherwise be missed.

Habitat & Range

In spring and summer, look for green herons along wooded streams and ponds, around lakes, at drainage ditches, and in marshes, often near woody cover. In winter, green herons move south from northern nesting areas, spending the winter in Florida and the Gulf States and south-ward into the tropics. Green herons also nest throughout the West Indies and in Central America south to Panama.

Feeding

Like stock-still balls of rust and greenish feathers, green herons wait patiently by the water's edge for fish, frogs, crayfish, various insects, and other small prey. They also slowly walk through the water and wait for prey to show. They have even been known to drop small baits, such as fish food pellets, bits of bread (from people feeding park ducks), or flower petals into the water to attract curious fish and other potential prey.

Nesting

Green herons nest in pairs or small clusters, but avoid large colonies. They nest in trees or shrubs that may either be near or fairly far from water and feeding areas. Three to seven eggs are laid in a stick platform nest primarily built by the female. Both parents incubate the eggs for about three weeks; both then feed their young, which can fly by three weeks of age.

Backyard & Beyond

Green herons may visit backyard ponds to investigate the goldfish or frogs. They also frequently fly over neighborhoods en route to golf course ponds, streams, lakes, or drainage ditches. Green herons are frequently overlooked until startled into flight.

Canada Goose
Branta canadensis

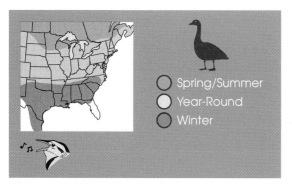

○ Spring/Summer
◐ Year-Round
○ Winter

*T*he Canada goose enjoys an almost iconic status with human observers (though large, nonmigratory flocks can wear out their welcome). Their huge, V-shaped flights mark the passing of seasons, their honking is reminiscent of wilderness itself, and their strong family bonds (they mate for life) endear them to us. Many non-bird watchers mistakenly call this bird the Canadian goose.

All About
The Canada goose's black neck and white cheek strap are unmistakable. In flight, Canadas beat their wings deeply and slowly and show a black-and-white tail. Their familiar call is a deep, two-syllable *ha-ronk* and is given by mated pairs as well as flocking birds. Canadas also give a variety of softer cackling calls to each other, especially when they are on the ground. More than a dozen different subspecies exist in North America, and their sizes vary from 25 to 45 inches in length.

Habitat & Range
The Canada goose is a habitat generalist when it comes to water, settling in lakes, bays, rivers, and city parks and ponds. The species has enjoyed unprecedented success in living with or near humans, and today it nests all across the upper two-thirds of North America. Some re-established populations of Canada goose are year-round, nonmigratory residents, though many birds nesting in northern North America migrate to the southern United States in winter.

Spring migration begins early, and many females are incubating by mid-March.

Feeding
Aquatic plants, grasses, grains, and seeds are the Canada's primary foods. To reach submerged food, it will tip its tail in the air and extend its neck below the water's surface. Flocks leave roosting areas in the morning to forage in nearby fields, meadows, and marshes. Urban populations often live on handouts of cracked corn near city park lakes and golf course ponds.

Nesting
Located on a high spot near water, the nest is a small mound made of surrounding sticks and vegetation and lined with down plucked from the female. Half a dozen or more eggs are laid and incubated by the female for nearly a month while the male stands guard and brings her food. Within two days of hatching, young goslings are herded by their parents to the nearest water. Families stay together until the following breeding season, though young birds become self-sufficient in about two months.

Backyard & Beyond
Some housing developments and golf courses find them (and their droppings) a nuisance. To best see Canadas, visit a wildlife refuge where large flocks congregate during winter and during spring and fall migration. Watching hundreds of loudly honking Canadas is quite a spectacle.

Wood Duck

Aix sponsa

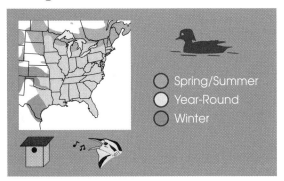

- ○ Spring/Summer
- ○ Year-Round
- ○ Winter

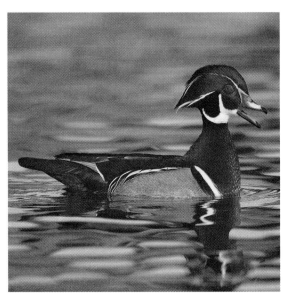

The up-slurred WHEEEP *of the wood duck is a familiar sound to anyone frequenting areas where woodland and fresh water mix. Patience and a bit of stealth will reward the birder seeking a good look at these cagey, dazzling ducks. Across much of the Midwest, wood ducks abound, finding ample habitat and welcoming nest boxes.*

All About

The male wood duck takes its colorful plumage to an extreme. In breeding plumage, it has a green crown and black face offset by white slashes reaching up from its white throat. The bill looks painted, a bright red-orange with black and white touches. Breast and undertail are chestnut, while the sides are adorned with vertical white and blackish slashes followed by a panel of butterscotch yellow. The male's back is metallic green. These colors fade during summer, as the birds molt into *eclipse*, or nonbreeding, plumage, but the bright bill and eye and face pattern remain. Both male and female have backward-facing crests that give them a helmeted look. The female wood duck is easy to identify, not only because of her head shape, but also because of her white, tear-shaped eye rings. Otherwise, females are grayish brown and generously flecked with whitish spots on their sides.

Habitat & Range

The perfect setting for wood ducks combines tranquil fresh water with plenty of trees—bottomland swamps, riverside forests, and tree-lined ponds and lakes. Wood ducks are permanent residents in much of the Midwest and South, except in the Appalachians, where populations withdraw during the cold months. Northern populations, from southern Canada through the Northeast, retreat south in winter.

Feeding

Wood ducks eat a variety of seeds and some fruits from aquatic and forest plants, including acorns. Sometimes, they eat grain. Insects and other small animals supplement their diet; though, for recently fledged birds, these are a mainstay.

Nesting

Wood ducks are cavity nesters, setting up house in holes high in mature or dead trees. They also nest down low in nest boxes. The nest is simply an accumulation of down placed on the cavity floor, where the female incubates her 8 to 15 pale eggs between $3^1/_2$ and 5 weeks. Chicks usually tumble out of their nest the day after hatching. Females accompany them for about six weeks, and they can fly at about two months of age.

Backyard & Beyond

If you live near fresh water, you may see wood ducks fly over your property. If your property includes a pond or wetland, you may attract wood ducks with a nesting box, which ideally would be set in the water on a pole fitted with a pole-mounted, predator baffle.

Mallard

Anas platyrhynchos

- ○ Spring/Summer
- ○ Year-Round
- ○ Winter

Of all the North American duck species, there's one that nearly everyone knows—the mallard. Abundant all across the continent, the mallard is known to interbreed commonly with black ducks and other wild duck species, as well as with domesticated ducks. Large numbers of semi-tame mallards exist on city park ponds, golf courses, and reservoirs, getting by on handouts from humans.

All About

The male mallard's green head and yellow bill are easily recognizable, but female mallards—with their overall dark brown coloration—can be confused with black ducks, mottled ducks, and other female ducks. Look for her orange and black bill and listen for the loud, raucous *quack, quack-quack, quack-quack* call, given only by female mallards. Mallards are fairly large ducks with a 23-inch body length.

Habitat & Range

Like other dabbling ducks, mallards prefer shallow bodies of fresh water at all times of year, including marshes, flooded woodlots, ponds, and swamps. They can be found year-round across most of the United States, but a large number of mallards breed in the far North and spend the winter in the Southeast.

Feeding

Mallards feed by scooping up seeds and plant material from the water's surface, by tipping up—tails in the air—to reach submerged plants, and by grazing for waste grain in agricultural fields. They eat everything from seeds and vegetation to insects, small fish, crawfish, and frogs.

Nesting

Mallards pair up well before the spring breeding season. The hen mallard chooses the nest site, usually in or near thick vegetation on the ground. She then builds a small bowl out of nearby plant material and lines it with her own down. Between 7 and 12 eggs are laid and incubated by the hen for a month. Like other ducks, mallard ducklings leave the nest within hours after hatching and follow their mother to the nearest water. Though ducklings feed themselves right away, it's nearly two months before they are able to fly. Predators take a heavy toll on nests and young, especially in parks where natural predators are augmented by domestic pets.

Backyard & Beyond

If you want to feed the mallards in your local park, don't bother with stale bread, which holds little nutritional value for birds. Instead, offer some cracked corn. This inexpensive food is available at most stores selling birdseed and is relished by mallards. When you've got a hungry flock of panhandling mallards nearby, take time to look at the birds' fine plumage. Look, too, for wild ducks of other species that may be "hanging out" with the local flock of tame mallards, as well as for the many interesting hybrids that result from the mallard's promiscuous nature.

Blue-winged Teal

Anas discors

Spring/Summer
Year-Round
Winter

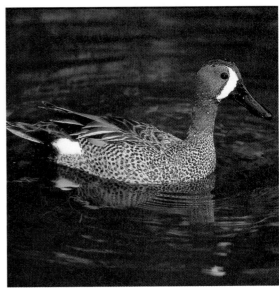

A *fast-flying, small (14 inches long) duck, the blue-winged teal shows the blue shoulder patch for which it is named only when the wings are extended. Blue-wingeds fly in tight flocks and seem to be wary as they pass repeatedly over a body of water before landing. However, they are not as skittish as other ducks when approached by humans, perhaps because they know they can explode off the water and straight into the air in seconds.*

All About

Males have a blue-gray head and a distinctive white face crescent and hip patch, making them easy to identify even from a distance. Females are a warm, gray-brown overall with a slight echo of the males' white face crescent. Identifying them is made somewhat easier by the fact that blue-winged teal pairs form in early winter and stay together through spring migration.

Habitat & Range

Blue-winged teal breed throughout the northeastern, central, and western United States. Most blue-winged teal spend the winter south of the United States, as far as South America. They are considered fair-weather ducks by many bird watchers because they stay far to the south until spring is in full force. Perhaps it is their later spring arrival and their earlier fall departure that has earned them the nicknames "summer teal" and "August teal." Their preferred habitats—at all seasons—are shallow, freshwater marshes and ponds.

Feeding

Teal feed on seeds and plant matter gleaned from the water's surface or by swimming with their heads submerged to find snails, aquatic insects, and crustaceans. Unlike other dabbling ducks, blue-wingeds do not "tip up" to feed on submerged vegetation.

Nesting

Like many other ducks, blue-winged teal nest on the ground in a spot concealed by thick vegetation. The female builds a shallow, basket-shaped nest out of dried grasses lined with her down. A clutch of nine or more eggs is laid and incubated by the hen for slightly more than three weeks. Teal ducklings leave the nest almost immediately and are able to feed themselves right away, but it will be six weeks before they are fully flighted.

Backyard & Beyond

The blue-winged's preference for shallow water means that it can show up almost anywhere—from farm or city ponds to marshes, mudflats, and sewage settling pools. If you see a flock of small ducks flying pell-mell, twisting and turning as one, chances are they are blue-winged teal. You can clinch the identification by looking for the male teal's white face crescent, or for the flash of blue, white, and green in the wings.

Ring-necked Duck

Aythya collaris

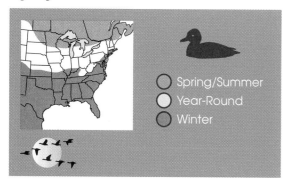

- ○ Spring/Summer
- ○ Year-Round
- ○ Winter

The ring-necked duck is fairly common all across the United States and Canada and a common migrant through the Midwest. Flocks of ringnecks frequent marshes, swamps, and sheltered and wooded corners of lakes. These birds are often found in areas where the only other regularly sighted ducks are wood ducks and mallards (in interior areas). Ringnecks are also found on open water and areas with a wider diversity of ducks.

All About

Closely related and superficially similar to the greater and lesser scaups, this diving bird has a few embellishments that easily set it apart from the scaup. Like the scaup, the male ringneck is blackish—in most light—on its head, chest, and back. However, even at a distance, the adult male ring-necked duck has a vertical white comma that edges its gray sides. Its bill is three-toned: The tip is black, followed by a white band, then much gray, then a white border where the bill meets the head. Like the scaup, the female ringneck is more somber in coloration and markings, but she has a noticeably dark crown compared with the rest of her head. She sports a white eye ring, and usually has a clearly three-toned bill. As with the red-bellied woodpecker, the ring-necked duck's name was poorly chosen by "dead-bird-in-the-hand" early ornithologists: Only in rare circumstances will you see its namesake rusty collar.

Habitat & Range

Most ring-necked ducks winter in the United States, below the northern tier of states, and south into central Mexico. Others winter in the West Indies, and a few are found as far south as Panama. Unlike scaup, ring-necked ducks frequent small or smallish bodies of water, and they rarely enter salt water. Summer finds them nesting in Canada, Alaska, and a good number of northern U.S. states in freshwater wetlands, usually surrounded by forest.

Feeding

Ring-necked ducks dive for their supper, snipping roots and stems of plants, eating seeds, insects, and mollusks. Like other waterfowl, their recently hatched young eat mostly insects.

Nesting

The female ring-necked duck usually lays between 8 and 10 eggs in a nest of grasses or other plants clipped from nearby. She incubates the eggs for almost a month. After they hatch, she accompanies her chicks until they can fly, shortly before two months of age.

Backyard & Beyond

Early in the morning or in well-protected areas, you may catch close-up looks at ring-necked ducks on small ponds or lakes. Even at a distance, though, the gray, white, and black markings on the male's sides help identify these birds as they dive underwater and pop back up to the surface.

Lesser Scaup

Aythya affinis

Spring/Summer
Year-Round
Winter

We have two scaup species in North America—greater and lesser scaup—both are medium-sized, black-and-white ducks, and they can be difficult to tell apart. The lesser scaup is by far the more commonly encountered of the two, especially on inland bodies of water. Both species are named for their characteristic skawwp! call, but the similarities don't end there. Both scaup species are excellent swimmers and divers, both have drab brownish mates, and both show lots of white in the wing in flight.

All About

Older field guides suggest that greater and lesser scaup can be identified based upon head color, but this is very unreliable in poor light. Separating scaup species in the field is most accurately done based on head shape—lessers have a thinner head with more of a peak on top, while greaters have a rounder head and larger bill. Female scaup are brownish gray overall with a white ring around the base of the bill. Hens can be identified based on the males with which they associate because the two scaup species are rarely seen in mixed flocks. All scaup show a blue-gray bill with a black tip—an important clue to separate the scaup from the superficially similar ring-necked duck, which has a white ring on its bill.

Habitat & Range

Lesser scaup are one of most common wintering ducks on inland bodies of water, with flocks sometimes numbering in the thousands. They are very late migrants in both spring and fall migration, arriving on the breeding grounds as late as mid-May and not leaving until just before the winter freeze-up.

Feeding

Specialists in diving for their food, lesser scaup eat snails, mussels, small clams, fish, and aquatic insects. They also rely on plant matter and seeds for food, especially in fall and winter.

Nesting

Preferring to nest in thick vegetation on dry ground or islands near water, the female lesser scaup does nearly all of the hard work. The nest is a scrape lined with dry grass and lots of the hen's down into which 8 to 10 eggs are laid. Hen scaup incubate their eggs for longer than three weeks before hatching. Hatchlings leave the nest within a day of emerging and are able to feed themselves immediately. Within two weeks they are diving for food, and two months later they are fully flighted.

Backyard & Beyond

Lesser scaup can be found on almost any open (ice-free) body of water in the continental United States in winter, but they are especially abundant along the Gulf and southern Atlantic coasts. Look for flocks of black-and-white ducks actively diving and bobbing to the surface of a pond, lake, or reservoir.

Ruddy Duck

Oxyura jamaicensis

○ Spring/Summer
○ Year-Round
○ Winter

This little dark duck is a familiar sight on marshes, bays, and ponds across North America where it often gathers in sizeable flocks in winter. Perhaps because they are rarely hunted they are among our least "spooky" ducks and thus can often be viewed from close range.

All About

Named for the ruddy-orange color of the breeding male, the ruddy duck is a compact-bodied bird with a big head. The long spiky tail is often held up at an angle, hence its alternate name, "stiff-tailed duck." Breeding males are a lovely blend of colors with rusty body, black head, white cheeks, and blue bill. Females and juveniles are drab gray-brown overall with a contrasting white face stripe. Males retain their white cheeks in winter plumage. In all plumages ruddy ducks are dark-capped and pale-cheeked. Ruddies are swift flyers with rapid wingbeats.

Habitat & Range

During the nesting season, most ruddy ducks are on small marshy lakes and wetlands of the western prairies and the interior West. They winter along the entire U.S. coast and across the eastern U.S., as far north as there is ice-free water. Ruddies migrate at night in small flocks and spend daylight hours during migration resting or sleeping on the water. Because many of North America's ruddy ducks use the prairie pothole region of the western Great Plains, drought years can have a devastating effect on this species.

Feeding

A diving feeder, the ruddy duck uses its large bill stir up food items from the bottom of a pond or lake. Aquatic insect larvae, invertebrates, seeds and plant matter make up the diet, nearly all captured as the ruddy strains the stirred-up mud through its bill. In summer the diet is primarily insect larvae while the winter diet may rely more heavily on seeds.

Nesting

The female weaves a platform nest out of cattails and grasses in thick vegetation suspended just inches above the water. She may also weave a partial roof overhead. She lays between five and ten eggs and incubates them for nearly about 25 days, during which time the male takes his leave and the female assumes all parental duties. Ducklings leave the nest a day after hatching and are able to swim and feed themselves immediately, though the female still cares for them. Young attain flight after seven weeks.

Backyard & Beyond

Look for ruddy ducks on marshy ponds and shallow lakes, along large rivers, and on reservoirs during their prolonged spring and fall migration. In spring, males perform amusing courtship displays with lots of head bobbing, tail spreading, and unusual posturing.

Common Merganser

Mergus merganser

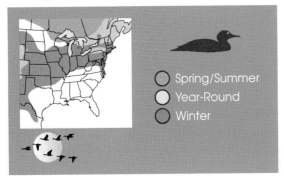

- ○ Spring/Summer
- ○ Year-Round
- ○ Winter

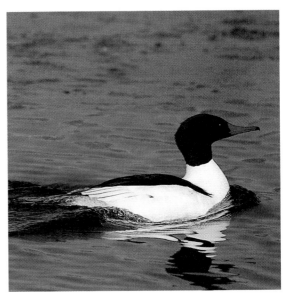

Mergansers are the only North American ducks that are primarily fish eaters; the common merganser is our largest, most boldly marked one. Like our two other mergansers, the common has a serrated bill enabling it to catch and grasp the fish it captures on underwater dives. This adaptation is why the mergansers are often called "saw-bills."

All About

The clean white body, dark green head, and bright-orange bill of the male common merganser are unmistakable identification clues, even at a great distance. The common merganser has the least obvious crest of any of the mergansers, but its large size and bold coloration separate it from the hooded and red-breasted mergansers. Female commons have a dark-brown head and a gray body with a white belly, but share the same bright orange bill color as the male. In flight, common mergansers appear slender and cleanly marked, showing lots of white.

Habitat & Range

Common mergansers breed near northern lakes and rivers that are surrounded by mature forests. Their breeding range covers much of Canada and tiny bits of northern Minnesota, Wisconsin, Michigan, and northern New England. Wintering birds will remain as far north as possible wherever clear, ice-free water is available. During most winters, this bird is the most-common merganser found across the Midwest on deep lakes, rivers, and reservoirs.

Feeding

Doing most of its feeding at morning and dusk, a common merganser will swim along with its head submerged (much like a loon), looking for fish. It pursues fish by diving and swimming after them; common mergansers have been observed swallowing foot-long fish head-first! They also consume mussels, crayfish, shrimp, and salamanders. When dive-feeding in deep water, they may stay under for 30 seconds or more.

Nesting

Common mergansers are cavity nesters, usually choosing a hole in a large tree near water. They will use nest boxes in proper habitat and successful adult females return to nest at the same site in successive years. A lining of wood chips and down is the only improvement made to a cavity and into this nest the female lays between six to twelve eggs. She incubates the eggs for a month or more before they hatch. Young mergansers leap from the cavity a day or so after hatching and follow their mother to the water. They can feed themselves immediately but do not attain flight for at least two months.

Backyard & Beyond

Look for common mergansers on lakes, rivers, and reservoirs from the onset of fall migration in September through spring migration ending in early April. In Europe common mergansers (called "goosanders" there) have increased significantly thanks to the availability of nest boxes.

Turkey Vulture

Cathartes aura

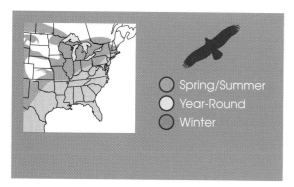

○ Spring/Summer
○ Year-Round
○ Winter

atharsis—a cleansing or purification—is the root of the turkey vulture's Latin name. It refers to this bird's invaluable service in ridding the landscape of animal carcasses—a necessity in the age of superhighways. The highway system, with its continual supply of shoulder fare, may have contributed to the turkey vulture's northward breeding range expansion.

All About

The tilting flight, with wings held in a shallow "V", immediately distinguishes a turkey vulture from most other large, dark birds in flight. At close range, the underwings appear two-toned, with the flight feathers having a reflective, pewter sheen. The small, naked head is red; the bill bone-white. On the ground, a turkey vulture appears to be all wing—a long blackish trapezoid, topped by a tiny red head. Hoarse hisses are their only sounds. Nestlings produce a continuous breathy roar when cornered in the nest.

Habitat & Range

Ranging widely as they search for food, turkey vultures prefer farmland pastures where carcasses might be found, and with nearby forests where they find nesting and roosting spots. Communal roosters, they may be seen warming themselves with wings spread open to the sun. Turkey vultures are migratory in the northern parts of their range, mingling with resident birds in the southern United States, some traveling as far south as Amazonia before returning in early spring.

Feeding

Powerful olfactory senses help the turkey vulture locate carcasses, and they may circle in groups, narrowing down the scent source, before spotting it. This allows them to find carrion in deep woods. One circling vulture brings sharp-eyed companions from miles around, and they share their plunder, rising with heavy flaps from roadsides when disturbed. Its bare head allows the vulture to reach into larger carcasses without fouling its feathers.

Nesting

Turkey vultures hide their nests on rock ledges, in hollow logs, under boulders, or in unused animal burrows. The female lays two eggs, which she and her mate incubate for around 28 days. The young are in the nest cavity and its vicinity for about 12 weeks, making first flights as early as 60 days of age. After a few weeks of exercising and being fed in the nest vicinity, they appear to be independent upon their first extended flight.

Backyard & Beyond

Turkey vultures have learned to exploit factory farms, especially chicken farms, for the inevitable carcasses they produce. They are closely attuned to spring calving and lambing times. Rather than being seen as harbingers of death, turkey vultures might be considered for their great beauty in flight and as a vital cleanup crew.

Cooper's Hawk

Accipiter cooperii

○ Spring/Summer
○ Year-Round
○ Winter

Cooper's hawks often perch in inconspicuous places, shooting through the branches or dropping from trees to nab unsuspecting prey. A flurry of fearful birds and a gray flash may mark the arrival of a Cooper's hawk to your backyard. Cooper's hawks are medium-sized hawks and formidable hunters that are usually seen singly except during migration, when they pass by in varying numbers at hawk-watching spots.

All About

Care must be taken to differentiate the Cooper's hawk from the similar sharp-shinned hawk. Adults of both species have similar markings, as do their brown-backed immatures and that of the northern goshawk (larger birds rarely seen south of Virginia, Indiana, and Missouri). Size is often not a trustworthy identification tool in the field—proportions and tail edges are more telling. Compared with the sharp-shinned hawk, the Cooper's has a proportionately larger head and neck and a rounded (not notched) or square-tipped tail (as does the sharp-shinned). Perched, adult Cooper's hawks often show a contrast between a blackish crown and gray nape and back. In flight, its head protrudes well beyond its often straight-held wings, and its tail usually looks rounded. Sharp-shinned hawks look like a capital "T" in flight, their shorter heads almost even with the leading edge of their wings.

Habitat & Range

In many areas, Cooper's hawks are uncommon nesters. Far-northern birds generally winter to the south. You can look for Cooper's hawks in any type of forest, along forest edges, and in woods near watercourses. But don't be surprised if you find one elsewhere, particularly in winter and fall. They seem to be adapting to suburban life, nesting near backyards or in city parks. During spring and fall, migrating Cooper's hawks gravitate toward ridges and coasts.

Feeding

These midsized hawks generally feed on midsized birds, including robins, flickers, and pigeons, but they also eat small mammals, including chipmunks and squirrels. Insects and reptiles sometimes feature on the menu.

Nesting

Cooper's hawks place their bulky stick nests high on horizontal branches in large trees, sometimes building them atop another large bird or squirrel nest. The female lays three to five eggs and incubates them for about five weeks. The male brings food, but the female feeds it to the young, which usually take flight about four or five weeks after hatching.

Backyard & Beyond

Cooper's hawks are attracted to what bird feeders attract—keeping intact natural predator and prey interactions, even in the suburbs. They will not scare birds from your feeders for long and, when successful, Cooper's hawks are usually weeding out the less-fit birds.

Red-tailed Hawk

Buteo jamaicensis

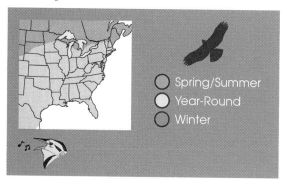

○ Spring/Summer
○ Year-Round
○ Winter

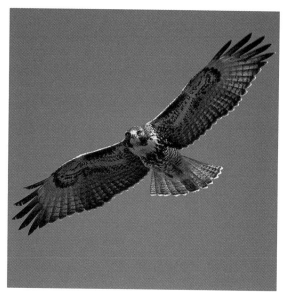

This bird is the large raptor people most often see doing "lazy circles in the sky." The red-tailed hawk inhabits open terrain across the continent and south to Central America. It thrives in habitats opened up by human activities, such as farming or forest clearing. They are also the large raptor most commonly seen perched along roadways and power lines.

All About
Red-tailed hawks occur across the continent in quite a variety of plumage colorations. In the East, however, count on a few easy field marks to help identify adult birds: the reddish-orange tail, a dark-streaked belly band, and a white chest. This hat trick of field marks can easily be seen in many soaring redtails, as well as in perched birds. Additionally, two chocolate-colored bars adorn the leading edge of the underwing. Overall, soaring red-tailed hawks are bulkier and more formidable in general appearance than slimmer red-shouldered hawks and broad-winged hawks, which have shorter tails. Red-tailed hawks younger than two years old lack the telltale reddish tail, but they still exhibit the belly band and white chest.

Habitat & Range
Look for red-tailed hawks along highway edges, over farm fields and forest clearings, and in almost any other open habitat with at least some telephone poles or trees on which they can perch and scan for prey. From tundra to tropical forests, the red-tailed hawk is a formidable pred-

ator. They breed as far south as Panama and on various Caribbean islands, thus the species name *jamaicensis*. For nesting, they usually avoid areas with a lot of human activity, even though they nest near New York City's Central Park and pass through suburbs during migration.

Feeding
Many farmers appreciate seeing red-tailed hawks flap over their acreage, as they eat many voles, mice, rats, rabbits, squirrels, and other small mammals. Other prey can include a variety of birds and reptiles. Red-tailed hawks may glide down from a perch to grab prey, dive down, or hover and then drop on prey.

Nesting
Nests are usually found in tall trees, although these birds will nest on cliffs and sometimes even buildings. Both mates build the large stick nest, which they line with softer materials. The female usually lays two or three eggs, which both parents incubate for about a month. The male hunts for food, passing it to his mate, who feeds their young. Nestlings fly after about 10 weeks.

Backyard & Beyond
You may hear the red-tailed hawk's blood-curdling cry around its nesting grounds. Because they range widely and some populations migrate short or long distances, you may see red-tailed hawks soaring or gliding over your home.

Northern Harrier

Circus cyaneus

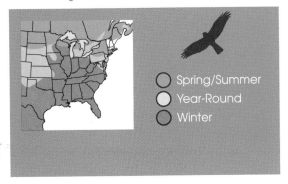

○ Spring/Summer
○ Year-Round
○ Winter

The slender, low-flying form of the northern harrier is associated with grasslands and marshes across most of North America during one season or another. Young birds, adult females, and adult males are very different in appearance and size—an unusual trait among raptors.

All About

The northern harrier's key field mark is a large white rump patch, but its shape—long slender wings and long tail—is also distinctive. First-year juveniles sport a rich chocolate brown on their back and wings accompanied by an unstreaked, rust-colored breast. Adult females, which can be twice as large as males, are the same colors as juveniles but have a heavily streaked breast and belly. Adult males are pale gray below and slate gray above, and are sometimes referred to by bird watchers as "gray ghosts." A ring of feathers surrounding the face form a facial disc, an owl-like adaptation that channels sound to the ears.

Habitat & Range

Present year-round in grassland habitat across the northern two-thirds of North America, the northern harrier is considered a locally common species. Their winter range includes most of the U.S. with the exception of high-mountain habitat in the East. Prairies, marshy grass- lands, wetlands, and old hayfields are home to the harrier. Unlike many other raptors, harriers will migrate and forage in rainy or snowy weather.

Feeding

Voles, mice, rats, shrews, rabbits, and other small mammals are the primary prey of the northern harrier, but small birds, snakes, other reptiles, and insects are also eaten. Harriers glide very low over grassy habitat, watching and listening for movement below them, and then wheeling to turn, hover, and pounce when prey is located.

Nesting

Harrier nests are built out of grasses, weed stems, and sticks placed on the ground, or on top of a platform built in cattails or other vegetation and suspended over water. The nests are always in dense vegetation and built primarily by the female. She lays a clutch of three to seven eggs and incubates them for about 30 days. The male delivers food to the female during incubation and after hatching, but she takes over when the chicks are about two weeks old. Five weeks after hatching the young harriers can fly.

Backyard & Beyond

Harriers prefer grasslands, rough meadows, and grassy marshes (the harrier was formerly called the marsh hawk) for foraging, though they can also be seen along grassy dunes, old strip mines, and airport fields. Look for a large bird with a small head flying low over the ground, wheeling and teetering like a vulture. When the white rump patch flashes, you'll know you've got your harrier.

Bald Eagle

Haliaeetus leucocephalus

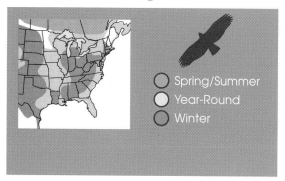

- Spring/Summer
- Year-Round
- Winter

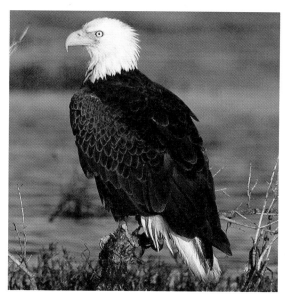

The bald eagle barely edged out the wild turkey when our founding fathers were voting on a national symbol. Skilled fishing bird, scavenger, and pirate, the bald eagle is an opportunistic raptor that's been given a second chance thanks to improved conservation and bans on DDT, which dramatically impaired the birds' breeding and sent their population into steep decline in the decades following World War II.

All About

There is no confusing the adult bald eagle, with its huge size and gleaming white head and tail. Adult plumage is not attained until after the third year. Until then, immature birds are dark brown with varying degrees of white mottling on their backs, wings, bellies, and, in older birds, heads. Depending upon age, the large bill is blackish or accented in the bright yellow seen in adults. Immatures and adults have strong, bright yellow talons.

Habitat & Range

Water plays a strong role where bald eagles hunt and nest. In the process of rebounding in many areas, bald eagles now nest in most states, where they are often local nesters tied to specific sites. They are particularly common from Florida to coastal South Carolina and around the Great Lakes, but the largest breeding populations are in Alaska and western Canada. During winter, bald eagles often congregate at wetland areas, rivers, and dams, where fishing or carrion feeding is particularly productive.

Feeding

Bald eagles hunt from perches or swoop down after sighting prey while soaring. Although fish are preferred prey (frequently grappled from the water in the eagle's mighty talons), eagles also eat a wide variety of other foods, depending upon individual, time of year, and location. Carrion—particularly dead fish, birds, and mammals—plays an important dietary role. Many live animals are also caught: muskrats, reptiles, amphibians, crustaceans, and birds—as large as great blue herons—have been documented. Bald eagles also steal fish from ospreys and other birds.

Nesting

Bald eagles nest high in large trees in huge, bulky stick nests that are often used again over the years. Both mates collect sticks, and nest building may take several months. The female usually lays two eggs, which she and her mate incubate for just over a month. Once the first chick hatches, both parents incubate and *brood*, or cover, the eggs and hatchlings. Both parents feed their young, which leave the nest between 8 to 14 weeks after hatching.

Backyard & Beyond

Recently, bald eagles have started nesting in closer proximity to human development, thanks to protection from disturbance. If you see a large, dark raptor soaring slowly in the sky, with flat wings, look for the other clues to the bald eagle's identity.

Osprey
Pandion haliaetus

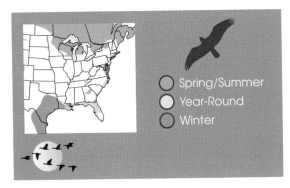

○ Spring/Summer
○ Year-Round
○ Winter

The bold chocolate and white "fish hawk," so familiar to boaters and fishermen, is happy to exploit artificial nesting platforms, from power poles to those built specifically for it. Though osprey populations declined by 90 percent from the 1950s to the 1970s (poisoned by persistent organochlorides), they have made a heartening rebound in recent decades.

All About

Chocolate-brown above and pure white below, the osprey is armed with long, pale green legs and grappling-hook talons for seizing fish. Fierce yellow eyes are ringed in black, making the bird look as though it is wearing aviator's goggles. A banded gray tail and ragged crest complete this gangly bird's unusual look. Females have streaked upper breasts and are larger than males. When disturbed, ospreys give a series of high, piercing, chicklike peeps and thin screams.

Habitat & Range

One of the most widespread species, the osprey inhabits rivers, lakes, and coastlines throughout much of the United States. It is still reclaiming territory in the interior United States, helped by osprey reintroduction programs. Lacking body down, ospreys must migrate to stay warm and to find sufficient food in unfrozen waters, traveling down both coasts of Mexico and Central America.

Feeding

The only North American raptor to feed exclusively on fish, the osprey soars and hovers over shallow, clear waters of estuaries, marshes, lakes, and rivers, searching for fish. Spotting prey, it folds its wings and plunges, feet first, often completely beneath the surface. Unique cylindrical, recurved talons and horny spikes on the soles of its feet hold the fish securely until the osprey reaches a "carving block," usually a dead snag, where it can eat. Fish are always carried with the head facing into the wind, and are sometimes eaten as a snack on migration, far from water.

Nesting

The huge stick nests ospreys build are a familiar site on channel markers, dead trees, and artificial nesting platforms along shorelines. Nesting pairs add sticks yearly until the nests assume enormous proportions. In the soft, grass-lined center the female lays two to three eggs, which she and her mate incubate for around 37 days. The male provides all the female's food during this time. Chicks stay in the nest for about 55 days, taking short flights, and are fed on or near the nest for around two weeks after first attaining flight.

Backyard & Beyond

Though artificial nesting platforms have had a positive influence on osprey populations, they are by no means out of danger. Overfishing, pesticide contamination, and persecution on Latin American wintering grounds (where they are shot by the hundreds at fish farms) continue to limit populations.

American Kestrel

Falco sparverius

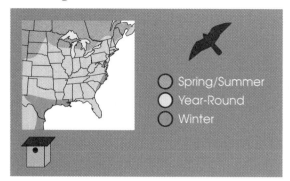

- Spring/Summer
- Year-Round
- Winter

North America's smallest falcon is also the most familiar to many, hovering over farm fields and air strips, perching on telephone poles and wires, and nesting in boxes put out by concerned land-owners, who welcome these insect and rodent eaters. In some regions, kestrel numbers have fallen in recent decades, probably due to large-scale landscape changes, as farm areas have reverted to forest and as cities and suburbs have stretched out to once-rural areas.

All About

In flight, the kestrel has sharp-looking, pointed wings and a slender, long tail. In comparison to the merlin and peregrine falcons, it is slim. Sharp-shinned and Cooper's hawks also have long tails, but their wings are broad, not pointed. While soaring, the kestrel's wings look more rounded and the tail fans. Adult males are brightly colored, with blue-gray wings and crown, rufous tail, and a rusty back embellished with black barring. Black spots speckle the underparts. Both sexes have two vertical stripes on the face and a black spot on the back of the neck. Adult females lack the male's blue-gray wings, have barred tails, and—instead of black spots—sport rusty lines of spots on their underparts.

Habitat & Range

The American kestrel is not strictly a farm bird, although many farms provide the ideal habitat for them. They also nest and hunt in open urban areas, open forest, clearings, and even deserts. They are truly American in the New World sense, nesting from Alaska to southern Argentina. In the North, numbers dwindle in winter, when northern birds move south *en masse* to winter in warmer areas.

Feeding

Grasshoppers and other large insects are important prey to kestrels, but voles, mice, and other rodents also play a part in their diet, as do small birds, reptiles, and other small animals.

Nesting

American kestrels are cavity nesters. Females usually lay their four to six eggs in a tree hole or other cavity, sometimes in a crevice in a building or cliff, or in a nest box. Both parents share the month-long incubation duties. Young fly about a month after hatching, and parents feed them until about two weeks after they leave the nest.

Backyard & Beyond

Provision of nest boxes in rural areas has helped American kestrel populations, and this is one potential way to attract kestrels to your property if you live in an open area. Kestrels also pass through suburban areas during migration. They may frequent open suburbs rich in grasshoppers and such prey as small birds and lizards. They will use snags placed in the middle of grassy meadows as hunting and eating perches.

Wild Turkey

Meleagris gallopavo

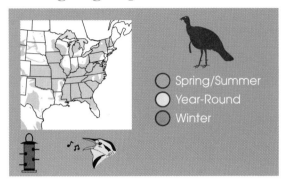

○ Spring/Summer
○ Year-Round
○ Winter

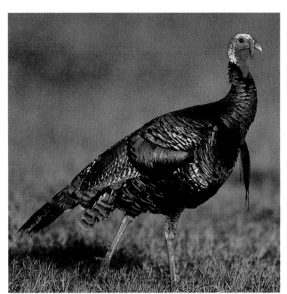

When restocking programs abandoned using farm-raised birds and turned to releasing wild-caught birds in the 1940s, the repopulation of wild turkeys into their former haunts took off. Today, the large dark forms of wild turkeys are a familiar sight along many highways, and the birds even come to backyard feeders.

All About

A tall, strong-legged bird, the wild turkey's feathers are iridescent with dark bronze, shot with hints of copper and acid green. Displaying in spring, the male erects its plumage in the strut posture, its enormous tail fanned, wings drooping, and wattles ablaze. A "beard" of wiry, barbless feathers sprouts from the center of his breast. Hens are visibly smaller and paler than gobblers, with a brown cast to their plumage and without distensible wattles. Along with the male's explosive gobble, turkeys employ a great variety of calls, including yelps and hollow *putt* sounds, in their intraflock communication.

Habitat & Range

Dense deciduous forests—either uplands or bottomlands—with some clearings are ideal turkey habitats. The nuts from oaks and other nut trees make up an important component of their diet. Some exploit agricultural fields for spilled grain. Wild turkeys are nonmigratory and may fast for more than a week in severe weather.

Feeding

The wild turkey's strong legs and feet help it scratch its way across the forest floor, raking away debris to uncover acorns, tree seeds, and invertebrates. Turkeys pluck buds and fruits as they walk or clamber through branches, and they strip grasses of their seeds by running stems through their bills. Young poults take a number of insects and invertebrates.

Nesting

Gobblers display—gobbling and strutting—in early spring to attract visiting hens. After mating, the hen lays about a dozen eggs in a feather-lined bowl in the ground at the foot of a tree or under brush. She incubates them alone for about 26 days. When all chicks have hatched and imprinted on the hen (from one to three days later), they leave the nest, following her every move. She feeds them for the first few days; after that they pick up their own food. She broods them on the ground until they are able to join her in a roost tree at night; she still shelters them with spread wings on the roost.

Backyard & Beyond

Wild turkeys may, in some rural and suburban situations, be attracted into yards with cracked corn spread on the ground. A small flock can consume as much as 50 pounds per week. Watching their fascinating social behavior and courtship behavior is a rich reward. Rotate feeding areas to prevent the spread of disease.

American Coot

Fulica americana

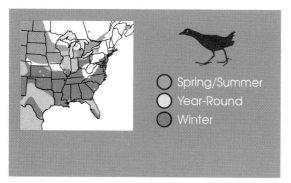

- ○ Spring/Summer
- ○ Year-Round
- ○ Winter

What looks like a duck and acts like a duck, but is not a duck? It's the American coot, of course. Coots are duck-like in many ways, but they are actually members of the rail family and are the most common (and most commonly seen) of all the rails. Like ducks, coots are excellent swimmers and use this ability to find and eat aquatic vegetation. However, coots are reluctant and awkward fliers—they must run, pattering across the water's surface and flapping madly to lift their heavy bodies into the air.

All About

Chunky and almost all black with a contrasting white bill and red eyes and forehead patch, the coot is hard to mistake for anything else. The common moorhen and purple gallinule are similar in shape, but both are more colorful (the gallinule much more so) and less common than coots. Coots swim using the lobed toes on their powerful feet, and when swimming they bob their heads back and forth with a "funky chicken" motion. Coots are raucous, loud birds that utter a variety of grunts, cackles, and croaks.

Habitat & Range

American coots are widespread across North America, especially in winter when they can be found in huge flocks on large bodies of water. They breed throughout the central and western portions of the continent, and they are year-round residents in parts of the Midwest and South. During the breeding season, coots prefer ponds, lakes, and marshes of almost any size, provided that they have large stands of tall reeds, such as cattails.

Feeding

Finding most of their food on or below the surface of the water, coots dabble, swim, and dive when foraging. They are equally at home on land, grazing on the grass of city parks and golf courses. Their diet is largely vegetarian with the main menu items being duckweed, algae, and various pondweeds and sedges.

Nesting

The female coot builds a floating, basket-shaped platform of vegetation with a lined cup to hold the eggs. She lays up to a dozen eggs and incubates them for about 23 days. Young coots have shiny, bald, red heads and golden down, an adaptation that is thought to trigger feeding by the parents. Babies leave the nest after a day or so and are able to find food on their own shortly thereafter.

Backyard & Beyond

Though they may not be a backyard bird, coots should be easy to find in nearby parks and on golf course water hazards. In winter, look for flocks of coots on almost any body of water, from reservoirs to sewage ponds.

Killdeer

Charadrius vociferus

Spring/Summer
Year-Round
Winter

The killdeer is a large, double-banded plover that screams its name across farm fields and other grass- and dirt-covered habitats. If you see an orange-tailed, stripe-winged bird calling KILL-DEEE, KILL-DEEE, you can rest assured that it's this plover. Despite their lousy-tasting flesh, many killdeer were shot during the late 1800s, along with a wide range of other shorebirds. These species are now protected from harm by federal and state laws.

All About

On its white breast, two black bands stand out. Other plovers—such as the smaller but similar semipalmated plover—have only one band or none at all. Otherwise, killdeer are wet-sand brown above and clear white below, with white around the front of the face and eye. The killdeer is one of our largest and longest-tailed plovers, so even mixed with a few other species on a mudflat, they stand out, especially when you spot those two breast bands. Much of the tail is orange, except the tip, which is black punctuated with white dabs.

Habitat & Range

Unlike most other plovers, killdeer often forage or nest far from water. You may find them on ball fields and airport runways, on turf, in pastures, and in farm fields, as well as on mudflats. They are found throughout North America, but northern birds head south for the winter.

Feeding

A farmer's friend, the killdeer spends its foraging time searching for beetles, grasshoppers, caterpillars, and other insects. Crayfish, centipedes, spiders, and other invertebrates are also eaten, as well as some seeds.

Nesting

A simple scrape in the dirt or gravel (including gravel-covered roofs) will do for a killdeer pair, although they sometimes add embellishments, such as a lining of pebbles, grass, or other small materials. Females lay three to five blotched eggs, which both parents incubate for just less than a month. Nesting in exposed habitats, killdeer rely on camouflage and deception to keep their eggs and chicks safe. If an intruder approaches the nest, an adult killdeer may feign injury—dragging a wing as if it is broken and exposing its bright tail—then lure the person or predator away from the nest. Adults watch over their hatchlings, little puffballs that can run around and find food by themselves shortly after hatching. They can fly before they reach one month old.

Backyard & Beyond

Killdeer are attracted to large areas of grass as well as to short-cropped fields, so you may see them on your property if it's relatively treeless and large. Their cries carry long distances, so you may also hear killdeer passing by or calling from nearby nesting grounds.

Lesser Yellowlegs

Tringa flavipes

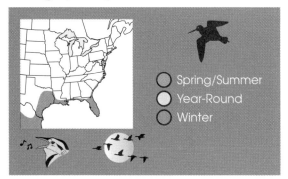

○ Spring/Summer
○ Year-Round
○ Winter

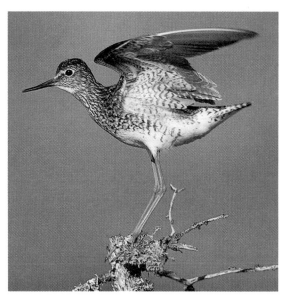

Lesser yellowlegs is a tall shorebird commonly seen in a variety of saltwater and freshwater situations. It winters in the Gulf States and along southern seacoasts, both east and west, so wherever you live in North America you stand a chance of seeing this species at some time during the year. Lessers often travel in large flocks and may be found together with greater yellowlegs.

All About

True to its name, this bird has bright yellow legs, which really stand out against its dark back and speckled underparts. The sexes are alike. When alarmed, it will take flight with a loud *tu* or *tu-tu* call, trailing its long yellow legs behind. The only species the lesser yellowlegs is likely to be confused with is the equally common greater yellowlegs, a nearly identical, but larger, close relative. In flight, both show white on the rump. The smaller lesser yellowlegs has a shorter, straighter bill than the greater, and overall it has a much more delicate appearance.

Habitat & Range

During migrations, the lesser yellowlegs is more likely than the greater yellowlegs to visit fresh water. It occurs widely and may stop at small ponds or wetlands, temporary rainwater puddles, marshes and mudflats, and flooded fields.

Feeding

Lesser yellowlegs feed in shallow water where they find their prey—aquatic insects, snails, small fish, and crustaceans—on or just beneath the water's surface. They sometimes swing their heads back and forth underwater in an effort to stir up food. On land, the lesser yellowlegs may snatch up terrestrial insects and worms from the ground, or pick flying insects out of the air.

Nesting

Breeding at the edge of the northern tundra, lesser yellowlegs nest in natural clearings with small clusters of vegetation. The nest is merely a scrape in the ground, softened with a few fallen leaves and placed next to a fallen log or under a low shrub, usually within 200 yards of a water source. Nesting starts as early as May, with the male calling loudly from the top of a tree or other elevated perch. The female lays three to four eggs, and both parents share the 18- to 20-day incubation. Within hours of hatching, the young are able to leave the nest. As soon as the chicks are self-sufficient—as early as July—the adults leave for the south. The youngsters start south a few weeks later.

Backyard & Beyond

Any marsh or wetland in your neighborhood might host lesser yellowlegs during migration. Look for lesser yellowlegs in spring from April through June, and in fall from July through September. You should be able to find it easily at mudflats and marshes, mingling with other shorebirds.

Spotted Sandpiper

Actitis macularia

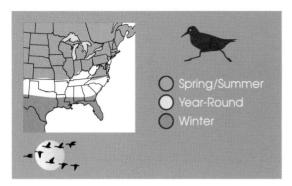

○ Spring/Summer
○ Year-Round
○ Winter

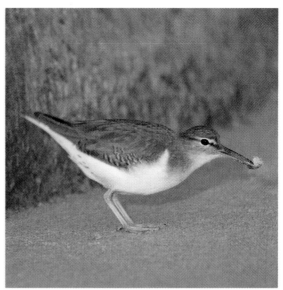

The spotted sandpiper is one of the easiest sandpipers to identify. Not only are its markings distinctive, but so are its mannerisms—the bird signals itself to birders by almost constantly bobbing its posterior. An inland nester across much of northern North America, the spotted sandpiper frequents waterways from creeks and streams to marshes, reservoirs, and mudflats during migration, and shoreline areas during winter.

All About

The wood-thrushlike breast spotting of breeding adult spotted sandpipers sets them apart from other sandpipers, but you can also easily identify spotless immatures (as shown in the photo) and non-breeders. For one thing, the spotted sandpiper's tail and rear end constantly bob up and down as the bird walks or pauses; this is true even in birds that have just left the nest. Also, look for a white crescent on the sides, which curls around the bend of the bird's folded wing, inching toward the back. Spotted sandpipers are about the length of a wood thrush and smaller than a robin—in other words, they are not the tiniest sandpipers, but they are rather small. Breeding individuals have bright orange bills; otherwise, spotted sandpipers have pale pinkish or orangish bills and legs.

Habitat & Range

Spotted sandpipers nest in freshwater habitats, both in forested and open settings across much of North America, except in the far South, where a good number winter. Find them at

pools where rainwater collects, along lakeshores, and at streams, rivers, or marshes. Many winter far to the south, from Mexico and Central America to as far south as northern Chile and Argentina.

Feeding

As would be expected of a bird that frequents a mixture of habitats, the spotted sandpiper captures a variety of prey in diverse ways. Insects, crabs, worms, small fish, and other creatures may be picked from the water or shore, caught in quick flights, or chased.

Nesting

Parental care in spotted sandpipers differs from that in many other birds. Female spotted sandpipers often pair up with more than one male, laying two or more clutches of eggs. Both parents build the nest, a depression in the ground usually sheltered by some plant cover and lined with plants or moss. There the female usually lays four eggs, which may be incubated by the male or by both parents for about three weeks. The nestlings teeter as soon as they hatch and can almost immediately scamper from the nest. Usually the male watches over the young, which can fly when they are about 18 days old.

Backyard & Beyond

Any park or backyard with a large pond, stream, or lake is likely to host a spotted sandpiper at one time or another.

American Woodcock

Scolopax minor

○ Spring/Summer
○ Year-Round
○ Winter

The male American woodcock's courtship display is one of Nature's most unusual and it may be performing it in or near your backyard on early spring evenings. Its nocturnal habits, amazing sky dancing, and camouflage coloration make it one of the most fascinating, weird, and mysterious North American birds.

All About

The American woodcock is a short, stocky shorebird with a long, straight bill and large eyes set far back on the head. This eye position gives it rearward vision, allowing it to watch for danger even when it is probing the ground for earthworms. The woodcock's plumage is a mixture of dark earth tones that hide it perfectly in its preferred woodland habitat. Males find a small clearing from which they repeatedly give a loud, nasal *peent!* call to announce themselves prior to launching into their impressive courtship display. They spiral upward for twenty or more seconds, wings whistling with each flap, then plummet to earth uttering a whistling twitter. Males perform this display before dawn and after dusk, hoping to attract watching females to mate.

Habitat & Range

During the spring and summer, woodcocks can be found in wet woodlands and swampy thickets all across the eastern half of the United States and southern Canada. At night they forage and display in open habitats such as old fields, meadows, and wetland edges.

Feeding

The tip of the woodcock's bill is sensitive and flexible—ideally suited to probing for earthworms and subterranean insects. When it senses an earthworm, the woodcock opens the tip of the upper mandible like a flexible tweezer to grasp the worm and pull it out. Other foods taken include spiders, snails, and some grass seeds.

Nesting

Several males may be displaying in one place while one or more females watch. A female will choose a male, mate with him, and leave. Males have no role in caring for the young. The nest is a simple scrape on the ground lined with and surrounded by dead leaves. Usual clutch size is four eggs and incubation lasts about three weeks. Downy hatchlings leave the nest almost immediately and are tended by the female for a few days until they can feed on their own. They are fully flighted and independent after five weeks.

Backyard & Beyond

On an early spring night at dusk, visit an old meadow surrounded by woods and listen for the low nasal call of the male woodcock and the whistling wings as he ascends for his display flight. If you look toward the western horizon, you may see his silhouette as he dances in the night sky.

Bonaparte's Gull

Larus philadelphia

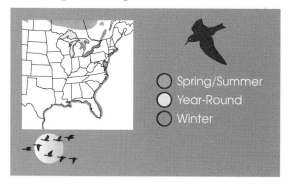

○ Spring/Summer
○ Year-Round
○ Winter

Though it breeds in the coniferous forests of the far North, the Bonaparte's gull is a common winter visitor across much of the U.S. Its small size and lilting ternlike flight separate it visually from other common winter gulls. This species is not named for famed French general Napolean Bonaparte, but for his cousin, French zoologist Charles Lucien Bonaparte.

All About

Between April and August, adult Bonaparte's gulls are in breeding plumage with a black hood and bill and a broken white eye ring. But it is the winter plumage (worn from September through March) that is most familiar to bird watchers. The only remnant of the dark hood is a dark ear spot behind the eye—giving the impressions that the bird is wearing earphones. The legs remain pink and the thin, straight bill remains black all year. In flight, the winter adult appears light overall with the wingtips outlined in black. First-winter birds show a faint black "M" pattern across the backs of their wings.

Habitat & Range

Bonaparte's gulls nest far to the north from east-central Canada into Alaska. Though they spend winters primarily on the ocean coasts, including the Gulf of Mexico, many birds linger inland, moving southward only if a freeze closes all bodies of water. They congregate in huge flocks at dam spillways, reservoirs, sewage lagoons, coastal estuaries, and along rivers, especially where food is abundant.

Feeding

Insects are a primary food during the breeding season, but Bonaparte's gulls also eat small fish, crustaceans, and grasshoppers. They forage while flying and can plunge into the water for a fish, pluck a morsel from the water's surface, or hawk insects in flight with equal skill. In winter you may often seen Bonies foraging among flocks of mergansers, grebes, or cormorants, seizing small fish and other items stirred up by these diving birds.

Nesting

Unlike any other North American gull, the Bonaparte's gull frequently builds its nest in trees, usually in a conifer adjacent to water. They may nest in small, loose colonies. The pair builds the nest of sticks lined with lichen or moss. Three or four eggs are laid and the shared incubation duties last about 24 days. Both parents care for the young until they are ready to undertake fall migration with the adults as early as late July.

Backyard & Beyond

Almost any large, ice-free body of water in winter can host a flock of Bonaparte's gulls. Bonies are usually found in single-species flocks—they rarely associate with other, larger gull species. Though they may be found hawking insects at sewage ponds, don't look for them at garbage dumps with other gulls.

Ring-billed Gull

Larus delawarensis

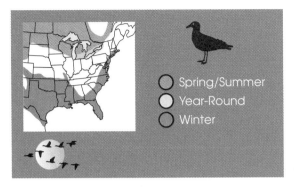

○ Spring/Summer
● Year-Round
○ Winter

This gull might almost be called the inland gull. Though found in coastal areas like most gulls, it is also the most numerous and widespread gull away from the seacoasts, sometimes found in huge flocks. At first glance it looks like a slightly smaller version of the herring gull, but it has a personality all its own.

All About

The ring-billed gull is a medium-sized (19 inches long) gull, and in adult plumage it has a light gray back and wings on a pure white body. Its wing tips are black with white spots, and it has a black ring near the end of its yellow bill. Males and females look alike. Young ring-billed gulls take three years to mature, during which time their bodies and wings are varying shades of mottled brown and gray, with a white tail that has a prominent, black terminal band. These gulls are smaller, lighter, and more graceful-looking than similarly patterned herring gulls, and they have a more buoyant appearance in flight.

Habitat and Range

In addition to the beaches and bays of the seacoasts, ring-billed gulls may be found at large inland lakes and rivers, in newly plowed fields and pastures, and at sod farms, garbage dumps, and parking lots throughout their range.

Feeding

Ring-billed gulls are omnivorous, thriving on whatever food is on hand. Fish are a favorite item, but insects and earthworms are high on the list, along with grains, refuse, and even small rodents. They will eat the eggs of other species, and they are not averse to taking handouts from humans at parking lots and picnic grounds. (French fries, caught in midair, are popular. Ketchup is optional.)

Nesting

After a courtship routine by the male (which includes bowing, throat-puffing, and a ceremonial walk around the female, enlivened by many odd gesticulations), the mated pair will build its nest on the ground in a fairly open area near water. The ring-billed is colonial, so there are usually lots of similar nests nearby. Both sexes build the flimsy nest of grasses, sticks, and moss; and both take turns incubating the two to four eggs for up to four weeks until hatching. The downy young are tended by their parents in the general vicinity of the nest until they attain flight at about five weeks of age.

Backyard & Beyond

Look for ring-billed gulls in large, open fields after spring or autumn rainstorms, or watch for them anywhere there is an infestation of large insects, such as grasshoppers or locusts. If there is a landfill or dam nearby, it may attract gulls from a wide surrounding area and can make for productive gull watching.

Herring Gull

Larus argentatus

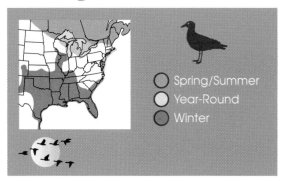

- ○ Spring/Summer
- ○ Year-Round
- ○ Winter

This is the bird that most people think of when they hear the term seagull. *Large, abundant, and widespread, the herring gull is an imposing bird— and, in its adult plumage, it is certainly beautiful. Picture a dozen or more sitting on a pier with ocean waves lapping below, and you have a perfect coastal postcard scene.*

All About

Measuring up to 26 inches in length, the adult herring gull has silver-gray wings tipped in black and white, a dazzling white body, bold yellow bill, and pink legs. Males and females are alike, and they are considerably larger than similar-looking ring-billed gulls. Immature herring gulls wear varying shades of brown or gray-brown and are not fully mature until their fourth year. All ages join in making the yelping or trumpeting calls, which are a constant fact of life throughout the herring gull's entire range.

Habitat & Range

Herring gulls are birds of shorelines, major lakes and rivers, garbage dumps, and, occasionally, farmlands—especially recently tilled fields. Their population, once confined to the northern states, has been spreading southward for decades. They nest across Canada and are found year-round throughout the Great Lakes. Winter flocks may be found along major rivers.

Feeding

Herring gulls eat almost anything, which is one reason for their success. Fish, along with all manner of other seafood, are a staple of the herring gull diet, but they also eat the eggs and chicks of other bird species (they can decimate a tern colony if given the opportunity), all kinds of garbage, large insects and grubs, and even carrion. They are smart and have learned to drop clams onto rocks or pavement to open them. They are quite willing to steal food from other birds. In the gull world, there is no such thing as a guilty conscience.

Nesting

Herring gulls nest on the ground, preferably in the lee of a rock or some other natural feature. Both sexes help scrape out a site and line it with grass, weeds, and feathers. Many nests contain a ball of some kind—whiffle ball, tennis ball— which may be a courtship gift from the male. The usual clutch is three eggs, and both parents share the month-long incubation. The young, downy and active from the start, depend on their parents at least until they fly at about 50 days of age.

Backyard & Beyond

Check the range map above to see when herring gulls might be expected in your area, and then visit the nearest beach! These birds also hang out at sewage outlets, dams, or anywhere that human activity may generate a reliable food supply.

Mourning Dove

Zenaida macroura

Spring/Summer
Year-Round
Winter

Whether you regard them as songbirds or living skeet targets, if you feed birds, you probably have mourning doves as constant companions. These tapered, graceful brown and pinkish birds whole-heartedly embrace human alterations of the natural landscape, finding their greatest abundance in agricultural and suburban areas. Doves love water, but may foul birdbaths by sitting around the rim, tails in.

All About

The mournful *oooahh, oooh, ooh, ooh* song of the mourning dove echos from power lines and treetops in early spring. Mourning doves travel in flocks, breaking rank only to nest and raise young. Males defend their mates as a kind of mobile territory, defending her and the immediate nest site—but not much else—from other birds.

Habitat & Range

The only habitat shunned by mourning doves is deep, contiguous forest. They are most common in agricultural areas with hedgerows and shelterbelts. They are also abundant in suburban areas as well, where visits to feeding stations are an integral part of their daily routines. Mourning doves migrate, especially far northern populations, but some individuals are resident year-round.

Feeding

Streamlined, fast, and powerful flyers, mourning doves travel in flocks, descending to feed on a great variety of grains and weed seeds that they peck from the ground. They are often seen in ranks on power lines over farm fields. A capacious crop allows mourning doves to gorge—sometimes to the point of being misshapen—and then digest their stored food later when resting.

Nesting

Mourning doves may mate and nest in any month of the year, but males begin to tune up their songs in late winter. They have a production-line breeding mode, following one brood with another as often as six times in a season. The twig nest platform, placed in a wide variety of tree species, but frequently in a pine, is often flimsy enough so that eggs show through from beneath. Two eggs are incubated by both members of the pair, and they hatch in 14 days. Young doves are fed first on crop milk, a secretion unique to the pigeon family, and later on regurgitated seeds. Young remain in the nest for another 15 days but may fledge much earlier. The male feeds them until about day 30, while the female re-nests. Immature birds are visibly smaller and have fine, buff feather edges overall.

Backyard & Beyond

Mourning doves take any seeds that might be offered at feeders, preferring sunflower seeds, cracked corn, millet, milo, and other grains found in seed mixes. They become adept at emptying hopper feeders into their ample crops, and then sitting for long periods afterward to digest their food.

Rock Pigeon

Columba livia

Spring/Summer
Year-Round
Winter

Originating in northern Europe, Africa, and India, rock pigeons—largely gone from their former wild haunts—have spread to cities and towns worldwide thanks to their domestication some five thousand years ago. Evidence of this domestication lies in their highly variable coloration; a flock may contain birds in every color from pure white to reddish to solid black.

All About

A substantial bird with a small head, deep chest, powerful wings, and a square tail, the rock pigeon is built for flight. Wild-type birds are slate-blue with a white rump, black terminal tail band, and two black bars on the secondary wing feathers. Pinkish green iridescence adorns the neck. Pigeons have short, reddish legs and a short, straight bill. Their song is a series of soft, resonant coos—*ooh-ga-rooogh*—and a harsh *Woogh!* serves as an alarm call. Pigeons can be found in flocks except when tending young.

Habitat & Range

It is rare to find rock pigeons in natural habitats, though there are still some cliff-nesting populations in North America. Most consider tall buildings, with their myriad ledges, to be ideal nesting grounds and are happy to take foods, such as bread and popcorn, from city sidewalks. Pigeons are nonmigratory, though their celebrated homing skills are exploited by pigeon racing clubs across the world.

Feeding

Walking and pecking with rapidly bobbing heads, pigeons find their preferred food—grains, seeds, and some fruits—on the ground. Urban birds have highly developed scavenging skills, raiding trashcans and fast food litter for high-carbohydrate fare, such as bread.

Nesting

It's easy to watch pigeons display and even mate; the male's spinning, bowing, and cooing may be conducted underfoot on city sidewalks. Pigeons mate for life, guarding females zealously. They may lay eggs and raise young anytime. Building ledges, highway overpasses, barns, bridges, and other structures may be selected as the site on which to build a stick-and-grass nest and lay two eggs. Both male and female incubate for about 18 days. The rubbery, black-skinned squabs stay in the nest for a variable period of 25 to 45 days. Fat at fledging, they may be forced to fend entirely for themselves upon leaving the nest.

Backyard & Beyond

Thanks to the flocking habit of pigeons, most feeder operators are less than delighted when they descend. The most effective deterrents seem to be sturdy feeders enclosed by wire caging that excludes pigeons while admitting smaller birds. Some people opt to spread food at a distance to keep pigeons from overwhelming seed feeders. Pigeons will eat anything that might be offered, but millet and cracked corn are special favorites.

Yellow-billed Cuckoo

Coccyzus americanus

Spring/Summer
Year-Round
Winter

The yellow-billed cuckoo is a furtive, skulking bird of thickets and brushy woodland edges and, though it is fairly large, its retiring habits make it far more easily heard than seen. It often hides deep within the foliage and, when perching in the open, it tends to remain very still. The yellow-billed cuckoo makes a unique repetitive clucking sound that is a sure clue to identification.

All About

Slender and long-tailed, the yellow-billed cuckoo has a plain brown back and creamy white breast. The underside of the tail shows a pattern of bold white spots against a black background, and bright rufous wing patches are visible in flight. The lower part of the bill is yellow. Male and female yellow-billed cuckoos look alike. The only other species they are likely to be confused with is the related black-billed cuckoo, which lacks the rufous wing color and has a black bill, among other differences.

Habitat & Range

Yellow-billed cuckoos inhabit deciduous woodland edges, thickets and tangles along watercourses or roadsides, willow groves, and overgrown orchards. Yellow-billed cuckoos are not generally found in deep interior woodlands, as they prefer some kind of "edge" to their habitat.

Feeding

Yellow-billed cuckoos eat great numbers of hairy caterpillars and many large insects such as dragonflies, cicadas, grasshoppers, crickets, and beetles. Small fruits are a minor but regular part of their diet in summer. Most yellow-billed cuckoos forage by slowly and methodically exploring branches, twigs, and leaves for hidden insects, but they occasionally may act like flycatchers, darting into the air for a meal on the wing, or hovering to seize a caterpillar at the edge of a leaf.

Nesting

Once paired, cuckoos survey the surrounding area for a leafy and secluded nest site, five to ten feet off the ground. Both help build a loose shell of twigs and stems, lining it with fine grasses. Three to five eggs are laid, and both parents share the incubation and feeding of the young. The entire process, from egg laying to fledging, takes only 17 days, one of the shortest such periods for any bird species.

Backyard & Beyond

If you have mature trees rimming your backyard, you may have an occasional yellow-billed cuckoo stopping by on migration—listen for its patented clucking calls. An old folk name for the yellow-billed cuckoo is "raincrow," because these *kowp-kowp-kowp* calls are so often uttered on hot summer afternoons, when thunderstorms are likely to follow. Knowing the cuckoo's call will be helpful in finding this secretive bird; otherwise, check the thickets and edges of your local woodland or park for a chance to find this species.

Great Horned Owl

Bubo virginianus

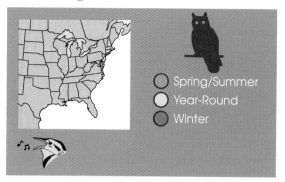

- Spring/Summer
- Year-Round
- Winter

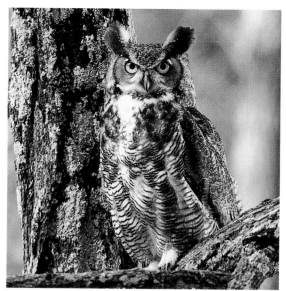

Huge, powerful, and widespread across North America, the great horned is the king of all of our owls. Armed with incredible vision, the great horned sees and pounces on prey, using its powerful talons and bill to dispatch its victim. The deep, hooting call of the great horned—whoo-who-o-o-o-who-who—a staple of movie and television soundtracks, is most often heard in nature just after sunset.

All About

The great horned owl is named for its large size (up to 24 inches tall, with a wingspan of 44 inches) and its long feathered head tufts (horns). A deep rusty brown and buff overall, this owl has large, golden-yellow eyes. Its thick, soft feathers provide excellent insulation from either heat or cold, permitting the great horned to nest as soon as early to midwinter even in regions with harsh winter weather.

Habitat & Range

A nonmigratory bird throughout the Americas, great horned owls can be found as far north as the tree line, and as far south as South America—and in nearly every conceivable habitat and setting. Great horned owls are equally at home in urban and suburban settings, as well as in deep woodlands, grasslands, and deserts.

Feeding

Mammals (rabbits, hares, and large rodents) are the primary prey item of great horned owls. They also eat earthworms, fish, snakes, and even birds as large as great blue herons. They are one of the few predators that will readily kill and consume skunks. Within a great horned owl's territory, it's unusual to find other, smaller owls—they may have been eaten by the resident great horneds. Their primary hunting mode is to perch, watch, and pounce on prey.

Nesting

Great horned owls most often take over an old stick nest built by a hawk, heron, or squirrel, but they will also nest on cliff ledges, in tree cavities, and even on the ground. Two to four eggs are laid and incubation by the female lasts slightly more than a month. The male brings food to his mate on the nest each night. Six weeks or so after hatching, the young owlets venture from the nest to nearby branches. They remain dependent on the adults for many months, but leave the nest area before the next breeding season.

Backyard & Beyond

If you live in or near older woodlands, chances are good that great horned owls are your neighbors. Though there is little you can do to attract great horned owls to your property, listen just after dusk and before dawn for their deep hoots, which carry for great distances. Watch for the great horned's silhouette at dusk along woodland edges, especially in treetops and on power poles.

Barred Owl

Strix varia

Spring/Summer
Year-Round
Winter

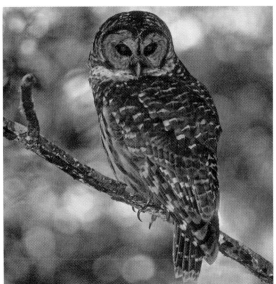

Who cooks for you? Who cooks for you all? *The wild hoots of the barred owl echo through swampy, deciduous woodlands throughout the eastern United States. Its dark, liquid eyes give it a deceptively gentle look, but this owl is a top-of-the-line predator, taking everything from fish to rabbits. Though it does some daylight hunting, most of the barred owl's foraging takes place at night.*

All About

A rounded, earless outline, smoky gray-brown plumage that is heavily mottled and barred with white, broad brown streaks on a white belly, and dark eyes distinguish the barred owl. Its bill and feet are yellow. Its familiar eight-hoot call gives way to raucous and sometimes frightening caterwauling in breeding season. This species is more apt to call in daylight than any other; it may call all day during overcast conditions.

Habitat & Range

Like its famous endangered cousin the spotted owl, the barred owl prefers old forest, probably in part because the large nesting cavities it requires occur in trees of ample girth. It is commonly associated with lowlands, but occupies upland sites as well. The barred owl does not migrate, but may wander in harsh winters.

Feeding

Anything it can kill is fair game for this medium-large owl. Small mammals, as small as mice and up to the size of rabbits, make up at least half the barred owl's diet. It makes acrobatic strikes after squirrels, sometimes turning completely over in flight. Birds, amphibians, reptiles, insects, and other invertebrates compose the rest of its diet.

Nesting

Most barred owls select large nest cavities, such as those formed when a large branch breaks off of a hollow tree. They will also use a hollow in a broken tree trunk, as well as the nests of other raptors or squirrels. Two to three eggs are incubated by the female alone. They hatch from 28 to 33 days later. The male feeds the family for the first two weeks of the chicks' life, after which the female leaves them and helps bring in food. Young owls, clothed in buff-colored down, begin venturing onto branches when they are around five weeks old, before they can fly. They give a hideous, rasping screech as a location call and may be found and observed discreetly from a safe distance. Fledglings are fed by their parents until early autumn, when they strike out to find new territory.

Backyard & Beyond

Surprisingly enough, the barred owl will accept nest boxes, because tree cavities large enough to contain them are hard to find. Plans for a wood duck nest box with a seven-inch entrance hole should accommodate them. This should be mounted as high as possible in a large tree.

Eastern Screech-Owl

Megascops asio

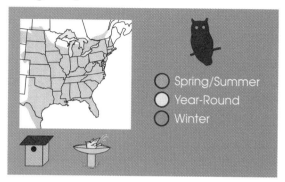

- ○ Spring/Summer
- ○ Year-Round
- ○ Winter

Eastern screech-owls are very acclimated to humans, but their nocturnal habits and cryptic coloration keep us from seeing them regularly. Even when perched in full view in daylight, screech-owls have a remarkable ability to conceal themselves. Found commonly in cities and towns, the screech-owl's success may be due not only to its secretive nature, but also to its ability to take a wide variety of small prey.

All About

A small bird (8½ inches long), the eastern screech-owl occurs in two color variations: reddish and gray, with gray being more common. The screech-owl's plumage appears very barklike. When a "screech" sits with its body elongated and ear tufts extended, it looks like a broken branch stub. This bird's name is misleading; a screech is rarely voiced. The call most bird watchers hear is a series of descending, whinnying whistles and tremolos on a single note.

Habitat & Range

A nonmigratory, resident bird throughout the eastern United States, the screech-owl is found wherever woodlands are mature enough to have cavities. Unlike many other owl species, the screech-owl is commonly found in urban parks and suburban backyards.

Feeding

Eastern screech-owls will eat almost anything—from mice and voles to moths, earthworms, crawfish, frogs, and fish. In spring and summer, they prey upon small and medium-sized songbirds, but during winter small mammals are more common prey. Screech-owls perch in a tree, waiting and watching for potential prey, most of which is captured with the owl's feet in flight or by pouncing on the ground.

Nesting

Screech-owls nest in natural cavities and will readily use nest boxes. They begin nesting early, from mid-December in the South to late March in the North. Two to six eggs are laid and a month-long incubation period ensues. The female incubates the eggs and broods the young owlets, while the male delivers all the food. Owlets remain in the nest for a month before venturing into nearby trees. They remain dependent on their parents for two months.

Backyard & Beyond

You may very well already have eastern screech-owls in or near your backyard. Spend some time outside at night—especially when the moon is full—listening for the screech-owl's wavering calls. Check natural tree cavities during the day for roosting or nesting owls—they may be peering out of the hole. You can attract screech-owls with an owl nest box. Boxes should be about 12 to 14 inches deep with an internal floor size of 7×7 inches and a 2³/₄-inch diameter entry. Place the box above 10 feet high in a shady spot on a tree trunk wider than the box's width.

Whip-poor-will

Caprimulgus vociferus

│*magine sleeping all day and flying around the woods singing all night. That's the life of the whip-poor-will. Like its relatives the common nighthawk and chuck-will's widow, the "whip" is most active at night and is often heard calling out its name repeatedly—whip-poor-WILL! whip-poor-WILL! In fact, they have been known to give this call continuously, more than a thousand times in a row. Because of its nocturnal habits and coloration, many bird watchers never get a good look at a whip-poor-will.*

All About

The whip-poor-will's body is just under 10 inches in length, and its wingspan is 19 inches—nearly 7 inches shorter than that of the chuck-will's-widow. The whip-poor-will's plumage is a subtle mix of charcoal gray, buff, black, and white. In flight, it shows prominent white corners on the tail. The large, dark eyes of the whip-poor-will are designed to function in the low-light conditions of dawn and dusk.

Habitat & Range

Whip-poor-wills prefer mixed woodlands with little underbrush, open farmlands, brushy fields, and rural roadways. These habitats all lend themselves to the pursuit of flying insects. Whips spend the winter in Florida, around the Gulf Coast, and into Mexico and Central America. They return each spring as early as March. In southern portions of the Midwest, the whip-poor-will is replaced by the closely related chuck-will's-widow.

Feeding

The whip-poor-will is an insect specialist, perching and watching for passing prey, which it pursues in silent flight. Stiff bristle feathers line its wide-opening bill and funnel flying insects into its mouth as it flies along. Primary food items include mosquitoes, moths, beetles, and grasshoppers. Most foraging is done in the half-light of dusk and dawn, and on brightly moonlit nights.

Nesting

A ground nester, the whip-poor-will builds no nest. As early as mid-April, two eggs are laid in a concealed spot on the ground and incubated by both sexes for about 20 days. After hatching, the young birds remain with the parents for two weeks, with both parents sharing the brooding. Young whips are able move around on the ground within a few days after hatching; they are able to fly at about 16 days old. This early mobility helps young whip-poor-wills avoid predators.

Backyard & Beyond

Whip-poor-wills are declining in some parts of their range due to the effects of pesticides and the loss of breeding habitats. If you are close to a calling whip-poor-will, listen for the *cluck* sound that it makes just prior to the *whip*. Perhaps the best way to see whip-poor-wills is to watch for them at dusk as they make their silent, batlike forays after insects along woodland edges and over meadows.

Common Nighthawk

Chordeiles minor

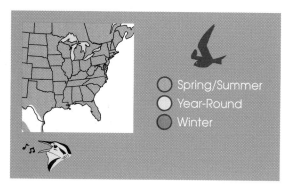

- ○ Spring/Summer
- ○ Year-Round
- ○ Winter

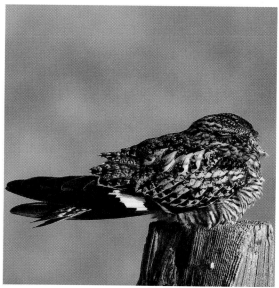

Peent! *is the nasal flight call of the common nighthawk, a familiar sound in cities and towns, though it is usually mistaken for an insect call. This call accompanies the batlike flight of the nighthawk as it courses through the sky, hawking insects. Despite its name, the nighthawk is not a hawk and is active both day and night.*

All About

The common nighthawk is a long-winged, dark bird with characteristic white wing slashes. Its distinctive bounding flight can be used to identify it from a distance as it forages over fields, towns, and woods. Nighthawks belong to the goatsucker family, a name based on the old myth that they drank milk from livestock at night.

Habitat & Range

A common breeding bird throughout North America, nighthawks can be seen in flight over almost any habitat. In cities and towns, nighthawks are attracted to the insects around streetlamps. Beginning in late July, nighthawks can be seen at dusk in large migratory flocks, sometimes numbering dozens of birds. Nighthawks winter in South America, returning to the southern United States by early April.

Feeding

A specialist in catching flying insects, the common nighthawk's mouth opens wide to capture its prey. The nighthawk sees its prey—most often flying ants, beetles, moths, and mayflies—and pursues and catches it. When a nighthawk needs water, it swoops low over a lake or river and skims a drink from the surface.

Nesting

Historically, nighthawk nests were found on the ground in grasslands and in open patches of soil, gravel, or sand. The nest is a shallow depression near a log or stone that helps to shade and conceal it. Now, nighthawk nests are more commonly found on gravel roads or on flat, gravel-covered rooftops in urban areas. The female selects the nest site, lays two eggs, and handles the 18-day incubation. Young nighthawks are brooded by the female for 15 days, protecting them from sun and weather. The male feeds both his mate and the young in the nest. After 20 days, the young birds are able to fly, and the male then takes over their care while the female starts a second nest.

Backyard & Beyond

Nighthawks have good success nesting on gravel roofs, but not so on roofs lined with rubber or foam, materials that pool water and retain heat. Watch and listen for nighthawks in the sky at dawn and dusk. You may hear their *peent!* before you see them. During courtship, male nighthawks perform a diving display near females, swooping swiftly toward the ground. As the male comes out of the dive, he flares his flight feathers, creating a booming sound much like a large truck shifting gears.

Chimney Swift

Chaetura pelagica

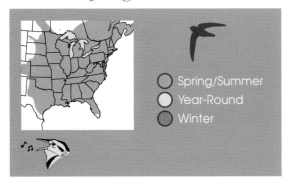

- ○ Spring/Summer
- ○ Year-Round
- ○ Winter

Known by bird watchers as "the flying cigar," the chimney swift is a familiar sight in the sky over cities and towns during the spring, summer, and fall. Its nickname aptly describes the swift's elongated flight silhouette. The twittering calls of chimney swifts are one of the most common bird sounds of summer. The chimney swift is named for its preferred nesting and roosting site—the inside of chimneys. This species spends much of its life on the wing, stopping only to sleep and nest.

All About

Chimney swifts are a dark charcoal-gray overall with a small black bill, eyes, and tiny feet. Indeed their feet are almost useless for walking, but are perfect for clinging to the inside of a chimney. The chimney swift is nearly all wing—with a 5-inch long body and a 14-inch wingspan. Four hundred years ago, all chimney swifts nested in hollow trees and caves, but the arrival of European settlers and their stone chimneys soon provided abundant nesting sites. Today most chimney swifts nest in chimneys and other human structures, such as unused smokestacks and abandoned buildings.

Habitat & Range

Widespread and common across the eastern half of the United States and southern Canada, the chimney swift is found wherever there are suitable nest sites. Fall migratory flocks of swifts are a magnificent spectacle as they form a swirling, chattering cloud descending to roost in a large chimney at dusk. In winter, this tiny bird migrates to South America, returning again in March to the southern United States.

Feeding

An all-insect diet is captured and consumed on the wing. Swifts often are seen flying high in the sky when foraging.

Nesting

A pair of swifts chooses a nest site—usually a chimney. The nest is a half-saucer shape made of sticks held together and made to adhere to the wall of cavity by the birds' saliva. Swifts break small twigs off trees, grabbing them with their feet as they fly past a tree. Two to five eggs are laid, and both parents share incubation (15 days) and brooding duties until the young swifts fledge at about 19 days after hatching.

Backyard & Beyond

Allowing chimney swifts to nest in your older, unused chimney is really easy—just let the swifts find it. They pose no danger and, if not for the sounds of hungry nestlings during a two-week period, you might not know they are there. If hosting swifts is not your cup of tea, check around your town or region for chimneys being used by swifts. Watch for them entering or leaving the large brick chimneys on schools and old factories. Modern chimneys with metal caps and flues are impossible for swifts to use.

Ruby-throated Hummingbird

Archilochus colubris

Spring/Summer
Year-Round
Winter

The only breeding hummingbird east of the Great Plains, the rubythroat enlivens many gardens and yards with its presence. Males are fiercely combative and will defend a single nectar source against all comers. Spectacular pendulum flights, constant chittering, the low hum of beating wings, and the occasional smack of tiny bodies colliding are familiar to anyone lucky enough to have rubythroats at their nectar feeders.

All About

Seen in direct sunlight, the male's ruby throat patch dazzles. Both male and female are iridescent green above. The female's underparts are white, and she sports white spots on her rounded tail. Males appear smaller and darker overall, with grayish-olive underparts and a slightly forked, all dark tail. A squeaky *chip* is uttered constantly while feeding. Males sing a seldom heard, monotonous song from exposed perches at daybreak.

Habitat & Range

Rubythroats prefer mixed deciduous woodlands with clearings, where wildflowers and abundant small insects can be found. They're fairly common in forested areas across the entire eastern United States, falling off abruptly at the Great Plains. Virtually all rubythroats leave for the winter, many making the arduous nonstop flight across the Gulf of Mexico on fat reserves alone. Rubythroats winter in Central America.

Feeding

Though they are usually regarded as wholly nectivorous, rubythroats take a great number of small insects, which they catch by gleaning or in aerial pursuit. They may even rob spider webs of their catch. They are strongly attracted to red or orange flowers, but rubythroats will take nectar from flowers of any color. They hover and probe rapidly, often perching to feed.

Nesting

Once a male rubythroat has mated, his investment in the offspring is over. The female constructs a walnut-sized, thick-walled cup of plant down and spider silk, bound tightly with elastic spider web and encrusted with lichens. This well-insulated nest protects the two lentil-sized eggs when she must leave to forage. The young hatch after about 13 days and remain in the nest for about 21 days. The female regurgitates small insects and nectar into their crops. They are fed for at least a week or longer after fledging.

Backyard & Beyond

Attract rubythroats with a 1:4 solution of white table sugar (sucrose) and water. Wash feeders with hot soapy water every few days and replace the solution. Boiling the solution briefly helps it keep longer. Artificial coloring in the solution is unnecessary (feeders have ample red parts). To thwart a bullying male, hang several feeders within a few feet of each other. He'll be unable to defend them all.

Belted Kingfisher

Ceryle alcyon

Spring/Summer
Year-Round
Winter

The belted kingfisher is a bird many recognize but few know well. Kingfishers take wariness to new extremes, uttering a loud rattle of alarm and swooping off at the slightest disturbance. The belted kingfisher's piercing rattle call, usually given as it takes flight, is more often heard than this wary bird is seen. They are a thrilling presence on streams, rivers, lakes, and marshes—wherever clear water and small fish abound.

All About

Almost comical in proportion, the belted kingfisher has an oversized crested head and a heavy spearlike bill, but diminutive feet. It cannot walk, but only shuffle, and it relies entirely on flight for most of its locomotion. Slate-blue upperparts, a stark-white collar and underparts, and a bluish breast band complete the ensemble. The female wears a "bra"—another rufous breast band below the blue one.

Habitat & Range

Because it is a sight hunter, the belted kingfisher seeks out clear water. Most often found along clear running streams, lakes, and ponds, it will also hunt drainage ditches and marshes. Nesting requires an exposed earthen bank. Kingfishers are migratory in northern latitudes. Though they can survive winter temperatures, they require open water year-round; thus, southern birds may migrate only as far as they must to find open water.

Feeding

Most of its hunting is done from a perch, but the belted kingfisher also hunts on the wing. Suspended in midair like an angel, it hovers, seemingly weightless, over a riffle. Spotting a minnow, it closes its wings and plunges bill-first into the water. It carries the fish in its bill to a sturdy perch (usually a dead snag or partially submerged branch), where it subdues its prey by whacking its head against the perch with sideways flips of its bill. The fish is then swallowed head first. Belted kingfishers also take crayfish and (to a much lesser extent) amphibians, reptiles, small mammals, and young birds.

Nesting

Kingfishers occasionally are forced to commute, if they are unable to find a dry earthen bank near their chosen feeding territory. They may use sand and gravel pits, landfills, or road cuts. This species excavates, digging rapidly with tiny feet straight into the bank, creating a round entrance hole and an upward-sloping tunnel that may extend as much as six feet into the bank. A chamber at the end holds five to eight eggs, which both male and female incubate for about 22 days. Young stay in the burrow for up to 29 days and are fed by their parents for three more weeks.

Backyard & Beyond

Any clear body of water, including backyard ponds with plump goldfish, can host a hunting kingfisher.

Red-headed Woodpecker

Melanerpes erythrocephalus

Spring/Summer
Year-Round
Winter

A striking combination of red, black, and white, the red-headed woodpecker is our most easily identifiable woodpecker and a favorite of many bird watchers. Though the species was first described in 1758, Native Americans had long used skins of the red-headed woodpecker as a battle ornament. Sadly, the red-headed has suffered population declines throughout its range, but it remains locally common in the proper habitat.

All About

The red-headed woodpecker could be called the red-*hooded* woodpecker because the red on adult birds forms a complete hood. Some mistakenly refer to the red-bellied woodpecker (which has a Mohawk stripe of red) as a red-headed woodpecker. The red-head's black back and tail are set off by a bright white breast and belly and an all-white patch of secondary (inner) wing feathers. The effect of these contrasting colors is stunning in flight. Red-heads give a variety of *churr-churr* calls as well as a loud, throaty *Queeah!*

Habitat & Range

Prior to the 1900s, red-headed woodpeckers were common in cities and towns. Today, red-heads are sparingly distributed across most of the eastern United States, usually in woods with mature oaks or beeches, in isolated woodlots along rivers, or in dead trees along flooded river bottoms and beaver ponds. Habitats affected by humans—strip mines, clear cuts, tree plantations, and farmlands—may attract red-headed woodpeckers as long as there are scattered, standing trees.

Feeding

Red-heads have the most varied diet of all woodpeckers, but they seem especially attached to acorns and beechnuts. They are excellent fly-catchers and are known to eat grasshoppers, fruits, corn, eggs, mice, and even bird nestlings. When nuts and insects are plentiful, red-heads will cache them for later consumption, hiding food items in bark crevices and knotholes. At bird feeders, red-heads eat sunflower seeds, peanuts, and suet, but they are particularly attracted to cracked corn.

Nesting

Avid excavators of nesting and roosting holes, red-heads thus provide homes for many other cavity-nesting creatures. Nest holes are almost always in dead trees or dead portions of living trees, though wooden telephone poles are also used. Five eggs is the normal clutch, and both parents share in the two-week incubation duties. Young birds spend three weeks in the nest cavity before fledging, and they emerge with gray, not red, heads.

Backyard & Beyond

Red-headed woodpeckers are very aggressive and can out-compete European starlings for nest cavities. Look for red-heads in large stands of trees (especially oaks) with little vegetation below them, as in a park or golf course. Reliable locations for seeing red-headed woodpeckers are becoming noteworthy as the species declines.

Red-bellied Woodpecker

Melanerpes carolinus

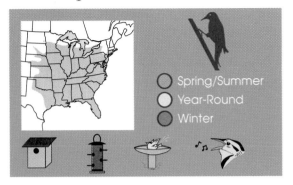

- Spring/Summer
- Year-Round
- Winter

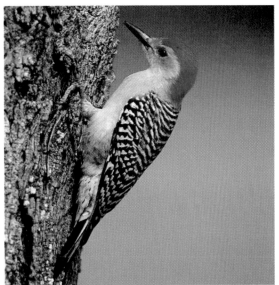

The red-bellied woodpecker is so common, vocal, and eye-catching that it might be elected "most familiar woodpecker" in a vote of bird watchers in the eastern United States. Although occasionally misidentified as a red-headed woodpecker because of the male redbelly's bill-to-nape stripe of bright red, the red-bellied woodpecker actually is quite different in appearance—and much more common—than the real red-headed woodpecker, which sports an all-red head.

All About

A medium-sized (9 1/4 inches long) woodpecker with a stout, chisel-shaped bill and a zebra pattern of black-and-white horizontal strips on the back, the red-bellied woodpecker is named for a feature we rarely see—a light wash of pink or red on its belly. Hitching up tree trunks with the aid of its strong feet and stiff tail, the bird's red belly is almost always obscured. Adult males have a solid strip of red from the top of the bill and head and down the back of the neck (the nape). Females have a red nape, but are brownish on the top of the head. The redbelly's loud, rich call sounds like *qurrrr*, and its longer version is more rattling and harsher—*chrr, chrr, chrchrchrchr*.

Habitat & Range

A year-round resident across the eastern United States, the redbelly is an adaptable bird, found wherever there are mature trees. They do not migrate, though some northern birds may move southward in winter.

Feeding

The redbelly is an expert at excavating insects from trees using its bill as a chisel and its long, barbed tongue to extract food items. It will also eat berries, fruits, nuts, tree sap, salamanders, mice, and even small nestling birds. At bird-feeding stations, redbellies relish peanuts, suet, sunflower seeds, and cracked corn.

Nesting

The male redbelly begins courtship by drumming (a rapid pounding with the bill) on a tree trunk or branch to attract the female's attention. Both male and female excavate the nest cavity, which is usually located in a dead tree below an overhanging branch. The 8- to 12-inch deep cavity will accommodate four eggs. Incubation duties are shared and last about 12 days. Nestlings are fed in the nest cavity by both parents for almost a month before they fledge; afterward, they remain near the nest and are fed by the parents for several more weeks. Nest hole competition from European starlings can be fierce and usually results in the redbellies being evicted and forced to excavate a new nest elsewhere.

Backyard & Beyond

Peanuts and suet are the redbelly's favored foods, but you can also offer apple halves stuck on a tree stub, sunflower bits, and grape jelly (in a small dish). Listen for the redbelly's loud, ringing calls and watch for its swooping flight.

Downy Woodpecker

Picoides pubescens

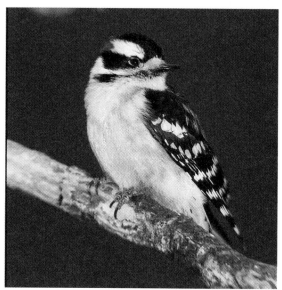

Downy woodpeckers are a favorite of backyard bird watchers because they are often the first woodpeckers to visit bird feeders. Common in any habitat with trees, downies are as equally at home in backyards as they are in remote woods. In all seasons, downy woodpeckers give a rattling whinny that descends in tone. They also utter a sharp pik! call regularly while foraging.

All About

The downy is the smallest (6³/4 inches long), most common, and most widespread woodpecker. Its black-and-white plumage is similar to that of the larger (9¹/4 inches long) hairy woodpecker. In both species, the males have a red patch at the back of the head. Downy woodpeckers have an all-white breast and belly and a white stripe down the middle of the back. The wings and tail are black with spots of white.

Habitat & Range

A common resident of woodlands throughout North America, the downy is a habitat generalist—found anywhere there are trees or woody plants on which to find food. Though their population appears stable, downies suffer from nest site competition and from the removal of dead trees, which they need for nesting and feeding.

Feeding

Downy woodpeckers use their stiff tails and strong, clawed feet to propel themselves along tree branches or trunks. As they move along,

downies probe and chisel at the tree's bark, searching for insects, insect eggs, ants, and spiders. They also eat fruits, such as sumac and poison ivy. At bird feeders, sunflower seeds and bits, suet, peanuts, and peanut butter are favorite foods.

Nesting

Like all woodpeckers, downies are cavity nesters. Each spring they excavate a new nest hole in the dead stub or trunk of a tree—usually one that is already rotting. The nest hole is placed underneath an overhanging branch higher than 12 feet above the ground. Excavation can take as long as two weeks—even with the male and female participating. Clutch size is usually four to five white eggs, with both sexes incubating. Hatching occurs at 12 days, and both parents feed the young for about three weeks until they fledge.

Backyard & Beyond

Telling the downy and hairy woodpecker apart can be difficult. A way to remember which is which is: *Downy is dinky; hairy is huge.* Downies have a small body, small head, and a small, thin bill. Hairies have a big body, a big head, and a large, chisellike bill. Though downies rarely nest in nest boxes, they readily use them for nighttime roosting, especially in harsh weather. Leave a dead tree or large dead branch on a tree in your yard (in a safe location), and you will be much more likely to attract woodpeckers.

Hairy Woodpecker

Picoides villosus

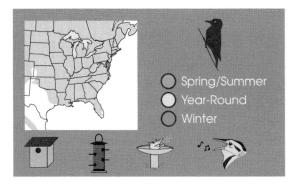

- ○ Spring/Summer
- ○ Year-Round
- ○ Winter

A familiar visitor to bird feeders, the hairy wood-pecker is named for the long, hairlike white feathers on its back. The hairy looks like a super-sized version of a downy woodpecker, but the best way to tell these two similar species apart is to compare the length of the bill to the length (front-to-back) of the head. The hairy's bill is always longer than the width of its head, and the downy's bill is always shorter than the length of its head. An easier way to remember is: Downy is dinky; hairy is huge.

All About

Hairy woodpeckers are medium-sized wood-peckers (9¼ inches long) with a long, sturdy, chisel-like bill that is used for finding food, for excavating nest holes, and for territorial drum-ming on hollow trees. Males and females look the same with white bellies, a white central back stripe, and distinctly patterned black and white on faces and wings. Adult males, however, have a red patch at the back of the head. Hairies utter a sharp *Peek!* call, as well as a loud ringing rattle on a single pitch.

Habitat & Range

Hairy woodpeckers are year-round residents across North America in mature forests and wherever there are large trees, including suburban backyards, urban parks, and isolated woodlots. They are one of our most widespread woodpeckers with a range extending into Central America.

Feeding

Using their bill, hairy woodpeckers can glean insects from tree bark or excavate them from beneath the bark's surface. Primary diet items include beetles, spiders, moth larvae, and ants, as well as fruits, seeds, and nuts. At bird feeders, hairies readily eat sunflower seeds, peanuts, suet, and cracked corn.

Nesting

It can take up to three weeks for a pair of hairy woodpeckers to excavate their nest cavity in the trunk or dead branch of a living tree. When completed, the nest cavity will have a 2-inch entry hole and will be 4 inches wide and as deep as 16 inches. Into this cozy space, four eggs are laid, and both parents share the roughly two-week incubation period. Less than a month after hatching, young hairies are ready to fledge from the nest, though the parents tend them for sev-eral more weeks. A new nest is excavated each spring, but old cavities are used for roosting at night and in winter.

Backyard & Beyond

If your neighborhood has large shade trees or mature woods, chances are good that you've got hairy woodpeckers nearby. Check large, dead snags and branches for woodpecker holes and listen for the birds' vocalizations and drumming in spring. Offer peanuts, sunflower seeds, or suet (in winter) in hanging feeders to attract hairy woodpeckers to your yard.

Yellow-bellied Sapsucker

Sphyrapicus varius

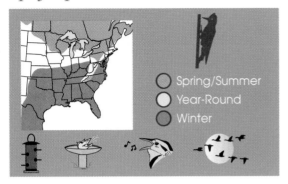

Spring/Summer
Year-Round
Winter

Even non-bird watchers know this bird's name, but few have ever seen this quiet member of the woodpecker family. Named for its habit of drinking sap running from the holes it drills in trees, the yellow-bellied sapsucker inadvertently provides sap to a host of other creatures, including hummingbirds, warblers, butterflies and other insects, squirrels, and chipmunks.

All About

The yellow-bellied sapsucker is a medium-sized woodpecker with extensive black-and-white barring over much of its back, wings, and tail. Adults have a brilliant red crown patch and adult males have a red throat patch outlined in black. Females have a white throat. The lemon-yellow belly can be difficult to see on perched birds. Juveniles are very dull-brown versions of the black-and-white adults. Winter and migrant sapsuckers are usually silent, but may give a cat-like, nasal *queeaah* call. In breeding season, sapsuckers are very noisy with lots of calling and staccato drumming.

Habitat & Range

Found in a variety of mixed-woodland habitats, but with a preference for aspen, maple, and fruit trees because of their sap production, the sapsucker will revisit and redrill sap holes from previous seasons and prior years. They breed across the entire breadth of Canada and across the northernmost tier of U.S. states from North Dakota to New England. They migrate to the southeastern quarter of the United States in winter, though some birds venture to Central America and to the Caribbean islands.

Feeding

Sapsuckers drill a line of small holes in the bark of a tree trunk, causing it to ooze sap, which the sapsucker returns to drink later. Insects from sap wells, gleaned from trees or captured in flight, are another important food source, as are fruits, berries, and tree buds. Ruby-throated hummingbirds visit sap wells to drink the sweet sap and eat the insects attracted to it. Suet, suet dough, peanut butter, and fruit are among the foods sapsuckers eat at feeders.

Nesting

Male sapsuckers excavate the nest cavity in a deciduous tree and the female lays up to six eggs on wood chips inside. Both parents share the two weeks of incubation as well as the month-long period of nestling care. After fledging, the adults teach the young for about ten days to forage and drill for sap on their own.

Backyard & Beyond

Because they are mostly silent in winter, you might miss a sapsucker as it sits quietly drilling small sap holes in your backyard. Inspect trees for evidence that a sapsucker has visited: a line of uniform, small holes drilled midway up a tree trunk. If a sapsucker has visited recently you'll see the liquid sap oozing from the holes.

Northern Flicker

Colaptes auratus

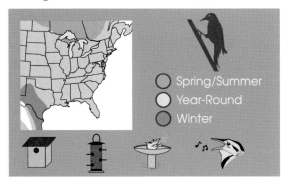

- ○ Spring/Summer
- ○ Year-Round
- ○ Winter

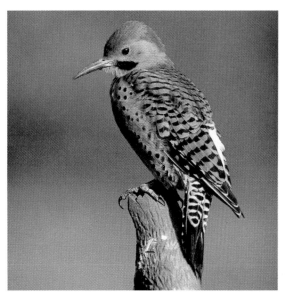

A familiar and fairly large (13 inches long) wood-pecker, the northern flicker is a distinctively marked bird that—unlike other woodpeckers—is often seen foraging on the ground. The eastern form of the flicker is known as the yellow-shafted flicker for its bright lemon-yellow underwing and tail color. A red-shafted form of the northern flicker occurs in the West. There are more than 130 different names by which the flicker is known, including high-hole, yellowhammer, and yawkerbird.

All About

The northern flicker is all field marks with its bright yellow wing flashes, white rump, spotted breast, and barred back. It is not easily confused with any other bird. In the East, both sexes have a red crescent on the back of the head, but only males show a black "moustache" mark on the cheek. The flicker has several calls including a single note *kleer*, a short *wickawicka* series, and a monotonous *wickwickwickwick* song. It also communicates by drumming on the resonating surface of a tree, pole, or even metal downspouts and chimney flues.

Habitat & Range

Widespread across North America, the northern flicker is found almost everywhere wooded habitats exist, though open woods and woodland edges are preferred. Flickers in the northern portion of the range migrate southward in winter, while southern birds are nonmigratory.

Feeding

Flickers feed on the ground where they specialize in eating ants. A flicker pokes its long bill into an anthill and uses its long, sticky tongue to extract the ants. They also eat other insects, as well as fruits and seeds. At bird feeders, they will eat suet, peanuts, fruits, and sunflower bits.

Nesting

Excavating a new nest cavity almost every year, flickers perform a much-needed service for many other hole-nesting birds—from chickadees to ducks—that use old flicker nests. Both sexes excavate the nest cavity in a dead tree or branch. The female lays between 5 and 10 eggs; both sexes share the 11-day incubation period. Young flickers leave the nest after about 25 days. Flickers will use nest boxes with an interior floor of 7×7 inches, an interior height of 16 to 24 inches, and a $2^{1}/_{2}$-inch entry hole. Because excavation is a vital part of courtship, boxes packed full of woodchips are more attractive. Competition for cavities from European starlings is fierce and may be causing a decline in flickers.

Backyard & Beyond

Offering suet, corn, or peanuts and nest boxes in your wooded backyard is one way to attract flickers. Equally important is the presence of ground-dwelling insects (leave those non-threatening anthills alone!) and dead trees or dead branches. A large, dead tree branch placed vertically in your yard may entice a flicker to stop.

Eastern Wood-Pewee

Contopus virens

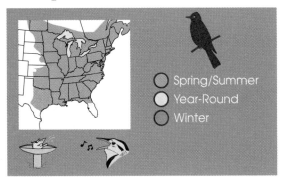

○ Spring/Summer
◐ Year-Round
○ Winter

PeeUWEEE? *and* PWEE-eehr *are plaintive sounds familiar to many forest hikers, bikers, and birders. Eastern wood-pewees call their name time after time, but it often takes a little effort to see them—unless you happen to be standing under a branch from which one flaps out, snaps up an insect, and then returns to the same spot.*

All About
Compared with smaller *Empidonax* flycatchers, the eastern wood-pewee is more sturdy, longer-tailed, and longer-winged. It is also generally grayer in appearance, with gray washed across its entire breast (the Acadian flycatcher is mostly whitish below). The wood-pewee lacks the prominent eye ring present in the Acadian and some other *Empidonax* species. Unlike the eastern phoebe, the eastern wood-pewee has two prominent wing bars and a two-toned black-and-orange (not all-black) bill, and it does not pump its tail. It usually feeds higher up than the phoebe, sallying forth from bare branches to grab its prey.

Habitat & Range
Common nesters across the forested eastern United States and southeastern Canada, eastern wood-pewees reach their southern breeding limits from northern Florida west to central Texas. They nest in deciduous forests and mixed deciduous and coniferous forests; they are often active at the forest edge and in clearings.

Feeding
Eastern wood-pewees pick their insect prey from leaves while hovering, but they are most noticeable when they sally forth from an exposed perch to capture flying insects (often the snap of bill meeting bug is audible). After the capture, they often return to the same perch to repeat the entire process—after ingesting their latest meal. They are most active and most vocal early and late in the day.

Nesting
Eastern wood-pewee nests are shallow cups made of weeds, grasses, bark, and other materials; they are placed on tree branches above or well above head level. On the outside, the nest is often festooned with lichens; inside, it is lined with such soft materials as plant fluff, hair, and fine grasses. There, the female usually lays three eggs. She incubates the eggs for just under two weeks. Both the male and the female feed the young, which leave the nest about two weeks after hatching.

Backyard & Beyond
In many areas, eastern wood-pewees are common migrants. It pays to learn this bird's field marks rather than just memorizing its song because wood-pewees don't usually sing while migrating to or from their South American wintering grounds. By "planting" snags—dead trees or large dead tree limbs—in your garden, you can provide hunting perches for migrating wood-pewees and other flycatchers.

Eastern Phoebe

Sayornis phoebe

Spring/Summer
Year-Round
Winter

A very adaptable flycatcher, the eastern phoebe often nests on human structures, such as on building ledges, inside barns, under bridges, and in culverts. Nesting in such proximity to humans, phoebes are used to our activity and this apparent tameness allows us to think of them as "our phoebes." Many bird watchers consider the early spring return of the phoebe (and not the American robin) to be the most reliable sign of spring's arrival.

All About

The eastern phoebe, unlike most other flycatchers, is relatively easy to identify. A medium-sized bird that constantly wags its tail, the phoebe also gives a vocal clue to its identity by softly uttering its name—*fee-bee*. Phoebes are a dark, drab gray-brown on the back, with faint wing bars and a light breast and belly, often washed with yellow.

Habitat & Range

Wherever there is a suitable nesting ledge (with abundant flying insects nearby), phoebes may be found. Natural habitats include woodland edges and small streams. Common throughout most of eastern North America during the spring and summer (eastern phoebes breed far into northern Canada), in winter many phoebes migrate to the southern Atlantic Coast and along the Gulf Coast into Mexico.

Feeding

The eastern phoebe is a perch-and-wait hunter, watching for flying insects from an exposed perch and making short flying forays to nab its prey. Phoebes consume vast quantities of flying insects, but will also pluck food items from the ground or vegetation. Wasps, bees, flying ants, moths, and butterflies constitute much of their prey. In fall and winter, when insects are scarce, phoebes will eat small fruits and berries.

Nesting

Phoebes are early nesters throughout the breeding range, and nest building often begins almost immediately after a male attracts a mate to a likely site. Favored natural nest sites include rock ledges and caves, but they also nest in barns or outbuildings, and on handy ledges or sills on house porches. The female builds the cup-shaped nest out of mud, moss, and grass. Four to six eggs are laid and incubated by the female alone, for just over two weeks. Young phoebes, unless disturbed earlier, fledge after about 16 days.

Backyard & Beyond

Bird watchers love phoebes not only because they are common, but also because they are so full of energy and seem willing to make their nests in close proximity to humans. To attract phoebes to your property, place nesting shelves (about 6×8 inches in size) about a foot below the eaves of your house, garage, or outbuilding. Choose a site that is away from human activity and is as safe as possible from predators, such as snakes, raccoons, and cats.

Great Crested Flycatcher

Myiarchus crinitus

Spring/Summer
Year-Round
Winter

Although one of the largest and most common eastern flycatchers, the great crested is raucous enough that it is usually heard before it is seen. A loud, enthusiastic wheeep! or whit-whit-whit-whit call is most often heard in woodland clearings during the summer months. The great crested is unusual among eastern flycatchers in that it is a cavity nester, relying on old woodpecker holes, hollow trees, and even birdhouses for nest sites. Adding to this bird's preference for the unusual is its habit of using shed snakeskin in its nest construction.

All About

One of our larger flycatchers at $8^1/_2$ inches tall, the great crested is a pleasing blend of colors with a lemon belly and underwings and a rufous tail, set off by a gray head and olive back. Males and females are alike in appearance, and both will aggressively defend their nesting territory against trespassing birds of almost any species.

Habitat & Range

Great crested flycatchers can be found in open woodlands, forest clearings, and even in wooded city parks throughout eastern North America during the summer months. Winter finds most of them in southern Mexico and southward to South America, though some spend the winter in south Florida. Fall migration starts in late August, with spring migrants returning to the United States as early as late March.

Feeding

Capturing flying insects is the great crested's main foraging mode, but it will also glean insects from vegetation and supplement its diet with small berries and fruits. Butterflies, moths, beetles, and grasshoppers are its most common foods. Great cresteds usually forage high in the treetops or from a high, exposed perch.

Nesting

A cavity nester that cannot excavate its own nest hole, it must rely on finding old woodpecker holes, naturally occurring hollows in trees, or human-supplied nest boxes. After inspecting possible nest sites with her mate, the female begins nest building using an incredible array of material, including animal hair, feathers, pine needles, string, cellophane, and shed snakeskin. Why great cresteds use such a variety of materials is a mystery. Five or more eggs are laid and incubated by the female for about two weeks. Two weeks after hatching, young flycatchers leave the nest.

Backyard & Beyond

Any backyard with large shade trees and adjacent woodland in the eastern United States has the potential to attract nesting great crested flycatchers. To encourage them, leave standing any dead or hollow trees, especially ones with knotholes or existing woodpecker holes. Nest box dimensions should be: interior floor of 6×6 inches, inside height of 12 inches, entry hole of $1^3/_4$ to 2 inches. Mount at a height of 10 to 20 feet.

Eastern Kingbird

Tyrannus tyrannus

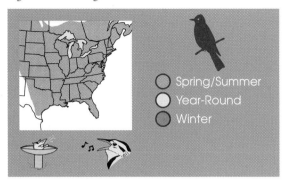

- Spring/Summer
- Year-Round
- Winter

High in the treetops a medium-sized, black-and-white bird flutters out to catch flying insects and aggressively attacks other birds in flight, all the while emitting a sputtery series of sharp notes that sound like the zapping of an electric current. This is the eastern kingbird, whose Latin name translates into "tyrant of tyrants," the most common kingbird found in the East.

All About

The eastern kingbird is an excellent flier, able to catch flying insects and aggressively defend its breeding territory with its aerial mastery. Both sexes are blackish above and white below. The female's chest is grayish. Male kingbirds have a small, red-orange patch of feathers on the crown, though this is rarely seen. A thin, white band on the tail margin clinches the identification.

Habitat & Range

Spending the breeding season in open areas with scattered trees, eastern kingbirds prefer locations near water, probably for the bounty of insects. Fairly common in agricultural areas, pastures, city parks, and suburban neighborhoods with large trees and open understory during summer, most eastern kingbirds migrate to Central and South America in winter. In migration, the kingbird travels in loose flocks, and it is not uncommon to see a dozen or more birds in one tree in spring or fall.

Feeding

The eastern kingbird, or beebird, is an insect eater, specializing in bees, wasps, moths, butterflies, and other large, flying insects. Sit-and-watch hunters, kingbirds find an exposed perch and wait for something edible to fly past. They then sally forth and grab the prey in their bill, returning to the perch to stun and eat the insect. Kingbirds also eat fruits at all seasons, including mulberries, cherries, and elderberries. Fruits make up the bulk of their winter diet in the tropics.

Nesting

The kingbird's nest is placed high in a tree and is a large, loosely woven cup of bark, twigs, and weed stems. Females do all of the nest building and incubation. A typical clutch is two to five eggs with a 15-day incubation period. Hatchling kingbirds spend about 16 days in the nest before fledging, after which they are attended to by both parents for several more weeks.

Backyard & Beyond

Kingbirds can often be seen perching high in a tree or along fences or power lines, hunting for insects. They are very active in their territories in summer, so watch for their fluttery flycatching flights and listen for their loud zapping calls. The old myth that eastern kingbirds prey primarily on honeybees resulted in many of these birds being shot. Studies have now shown that kingbirds eat relatively few honeybees, mostly drones.

Red-eyed Vireo

Vireo olivaceus

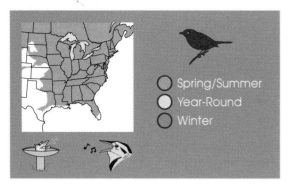

○ Spring/Summer
○ Year-Round
○ Winter

Easy to hear and hard to see, the red-eyed vireo is one of the most numerous summer birds of the eastern American woodlands. It arrives in April or early May from its South American wintering grounds, and its song rings out from every wooded tract. Foraging high in the emerging leaves, the vireo sings almost endlessly—one patient listener counted 22,197 songs from the same bird in one summer day!

All About

The red-eyed vireo is about 6 inches long—an olive-backed, white-bellied bird with a gray cap and bold white stripe over its bright red eyes. Males and females are similar. They have sharp, slightly hooked bills designed to catch insect prey. Despite their small size, they are strong fliers; their twice-yearly migration carries them to the Amazon and back. Red-eyeds, like all vireos, are more deliberate in their movements than warblers.

Habitat & Range

Red-eyeds are usually found in open deciduous or mixed woodlands with a strong understory of sapling trees. They sometimes occur in large city parks, orchards, or even wooded suburban backyards.

Feeding

Like many small neotropical migrants, the red-eyed vireo feeds mostly on insects. It gleans its food from the upper branches of tall deciduous trees, singing as it moves slowly along the branches, peering under and around the leaves. Occasionally, it hovers to snatch a bug from an otherwise unreachable surface. In late summer, the red-eyed vireo will supplement its diet with berries of many kinds.

Nesting

The female selects a suitable site, usually 5 to 10 feet off the ground on a horizontal forked twig. She builds a tightly woven nest of fine grasses and strips of grapevine, suspending it below the fork and decorating it with bits of lichen on its outer surfaces. Here she incubates her four eggs for 11 to 14 days. Both parents feed the nestlings for 10 to 12 days until they are ready to fledge. Red-eyed vireos are frequent victims of nest parasitism by cowbirds and only rarely do they fight back by building a floor over the cowbird egg and laying another clutch. Most of the time they simply accept the cowbird chick, to the detriment of their own.

Backyard & Beyond

The best way to find a red-eyed vireo is to learn its song, then listen for it in the spring and summer woods. It is sometimes written as *Here I am, look at me, over here, here I am* sung over and over in a clear sweet voice, usually from high in a tree. Finding the singer will take some persistence and a good pair of binoculars. In fall, silent red-eyed vireos may be spotted in hedgerows and tangles, looking for berries.

Warbling Vireo

Vireo gilvus

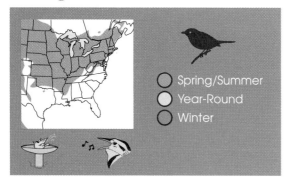

- Spring/Summer
- Year-Round
- Winter

This persistent singer is much more impressive to the ear than to the eye. The warbling vireo is a dull greenish-gray overall, yet it has a vocal repertoire to match the most brilliant of warblers—it's as if the vireo wants to make up for its dull plumage by singing enthusiastically throughout spring and summer. This is one of the few vireos that has benefited from forest fragmentation, and it is far more common now than it was in Colonial times.

All About

A plain little bird, stockier and duller than the equally common red-eyed vireo, the warbling vireo has few obvious field marks. It has a gray-brown back and light belly, offset by yellowish sides, a dark crown, and a white eyebrow line. The warbling vireo's song is described as *If I sees you, I will seize you, and I will squeeze you 'til you squirt!* It is sung repeatedly in a hoarse warble.

Habitat & Range

The warbling vireo's breeding range covers much of the U.S. and western Canada, with the exception of the Southeast and arid regions in the Southwest. It occupies a variety of habitats from mature deciduous forests to urban parks and recovering clear-cuts. In the breeding season, the warbling vireo's habitats of choice are often associated with water; many bird watchers associate this bird's song with large shade trees along streams and rivers. Warbling vireos spend the winter along the western edge of Mexico and Central America.

Feeding

An insect-eating specialist, the warbling vireo gleans moths, caterpillars, beetles, and other insects from foliage as it works its way along the outer branches of a tree. It also captures flying insects during short aerial forays. Large prey items are subdued by whacking them against a tree branch before they are eaten. During fall migration and in winter, warbling vireos eat fruit.

Nesting

The female warbling vireo chooses a nest site, often high in a tall deciduous tree, such as a poplar, maple, or elm. A nest woven of grass, bark strips, and leaves is suspended from a forked branch. The female lays four eggs and both parents share the incubation duties, with the male often singing from the nest—an unusual behavior for a songbird. The young hatch within two weeks, are fed by both parents, and fledge about two weeks later.

Backyard & Beyond

Warbling vireos can be most easily located by listening for their song during spring and summer. Listen for them along wooded waterways, around lakes, and in other places where large shade trees and water are present. Scan the treetops for this plain little songster with the bright, warbling song.

Blue Jay

Cyanocitta cristata

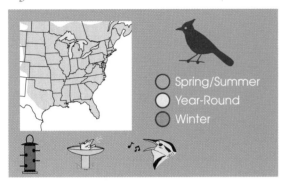

○ Spring/Summer
● Year-Round
○ Winter

Blue jays are smart, adaptable, and noisy birds. They will often mimic the call of a red-tailed or red-shouldered hawk as they approach a bird feeder, in an apparent attempt to scare other birds away from the food. Sometimes persecuted by humans as nest robbers or bullies at the feeding station, blue jays are one of our most ornate and lovely birds. Bird watchers visiting the United States from abroad are astounded that such a beautiful bird is common in our suburban backyards.

All About

No other eastern bird is blue and crested, making the blue jay almost unmistakable. Males and females are similar. Besides the standard *jay jay* or *jeer jeer* call often used as a scold, blue jays also emit a variety of squeaks, rattles, and croaks, in addition to mimicking other birds' calls. If you hear a sound in the woods that is loud and unmusical, chances are good that it's coming from a blue jay.

Habitat & Range

Blue jays are common in wooded habitats, especially those with oaks. Indeed the blue jay has a special relationship with oaks, burying as many as 5,000 acorns in fall caches for future consumption. Many of these acorns are never retrieved, so jays are credited with helping with forest generation. Resident throughout their range, blue jays in northern latitudes migrate southward in early fall, traveling by daylight in flocks of 10 or more birds, many carrying acorns in their bills.

Feeding

Blue jays will eat almost anything. Grasshoppers and other insects, and acorns and other nuts are their primary foods. Bird eggs or nestlings, mice, frogs, and a variety of human-supplied foods are also eaten. When storing acorns, blue jays will carry as many as five acorns in the throat and bill to the cache site, drop them in a pile, and bury them one at a time. They will return to recover only some of these acorns.

Nesting

Males help gather nesting materials, but females do most of the building in a tree. The twig nest is woven into a cup and lined with wet leaves and rootlets. Suburban blue jays often incorporate string, plastics, and paper (human trash) into nests. The female lays four to six eggs and incubates them for 18 days, followed by about 20 days of nestling care before the young jays fledge.

Backyard & Beyond

A common feeder visitor, blue jays are attracted to suet, peanuts, sunflower seeds, and even dog food. A source of water is highly attractive to blue jays, too. Look for blue jays along woodland edges and listen for their raucous cries, almost always the first clue to their presence.

American Crow

Corvus brachyrhynchos

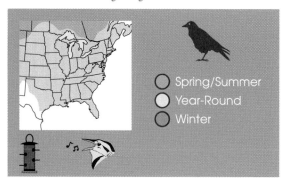

- ○ Spring/Summer
- ○ Year-Round
- ○ Winter

Noisy, sly, opportunistic, and ubiquitous, the American crow lives among us; yet, comparatively little is known about it. Like other bold, brash corvids (the blue jay being a prime example), the crow is downright sneaky where its personal life is concerned. Few people know that crows may breed cooperatively in groups of up to a dozen birds, helping tend the dominant pair's nest.

All About

An unrelieved glossy black from bill to toenail, crows are armed with a stout, strong bill that acts as a chisel, axe, shovel, or forceps, among other uses. Its distinctive wingbeats appear to row the bird through the sky. Crows are well known for their raucous *caw*. Evidence suggests that crows have different "words" for different situations (assembly, dispersal, mobbing); their language is complex, as is their social behavior. Few people are privileged to hear the crow's song, given by both sexes, which is a long recitation of rattles, coos, growls, and imitations of sounds.

Habitat & Range

Though they are strongly associated with agricultural areas, crows find perfect conditions in cities and suburbs, where they raid pet dishes, bird feeders, and garbage cans. In the northern part of their range, crows are migratory, but all spend the winter within the continental United States. Throughout their range, crows use communal roosts when not breeding, and these can swell to massive proportions by late winter.

Feeding

There's almost nothing edible an American crow will not eat. At roadkills, landfills, and compost piles, crows will load their distensible throat with food and fly heavily off, often caching it under leaves or sod for later enjoyment. Crows forage by walking slowly on the ground—hunting invertebrates and vertebrates alike—and are constantly scanning roadsides and fields as they fly, descending to investigate anything that might be edible.

Nesting

Crows stay in family units composed of a pair and their young from the previous year. These yearlings may help build the nest, incubate, or feed the incubating female or her young. Four or five eggs are laid in the bulky twig nest, which is usually hidden high in a pine. The female incubates for around 17 days, and young fledge at around 36 days of age. Their strangled, nasal calls sometimes betray the nest location.

Backyard & Beyond

Crows are always up to something, and feeding them gives us an opportunity to observe their always-intriguing behavior. To find something a crow might like, open the refrigerator. Freezer-burned meat is a favorite. Cracked or whole corn is irresistible as well. Neighbors may wonder, but crows are well worth watching.

Horned Lark

Eremophila alpestris

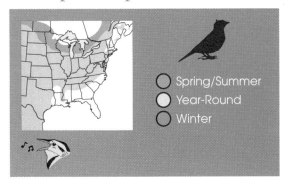

- ○ Spring/Summer
- ○ Year-Round
- ○ Winter

The "horns" on the head of this small bird are not horns at all, but feather tufts that can be raised and lowered. In spite of this conspicuous field mark, horned larks can be surprisingly difficult to see when they are on the ground. Your first clue to their presence may be their high, tinkling call, or when a small flock is startled into flight.

All About

Horned larks are sleek-looking birds of open ground where they are often found in flocks. Males show a yellow face and throat, and a bold black mask or moustache and breast band. The back and wings are a blend of tan and rust. The female's plumage is a paler version of the male's. Their flight style is light and undulating, providing glimpses of the black tail panels, and often accompanied by twittering call notes.

Habitat & Range

Found in all types of wide-open, barren terrain from beaches and dunes to tundra, short-grass prairie, overgrazed fields, gravel roadways, recovering strip mines, and airport runways, the horned lark is widespread across North America. Its population and range have both expanded in the last half-century and the species is now found year-round in nearly every state. Breeding birds from the far North begin fall migration in September.

Feeding

In winter, when horned larks commonly mingle in large flocks with longspurs and snow buntings, seeds are the primary food. During the breeding season and migration, insects are added to the larks' menu. Horned larks forage by walking over the ground, looking for food items. This type of foraging is especially productive in fields where manure has been spread or where the soil has recently been tilled or grain recently harvested.

Nesting

Horned larks may nest very early in spring in the Midwest, but later in the far North. The female chooses the nest site on the ground and digs out a shallow scoop. Into this depression she weaves a nest from grass, rootlets, and other plant material. She lines it with soft materials such as fur or feathers and lays from two to five eggs into it. She alone incubates the eggs for 11 days. Young hatch with a warm down covering and stay in the nest until fledging about 10 days later

Backyard & Beyond

Winter flocks of horned larks can be easier to find than breeding birds. Check in and around agricultural feedlots, in muddy farm fields, active pastures, and anywhere waste grain or seed might be scattered. Scan the ground carefully for the larks' movement—one or more birds may catch your eye as they flutter across the open ground.

Purple Martin

Progne subis

Spring/Summer
Year-Round
Winter

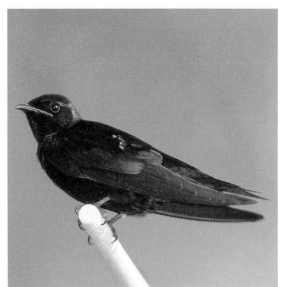

No other North American bird has a closer association with humans than the purple martin. For more than four hundred years, martins in eastern North America have nested in human-supplied housing, at first in hollow gourds offered by Native Americans and today in a variety of specialized housing. Generations of people and martins have grown up together. Even non-bird watchers can appreciate this friendly and familiar bird.

All About

Our largest swallow (at 8 inches), the purple martin is a graceful flyer with a bubbly, liquid song. The adult male has a deep blue body and black wings and tail. Females and youngsters are gray and black with some blue on the back. In flight, martins can be confused with European starlings, but martins have a notched tail and call out almost constantly.

Habitat & Range

Purple martins breed across eastern North America, except for the extreme north. They spend winters in South America but return to the southern United States in mid-January, their arrival eagerly anticipated by their human landlords. Because of their reliance on human-supplied housing, most martins are found around cities, towns, and settlements.

Feeding

Martins eat flying insects almost exclusively, but—contrary to popular opinion and marketing hype—martins do not eat many mosquitoes. Instead, their diet includes larger flying insects, such as beetles, flies, dragonflies, wasps, butterflies, and moths. In cold, rainy weather, martin landlords often resort to feeding them mealworms and bits of scrambled egg in an effort to keep their beloved birds alive. Some landlords even shoot mealworms into the air with a slingshot just so the martins can catch their food.

Nesting

Martins are rather selective in choosing colony nest sites, but one thing is certain: They like to be with other martins. Research has revealed that they prefer white housing with a large (8×8×8-inch) interior and an 1½-inch entry hole. The housing should be mounted near a human dwelling in an open area. Martins build a loose cup nest inside the cavity out of pine needles and grass, lined with green leaves (which limit parasites). The female lays four to six eggs and does most of the incubation, lasting about 16 days. Both parents feed the nestlings for the month-long period before fledging.

Backyard & Beyond

The most successful martin landlords are those willing to put in the extra effort to care for their tenants with predator-proof housing, elimination of competing house sparrows and starlings, and regular monitoring. Your chances of attracting martins are greatly enhanced if there is an existing colony within a mile of you.

Tree Swallow

Tachycineta bicolor

T he lovely tree swallow is making a breeding range expansion in many areas of the U.S. Once limited by the availability of the nesting cavities they require, tree swallows are benefiting greatly from artificial nest boxes erected to attract bluebirds. Their liquid twitters, sharp blue-and-white coloration, and trusting ways make tree swallows a welcome addition to our birdlife.

All About

Long triangular wings, snow-white underparts, and glossy teal-blue upperparts make the tree swallow a beautiful signal of spring. Soaring kitelike, then rising with rapid flaps, they course and dive over meadows and ponds in search of flying insects. Their jingling calls have been likened to the sound of someone shaking paperclips in a glass tumbler. Females are somewhat browner above and a duller blue than males.

Habitat & Range

Tree swallows prefer open fields, preferably near water, for nesting, though they will inhabit upland sites. Marshes also provide the flying insects they require. The tree swallow's breeding range extends across Canada and the northern tier of the U.S. and is expanding southward at a good clip. Tree swallows winter in coastal areas from South Carolina to Florida and along the Gulf Coast into Mexico and Central America. One of our heartiest swallows, the tree swallow often surprisingly shows up early in spring.

Feeding

Eighty percent of a tree swallow's diet is insects; fruits make up the other portion, mainly bayberries that sustain them in adverse winter weather. "Myrtle swallow" would be a more apt name for these birds, as myrtle is another name for bayberry. This ability to eat fruit helps tree swallows survive cold snaps as they make their way northward to breed. During breeding season, insects are caught on the wing in spectacular zigzag flights and are stored in the throat to be fed to nestlings.

Nesting

A foundation of coarse grass leaves and stems is lined with large body feathers, usually white. Tree swallows are mad for feathers in nesting season and can often be induced to take soft white feathers from the hand. The female incubates four to seven eggs for an average of 14 days. Young leave the nest 15 to 25 days later, flying strongly. Second broods are rare.

Backyard & Beyond

Before the advent of artificial nest boxes, tree swallows were limited to old woodpecker holes—a hotly contested resource. A nest box with a 1 9/16-inch hole, mounted on a predator-proof pole in an open meadow near water, is the best bet for attracting tree swallows. Look for tree swallows hawking insects over ponds, lakes, and rivers during the summer months.

Barn Swallow

Hirundo rustica

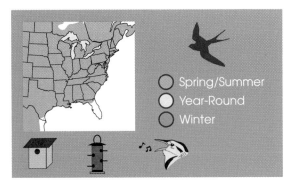

- ○ Spring/Summer
- ○ Year-Round
- ○ Winter

One early naturalist estimated that a barn swallow that lived 10 years would fly more than two million miles, enough to travel 87 times around the Earth. This species seems to define what it means to be at home in the air, and it has been compared to an albatross in its ability to stay effortlessly aloft. One of the most familiar and beloved birds in rural America, the barn swallow is welcomed everywhere as a sign of spring.

All About

Glossy blue-black above and orange below, the barn swallow is the only American swallow that has a true "swallow tail," with an elongated outer pair of tail feathers. Males and females are similar, but females are not quite as glossy or highly colored, and the fork in their tails is not quite as pronounced. Like all swallows, they have short legs and rather weak feet used for perching, not walking.

Habitat & Range

A bird of rural areas and farmlands, the barn swallow may be found over any open area, such as pastures, fields, and golf courses, as well as lakes, ponds, and rivers. It has adapted well to humans and is not shy of people, nesting close to settled areas as long as it has open space for feeding. Barn swallows travel in great flocks during migrations, often in company with other swallow species. They arrive in most of their U.S. range in April and leave in early to midfall.

Feeding

Foraging almost entirely on the wing, the barn swallow takes a variety of insect prey, from flies and locusts to moths, grasshoppers, bees, and wasps. Occasionally small berries or seeds are added to the diet, but this is uncommon. Only in bad weather will barn swallows feed on the ground.

Nesting

Nothing says "country" more than a pair of barn swallows zipping in and out of the open doors of a working barn, darting after insects and chattering incessantly. Sometimes two or three pairs will share a favored site. The nest itself is a cup of mud and grass, lined with feathers and placed on a rafter or glued under an eave. Besides barns, barn swallows may use other open buildings, covered porches, or the undersides of bridges or docks. During second nestings, immatures from the first brood help feed and care for their younger siblings.

Backyard & Beyond

During breeding season, you may bring barn swallows into close range by throwing feathers into the air near a flock of soaring birds; the graceful fliers will swoop in to snatch them up for nest linings. Barn swallows also enjoy eating bits of baked eggshells (crumble them first) during breeding season.

Tufted Titmouse

Baeolophus bicolor

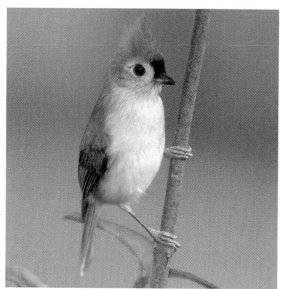

From deep mixed woods to old orchards, from city parks to leafy suburban backyards, this friendly and active little bird makes itself at home throughout the year. It is noisy and sociable, quite tame in human company, and fearless among other small birds with which it associates. Its cheerful calls of peter, peter, peter ring out even in midwinter, chasing away the January blahs.

All About

The tufted titmouse is 6½ inches long and dressed primly across its upperparts in gray, with a creamy breast and rusty flanks. A black-button eye stands out against its white cheek, and a crest adorns its head. Its small, sharp bill is black, as are its legs and feet. Titmice are very vocal and, besides their signature *peter* calls, they have a variety of whistled notes—similar to those of the cardinal and Carolina wren. Their harsh, raspy, scolding notes are similar to the chickadee's.

Habitat & Range

The tufted titmouse was originally considered a southern woodland bird, but for the past 50 years it has been expanding its range northward. The species' affinity for bird feeders and nesting boxes has played a part in this expansion. Titmice are nonmigratory and able to survive harsh weather if sufficient food is available.

Feeding

Tufted titmice eat mostly insects and seeds, depending on time of year. Caterpillars are a popular item in summer, but they also take wasps and bees, scale insects, beetles, the larvae of many species, and, in winter, insect eggs. Acorns are a mainstay in fall and winter. At feeders, titmice relish sunflower seeds, suet, suet dough, and peanuts.

Nesting

The natural nesting choice of the tufted titmouse is a tree cavity—an abandoned woodpecker hole, or crack caused by a lightning strike. Other sites include rotted fenceposts, drainage pipes, and nest boxes. The female builds the nest of grass, moss, bark, and leaves, filling up whatever size hole they have adopted. When the main structure is completed, the birds line it with hair—often plucked from a living animal—woodchuck, rabbit, dog, or even a handy human. Five or six eggs are laid, incubated by the female for 12 to 14 days. Both parents feed the young, which fledge at about 15 days. The family group stays together, sometimes into the next year, and year-old birds may help their parents care for the nestlings of the newest brood.

Backyard & Beyond

Tufted titmice sometimes breed in nest boxes, especially those with an entrance hole in the 1½-inch range. In winter they travel in mixed flocks with chickadees, sparrows, woodpeckers, and kinglets. Tufted titmice are easy to locate in woodlands by their noisy scolding calls.

Black-capped Chickadee

Poecile atricapillus

Spring/Summer
Year-Round
Winter

In the southern portions of Ohio, Indiana, Illinois, and Missouri, the resident chickadee is actually the Carolina chickadee (Poecile carolinensis), a slightly smaller but otherwise quite similar cousin of the black-capped chickadee of the northern half of the U.S. Chickadees travel in noisy little bands and draw attention to themselves with their frequent scolding chatter.

All About

Both chickadees have black caps and bibs as well as white cheek patches; gray backs, wings, and tails; and pale underparts with buff-colored flanks. The bill is tiny and dark, and the legs and feet are black. Males and females are alike, and there are no seasonal differences in plumage. In general, black-capped chickadees are larger (5 1/4 inches long), bigger-headed, with brighter white cheeks. Carolina chickadees are drabber gray overall, smaller (4 3/4 inches long), with less white in the wings. Vocal clues can be helpful. Black-cappeds sing *fee-bee* (two notes) while Carolinas sing *soo-fee, soo-fay* (four notes). The common *chick-a-dee-dee-dee* call is lower, hoarser, and slower from black-cappeds, and higher and more melodic from Carolinas.

Habitat & Range

The Carolina chickadee is resident (nonmigratory) and through most of its range it is the only chickadee present. It is generally replaced by the black-capped chickadee in the northern half of the Midwestern states. Black-cappeds will occasionally move south in winter. Where the two species overlap they may occasionally interbreed, so identifying individual birds under such circumstances is tricky.

Feeding

Both chickadees have a varied diet. Nearly half of the food taken in the wild consists of insects, such as aphids, ants, moths, and leafhoppers. They also eat spiders, weed seeds, and the seeds and small fruits of many trees and vines. At feeders they are partial to sunflower seeds, suet, and peanuts.

Nesting

Cavity nesters, Carolina and black-capped chickadees seek out natural holes in woodland trees, often adapting old woodpecker holes. They readily accept nesting boxes. The nest (made by the female) is a thick mass of mosses, bark, and grasses, enclosing a cup of soft hair. One side is built up higher than the other and can be pulled down like a flap to cover the young when both parents are away. As many as eight eggs are laid and incubated by the female for 11 to 13 days; both parents then share the feeding of the young until they fledge after two weeks.

Backyard & Beyond

To lure chickadees, offer black-oil sunflower seed in hanging tubes or hopper feeders, suet, or other fats such as "bird pudding." To induce a pair to stay and nest, install one or more nest boxes with entrance holes that are 1 1/4 to 1 1/2 inches in diameter.

White-breasted Nuthatch

Sitta carolinensis

Spring/Summer
Year-Round
Winter

Nuthatches are universally referred to as "upside-down birds," because they forage by probing the bark of tree trunks with their heads downward. During their journeys down the trunk of a tree, they often pause, and then raise their head so that it is parallel to the ground—an absolutely unique posture among birds. The most well-known member of the family is the white-breasted nuthatch, a bird of deciduous woods and well-treed backyards.

All About

At nearly 6 inches in length, the white-breasted nuthatch is the largest of its tribe. Males have gray backs with black caps, white underparts, and a beady black eye on a white face. Females are similar but wear gray, not black, on their heads. White-breasteds are thick-necked and short-tailed, with a stocky appearance. White-breasted nuthatch calls—uttered frequently in all seasons—are a nasal and repetitive *ank-ank*.

Habitat & Range

White-breasted nuthatches prefer deciduous woods, but are also found in large parks and leafy backyards. In northern coniferous woods, and at high elevations along the Appalachian chain, they are replaced by the smaller red-breasted nuthatch, while the brown-headed nuthatch displaces them in the dry pine woods of the South.

Feeding

The white-breasted nuthatch eats both insects and seeds, varying its fare with the seasons. Insects make up nearly 100 percent of their summer diet, with seeds being added in fall and winter. Autumn's extra seeds and nuts are sometimes stashed—or "hatched away"—in tree bark crevices, to be retrieved later—a habit that has given these birds their name. White-breasted nuthatches will come to feeders for sunflower and other seeds, or suet, but they tend to abandon backyard feeders almost entirely in spring and summer when insect prey is plentiful.

Nesting

Nuthatches maintain their pair bond and territory all year long. The nest is placed in a natural cavity, old woodpecker hole, or more rarely a nest box. Built by the female, it is a cup of grasses, bark strips, and twigs and is lined with hair. When the nest is finished, the nuthatches "sweep" the entrance with their bills, rubbing a crushed insect against the wood—the chemicals released may aid in repelling predators. The female incubates a clutch of eight eggs for two weeks. Both parents feed the young for at least two weeks until fledging.

Backyard & Beyond

Nuthatches are irregular feeder visitors, but they like black oil sunflower seeds and suet, peanuts, or peanut butter mix. In woodlands, listen for the nuthatch's nasal calls anytime. Male and female always forage near each other and, in winter, with other species in a mixed flock.

House Wren

Troglodytes aedon

Spring/Summer
Year-Round
Winter

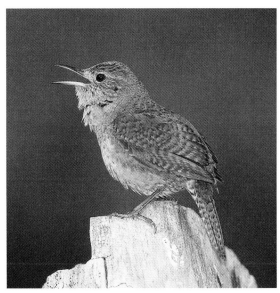

The rich and burbling song of the house wren is surprisingly loud for such a tiny (4³/4 inches long) bird. House wrens are named for their preference for living in close proximity to humans, often in tiny houses we provide for them. This mostly plain brown bird makes up for its small size and drab coloration by being a fierce competitor for nesting sites.

All About

House wrens are notable for their lack of field marks—the warm-brown upperparts and tail are matched by a grayish breast. Look closely at the house wren, and you'll see a variety of small white and black spots, the only variation in the bird's plumage. Males and females look alike and both have the wrenlike habit of cocking their tails up when perched. The thin, slightly curved bill is ideal for capturing and eating the house wren's insect prey.

Habitat & Range

Spending the summers in thickets and brushy edge habitat adjacent to woodlands, the house wren is a familiar bird in parks, backyards, and gardens, often—but not always—near human settlements. Some house wrens winter in the southernmost states in the United States, but many travel beyond our borders farther south.

Feeding

Insects make up the house wren's diet (grasshoppers, crickets, spiders, and moths are on the menu), but they will also eat snails and caterpillars. Most of their foraging is done in thick vegetation on or near the ground.

Nesting

House wrens nest in a variety of cavities from woodpecker holes to natural cavities and nest boxes. Like Carolina wrens, house wrens will also nest in flowerpots, drainpipes, and other such sites. They are very competitive about nesting sites, often filling all or most available cavities with sticks. The male builds these "dummy" nests, and the female selects one in which to nest. The twig structures are lined with soft materials, such as grass or hair, and the female lays six to eight eggs. She performs the incubation duties, which last from 12 to 14 days. Fledglings leave the nest two or more weeks after hatching. House wrens are known to pierce the eggs of other cavity nesting birds in their territories.

Backyard & Beyond

House wrens will readily accept nest boxes with interior dimensions of 4x4 inches and entry holes of 1¹/4 inches in diameter. Nest boxes placed adjacent to brushy habitat or a wood's edge seem to be most attractive. The house wren's song and scolding calls are heard often wherever they are present. Nest boxes for bluebirds and tree swallows should be placed far from edge habitat, in the open, to avoid conflict and competition from territorial house wrens.

Ruby-crowned Kinglet
Regulus calendula

Spring/Summer
Year-Round
Winter

The appearance of this perky little bird within mixed songbird flocks is a sure sign that fall is on the way. Ruby-crowned kinglets nest in the north and northwest of the continent in mixed coniferous forests. They winter in abundance from the South into Mexico.

All About

After hummingbirds, ruby-crowned and closely related golden-crowned kinglets rate as North America's smallest birds. Like the golden-crowned, the ruby-crowned kinglet is restless, briefly hovering by the tips of branches and constantly flicking its wings—a behavior that sets them apart from larger, longer-tailed warblers. Two other field marks are the bird's wide white eye ring and single, wide wing bar. Otherwise, the ruby-crowned kinglet is a study in olive-drab. Its namesake red crown patch is usually concealed.

Habitat & Range

This bird abounds from northern Maine, New Hampshire, and Vermont west across the upper reaches of the Great Lakes, through central Canada, then south through the western mountain states. Some even nest in a few spots in Arizona and New Mexico. As cold months approach, ruby-crowned kinglets migrate south, spending the winter from southern New England south through the Southeast. In the West, the wintering range extends from the Pacific Northwest south and east across Oklahoma and Texas. Many ruby-crowned kinglets winter in Mexico, but rarely as far south as Guatemala.

During migration and in winter, kinglets are found in a wide variety of habitats, feeding in trees from pines to oaks and in tall shrubs.

Feeding

Much of a ruby-crowned kinglet's life is spent in the relentless pursuit of invertebrates, punctuated here and there in winter by the procurement of a seed or berry. In winter, these birds pick among branches and crags to find dormant spiders and insects and their eggs. In warm months, they feed exclusively on small invertebrates.

Nesting

Surprisingly for such a small bird, the ruby-crowned kinglet may lay up to a dozen small white, brown-speckled eggs—the largest clutch of a North American bird its size. Seven to eight eggs is a more typical clutch, which a female lays and incubates for about two weeks in a tightly bound nest of lichen, moss, spider web, hair, and various plant materials. The nest is usually suspended from a branch close to the trunk and protected from above by overhanging branches. Both parents feed their young, which leave about 16 days after hatching.

Backyard & Beyond

In many parts of the country, October and April are peak months for spotting migrating ruby-crowned kinglets. They may accompany chickadees and titmice that come to your feeders, or be seen with migrating warblers.

Blue-gray Gnatcatcher

Polioptila caerulea

Spring/Summer
Year-Round
Winter

The blue-gray gnatcatcher is the birder's "mini-mockingbird," always in motion and usually talking about it. This graceful, delicate, miniscule bird seems to arrive too early in spring, sallying into swarms of midges from still-budding branches. Its slender, elongated form and flashy black-and-white paneled tail are hard to mistake, though the gnatcatcher often goes unnoticed. It's most likely to be spotted on its early spring migration, for it is a woodland denizen, often hidden by foliage after the trees leaf out.

All About

It's often the gnatcatcher's twangy, whining call—like a miniature banjo being tuned—that alerts us to its presence. Its song is a sputtering, wheezy, petulant-sounding jumble, punctuated by *mews*. The blue-gray gnatcatcher has been recorded mimicking other species, a talent not widely appreciated, perhaps because its high, whispery voice is beyond the hearing register of many bird watchers. A white eye ring and neat black eyeline, blue-gray upperparts, and a long, slender tail edged in white distinguish this elegant bird. Females are similar, but lack the black eyeline.

Habitat & Range

Blue-gray gnatcatchers are strongly associated with oaks in a wide range of habitats, sticking to woodlands dominated by broad-leaved species. They are more often seen along woodland edges than in yards and gardens, except during migration. Gnatcatchers winter in the western coastal scrub of Mexico and Central America.

Feeding

Perching on the outer twigs in the mid- to high canopy, gnatcatchers go out after flying insects or glean the outer foliage for insects and spiders. As they forage, they flick their white outer tail feathers, which is thought to create bursts of light that startles UV-sensitive insects into flight. The bill is a fine black forcep, good for grasping tiny prey.

Nesting

Gnatcatcher nests are often mistaken for those of hummingbirds, being neat, compact cups of silk (often gathered from tent caterpillar nests), plastered with lichens. They are usually saddled on a horizontal limb. It is often possible to witness construction because the male gnatcatcher escorts the nest-building female with much fanfare and conversation. Both male and female incubate four eggs for 13 days, and young birds leave the nest 13 days after hatching. They are still being fed by their parents three weeks after departing the nest but gain independence soon thereafter.

Backyard & Beyond

This species has expanded its range explosively over the past three decades, pioneering into the Northeast and southeastern Canada. However, its range expansion cannot be attributed to feeding stations, as has been postulated for the northward movement of tufted titmice, northern cardinals, and red-bellied woodpeckers. The gnatcatcher relies solely on insects for sustenance.

Eastern Bluebird

Sialia sialis

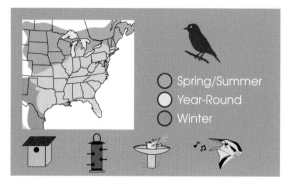

○ Spring/Summer
○ Year-Round
○ Winter

The eastern bluebird is our most famous thrush, even more popular than its cousin, the American robin. Its beauty, its song, and its willingness to live close to us has inspired many poets, songwriters, artists, and bird watchers. You can attract bluebirds to your property if you have a large open lawn, especially if you provide housing. Thanks to a concerted effort by bluebird lovers to provide nest boxes, the eastern bluebird has rebounded from its low population in the 1960s.

All About

The sky-blue back and rusty breast of the male bluebird are echoed in the female's more muted tones. There are three bluebird species in North America, but only the eastern is commonly found in the eastern United States. Bluebirds are often seen perched along fence lines, on wires, or high in trees. They may appear all dark in bright sunlight, so many observers miss seeing them. During spring courtship, paired bluebirds can be seen fluttering their wings near a prospective nesting site, uttering their rich *turalee turalay* song.

Habitat & Range

Bluebirds are resident (nonmigratory) throughout the eastern United States in open habitats, such as pastures, grasslands, parks, and large suburban lawns (especially where bluebird nest boxes are available). The two habitat requirements of bluebirds are large, open, grassy areas for foraging and cavities for roosting and nesting. In harsh winter weather, bluebirds may migrate short distances to find food or shelter.

Feeding

From an elevated perch, bluebirds watch for moving insects and then drop to the ground to pounce on them or to capture flying insects in midair. They eat insects year-round and will shift to fruits and berries when insects are scarce. Bluebirds visit feeders for mealworms, berries, and suet or suet dough.

Nesting

Bluebirds are cavity nesters and will use old woodpecker holes or natural cavities in trees where available. Human-supplied nest boxes are an important resource for the eastern bluebird. The female bluebird builds the nest inside the cavity using bark strips, grass, and hair. She lays four to six eggs and incubates them for 12 to 16 days. Both parents care for the nestlings until fledging occurs after 14 to 18 days.

Backyard & Beyond

If you offer housing, it's important to monitor and manage it to keep non-native house sparrows and starlings from usurping it and to keep predators from accessing the eggs or young. Place the houses (with 1$\frac{1}{2}$-inch entrance holes) on metal poles with a pole-mounted baffle beneath the house. House location should be in the middle of a large, open, grassy lawn or field. Bluebirds catch insects on the ground in grassy areas, so they are particularly vulnerable to lawn chemicals.

American Robin

Turdus migratorius

Spring/Summer
Year-Round
Winter

Almost all North Americans have grown up having a fairly intimate acquaintance with a thrush. The American robin, the largest, most widespread, and most abundant North American thrush, has followed the watered lawn—with its plentiful earthworm prey base—westward across the continent. Only parts of Florida, Texas, and the Southwest, where the soil is too sandy to support the introduced common earthworm, lack robins.

All About

The robin's simple yet evocative *cheerily-cheerio* song meshes well with the thunk of basketballs and the drone of lawnmowers in suburban neighborhoods all across North America; yet, they also hide their nests in mountaintop spruce and fir forests, where they are as wary as any hermit thrush. Males sport brick-red breasts and black heads with broken white spectacles and a streaked white throat and lower belly. Females are paler.

Habitat & Range

The robin is primarily a bird of lawns with trees and shrubs, though it also breeds in high mountain forests near clear-cuts or openings. Few other species show its adaptability to diverse habitats, from landscaped parking lot islets to dense, secluded forests. Migration is marked in northern climes, but is less so in southern ones.

Feeding

Running, then standing erect and motionless on a lawn, the robin watches and listens for earthworms and other invertebrates crawling in the grass. A quick stab captures them, sometimes resulting in a tug-of-war with a recalcitrant night crawler. Robins flock in fall to exploit fruiting trees and shrubs, fluttering and giggling as they reach for food.

Nesting

Most bird watchers are familiar with the robin's sturdy mud-and-grass cup, often nestled in an evergreen, a climbing vine, on a horizontal branch, or even on a windowsill. The female incubates three to four eggs for 12 to 14 days. Adults can be seen foraging with bills full of earthworms as soon as the young hatch. Young leave the nest, barely able to flutter, on about the thirteenth day. They are distinguished by their spotted, whitish breasts and reedy, begging calls. The male feeds them for another three weeks, while the female usually starts a second brood.

Backyard & Beyond

By mowing the lawn regularly and planting dense evergreens and fruit-bearing shrubs and trees, we unwittingly provide perfect conditions for robins. Robins seldom visit feeders, but will take bread, chopped raisins, and crumbled moistened dog chow in severe winter weather. Oddly enough, the American robin is the only member of its genus, *Turdus*, that breeds in any numbers in North America. The closely related clay-colored robin, which looks like a washed-out, American robin, breeds sparingly in south Texas.

Wood Thrush

Hylocichla mustelina

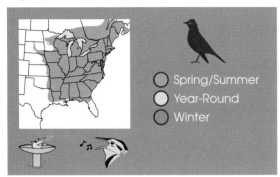

○ Spring/Summer
○ Year-Round
○ Winter

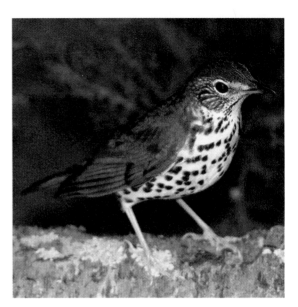

The lilting flutelike song of the wood thrush inspires bird watchers, naturalists, poets, musicians, and humankind in general. Few things are more beautiful than the evening song of the wood thrush as it echoes from deep within the forest. However, this species has suffered severe declines in population during the past thirty years due to loss of habitat, forest fragmentation, and nest parasitism from the brown-headed cowbird.

All About

This medium-sized (7³/4 inches in length) brown thrush has a bright rufous head and neck, olive-brown back and tail, and a white breast with large dark spots. Erect and robinlike in its posture, the wood thrush sings a multi-pitched and highly variable *eeeolay* song and utters a *whit-whit-whit* call when agitated. Wood thrush males do most of their singing at dawn and dusk, and usually from a midlevel perch in the forest.

Habitat & Range

Wood thrushes only spend their summers with us in eastern North America, arriving as early as April, but departing for the tropics by mid-August or later. Many make the flight across the Gulf of Mexico in both spring and fall. During the breeding season, they can be found in mixed deciduous forests with tall trees and a thick understory. Fragmented forest plots or those with cleared understory (due to deer browsing or human landscaping) are far less attractive to wood thrushes.

Feeding

Feeding much like a robin on the forest floor, the wood thrush sweeps aside leaf litter with its bill to uncover insects, larvae, millipedes, moths, ants, and even salamanders and snails. In fall, wood thrushes will feed in forest edge habitats to take advantage of fruits and berries.

Nesting

The female wood thrush builds a cup-shaped nest out of grasses, leaves, and rootlets, usually held together with mud, in the fork of a tree branch within 20 feet of the ground. She lays three to four eggs and incubates them for about 12 days before they hatch. Young wood thrushes are ready to fledge two weeks later. Wood thrush nests in fragmented forest habitats are more likely to be parasitized by the brown-headed cowbird, which does not build its own nest, but rather lays its eggs in the nests of other songbirds—often at the expense of the host species.

Backyard & Beyond

From spring through fall your best chance of locating a wood thrush is to listen for a male singing from patches of dense forest. Once you hear the song, patiently scan the upper, inner branches of the forest for this rusty-brown master singer. If you live in wooded habitat that is home to wood thrushes, be a good neighbor and keep pets restrained during breeding season.

Veery
Catharus fuscescens

Spring/Summer
Year-Round
Winter

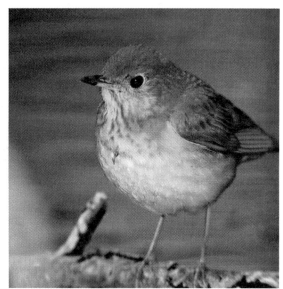

The spiraling, almost unearthly song of the veery captivates most people who hear it. Actually seeing this shade-loving songbird is far more challenging. Although still a common nester in many areas, the veery has declined in many parts of its range, perhaps due to destruction of its winter habitat and, on its nesting grounds, from nest parasitism by cowbirds combined with the paring down of underbrush by surging deer populations.

All About
Of all North American thrushes, the veery shows the greatest contrast between rich rustiness above and plainness below. A "typical" veery has a rusty wash on its breast and cheeks and a head lacking strong markings. Diffuse spotting punctuates the breast's rusty wash, but the remaining underparts are white. Western and Newfoundland birds are darker and more heavily spotted below, but the face is still plain, lacking the distinctive eye rings found on similar Swainson's and hermit thrushes.

Habitat & Range
The veery nests across much of southern Canada, in the western mountains down to Colorado, across the Great Lakes states and throughout the Northeast, as well as in the Appalachians. Favored nesting habitat is moist deciduous forests with plenty of bushy undergrowth. In fall, most veeries migrate across the Gulf of Mexico and western birds apparently migrate through the East before taking this southbound flight. Veeries winter in tropical forests from Colombia to Brazil. Studies indicate that older second-growth forests are far more attractive to nesting veeries than those cut in the last decade or two.

Feeding
The veery spends most of its time on or near the ground, feeding on a mix of berries and insects that it finds by hopping, flycatching, or flipping over dead leaves. Prey includes beetles, snails, ants, wasps, caterpillars, and spiders. Berries and other small fruits are particularly important in late summer and fall. The veery spends more than half the year outside the U.S. and Canada. Its diet during this time is not well documented.

Nesting
A female veery builds a nest on or near the ground. Using dead leaves as a base, she later constructs a cup of small bark bits, weeds, and leaf mold. The female incubates her clutch of four, sometimes three or five, blue-green eggs, which hatch after 12 days. Young leave the nest about 12 days after hatching, and are fed by both parents.

Backyard & Beyond
Migrating veeries put in appearances in backyards, not at feeders but often in berry-bearing shrubs and trees including spicebush, elderberry, dogwood, and blackberry. These birds migrate primarily at night and many die after colliding with tall buildings and communications towers.

Gray Catbird

Dumetella carolinensis

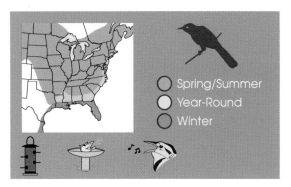

○ Spring/Summer
○ Year-Round
○ Winter

Named for its mewing catlike call, the catbird is actually a multitalented singer that is almost comparable to the mockingbird in its vocal versatility. Able to operate both sides of its syrinx, or vocal organ, independently, it can actually sing two different songs at once, and it's a mimic, too—not a bad resume for an otherwise plain gray bird.

All About

A slim, slate-gray bird about 9 inches long, the catbird is distinguished by a solid black cap and a bright chestnut patch under its tail. Because of its habit of cocking its tail, this patch is often visible. Catbirds are easy to recognize because—no matter what age, sex, or season—they all look the same. Very vocal, the male catbird makes an almost endless array of sounds, one after the other; some are his own and others are "stolen" from other birds or even from frogs, domestic animals, or mechanical devices heard in his travels. You can usually tell a catbird's song from that of other mimics, though, because each phrase is repeated only once, and the telltale *meouw* is thrown in from time to time.

Habitat & Range

In most of its U.S. range, the catbird is migratory, moving southward in winter, away from the coldest weather. Flying at night, migrant catbirds are often victims of collision, striking tall buildings or communication towers with distressing frequency. A few avoid the dangers of migration by remaining in their northern territories, a tactic that works if they are well fed and the season is not overly harsh.

Feeding

Foraging in thickets and brambles, the gray catbird eats mostly insects in spring and summer, adding small fruits as fall approaches. Favored insects include caterpillars, ants, aphids, termites, cicadas, and dragonflies. Among fruits it chooses grapes, cherries, and berries, followed by such late-lingering items as multiflora rosehips, catbrier, privet berries, bittersweet, and mountain ash.

Nesting

Singing from deep within a thicket, the male catbird courts his female in spring. After mating, she builds a bulky cup of twigs, weeds, and leaves, sometimes adding bits of paper or string and then lining it with fine grasses or hair. She incubates her three or four eggs for about two weeks; both parents then feed the nestlings for 10 to 12 days until they fledge. Two broods are common.

Backyard & Beyond

If a catbird remains in your neighborhood during winter it may be attracted by offerings of dried or fresh fruit, suet, doughnuts, peanut hearts, or table scraps. These birds are easily intimidated by other species, so they are more likely to respond to food scattered on the ground than concentrated in a small feeding dish.

Brown Thrasher

Toxostoma rufum

Spring/Summer
Year-Round
Winter

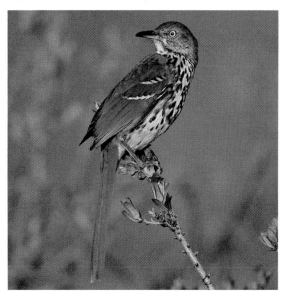

The brown thrasher has a lush resounding voice, and sings a seemingly endless train of melodies—its own and others'—from one end of a spring day to the other, and it may stay hidden in a deep shrub all the while. The brown thrasher is common throughout its range, but not as well known as it ought to be. This mimic is a cheerful and friendly addition to any backyard.

All About

Nearly a foot long, the brown thrasher is a strong and handsome bird, equally at home in woodland edges or shrubby backyards. Its upperparts are bright cinnamon, broken only by two, thin, white wing bars; its white breast is heavily streaked in brown. It has a long tail, a long slightly curved bill, and strong sturdy legs well suited to "thrashing" about on the ground. Beginning birders may confuse a thrasher with one of the thrushes, or perhaps a fox sparrow, but the thrasher is much larger, with a longer bill and tail. The thrasher's song is almost as rich and varied as a mockingbird's, and it is very similar in quality, but where the mocker usually sings its phrases three times each, the thrasher utters his only twice.

Habitat & Range

Often seen on the ground, the brown thrasher is a bird of woodland edges, thickets, hedgerows, brushy riversides and parks, and shrubby backyards. It retreats from the northern reaches of its breeding range to spend the winter in less frigid areas, usually returning sometime in April. In most of the South, it is a year-round bird.

Feeding

More than half the brown thrasher's diet consists of insects—beetles, grasshoppers, cicadas, and caterpillars—most of which it finds on the ground as it rummages with feet and bill among the leaf litter. Brown thrashers also eat fruits, nuts, seeds, and acorns.

Nesting

The male brown thrasher sings vigorously upon first arriving at its breeding grounds, both to establish territory and to attract a mate. The mated pair builds a large, twiggy nest in deep cover, usually quite close to the ground. Both parents incubate four eggs for nearly two weeks. Chicks are fully feathered and ready to fly in just nine days, an adaptation to avoid predators, which are especially dangerous to low-nesting birds. Two and sometimes three broods are raised each year.

Backyard & Beyond

Brown thrashers will visit feeding stations for seeds and grains that are scattered on the ground. Nuts are popular, as are suet mixtures, cornbread, doughnuts, and raisins. Thrashers are not particularly shy of humans, but do require some shrubs or hedges nearby where they can retreat if they feel threatened.

European Starling

Sturnus vulgaris

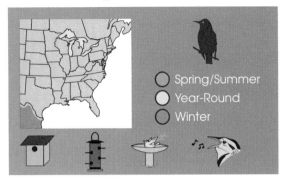

- ○ Spring/Summer
- ○ Year-Round
- ○ Winter

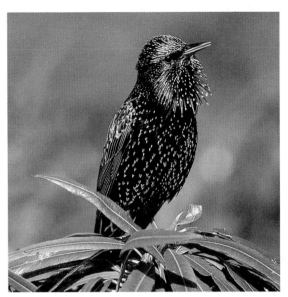

In 1889, there were no European starlings in North America, yet today—just over a century later—we have more than 200 million. Blame a fan of William Shakespeare. In 1890, a flock of a hundred starlings was released in New York's Central Park in an attempt to bring to America all the bird species mentioned in Shakespeare's plays. The adaptable starling soon spread westward in history's greatest avian population explosion.

All About

Glossy black overall, with a yellow bill during breeding season, the starling is one of the most familiar birds—not only because it is so common, but because it almost always lives close to human settlements. In winter, starlings are duller overall, covered with white spots (little stars, or "starlings") and with a blackish bill. In all seasons, starlings are very vocal, displaying an astonishing ability to mimic other bird songs, sirens, voices, barks, or mechanical sounds. In flight, starlings flap their triangular-shaped wings rapidly.

Habitat & Range

Starlings cover the entire North American continent year-round, except for the far North in winter. In fall they form gigantic, noisy flocks roaming in search of food and roosting sites. Every habitat type can host starlings, but they prefer those altered by humans (farmland, urban, and suburban areas) and tend to avoid remote, pristine habitats except where humans are present.

Feeding

Insects, berries, fruits, and seeds are the starling's regular diet, but they are highly adaptable—as willing to eat French fries from a dumpster as they are to find bugs in our lawns or suet at our feeders. The starling's traditional foraging technique is to insert its long, sharp bill into the ground and then open it to expose beetle grubs and other prey.

Nesting

Starlings are cavity nesters that cannot excavate their own holes, so they use existing cavities, such as woodpecker holes, pipes, crevices in buildings, and birdhouses. Sites are often usurped from other, less aggressive cavity nesters, such as bluebirds or purple martins. Once a male has a site, a female will help finish the nest—a messy affair of grass, feathers, paper, and plastic. Between four and six eggs are laid and incubated by both parents for about 12 days. Young starlings leave the nest three weeks later.

Backyard & Beyond

Most Americans can see a starling simply by looking out their window. Many bird watchers consider them a pest at their feeders and birdhouses. To discourage starlings at your feeders, simply remove the foods they prefer: suet, peanuts, bread, and cracked corn. At nest boxes, an entry hole diameter of 1⁹/₁₆ inches or less will exclude starlings. Frequent removal of their nesting material will also discourage them.

Cedar Waxwing

Bombycilla cedrorum

Spring/Summer
Year-Round
Winter

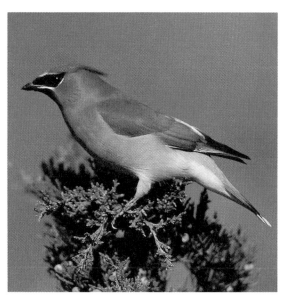

A beady, insectlike trill first alerts many bird watchers to the presence of cedar waxwings, so completely do they blend into canopy foliage. These wandering fruit-eaters appear and disappear seemingly without rhyme or reason, descending to strip a tree of its fruits, then whirling off to parts unknown. Fermented fruits may cause entire flocks to stagger about on the ground until the intoxication wears off.

All About

"Sleek" is the word most often used to describe the silky fawn plumage of the cedar waxwing. A velvety-black bandit mask hides the eyes, and a bright yellow band tips the gray tail. Older birds have red tips on the secondary wing feather shafts, which look like shiny drops of sealing wax. Cedar waxwings are most often seen in flocks in fall and winter.

Habitat & Range

The cedar waxwing's only real habitat requirement is the presence of fruit-bearing trees and shrubs; thus, it can be found everywhere except grasslands, deserts, and deep interior forests. Thought to be nomadic, the species does make a poorly understood migration that takes it as far south as southern Central America.

Feeding

Cedar waxwings travel in tight flocks to locate and feed on small fruits. They may be completely hidden in leaves as they flutter and pluck fruit, only to explode out with reedy calls and a rush of wings when startled. In late summer, they may be seen in twisting, dodging pursuits of winged insects over water.

Nesting

Though they defend no territory and in some places are semicolonial, cedar waxwings are monogamous. Both sexes help build a bulky, cup-shaped nest in the outer canopy of a tree. Leaves, straw, twigs, and string, often in a trailing mass, comprise the nest. The female lays four eggs and incubates them for 12 days, while the male feeds her. Young are fed on insects for the first two days, then solely on regurgitated fruits, leaving the nest around 15 days later. This fruit-based diet ensures that any parasitic brown-headed cowbirds hatching in their nests do not survive. Large flocks of immature birds (identifiable by their yellowish, streaked bellies) linger near breeding grounds for one or two months after the adults leave.

Backyard & Beyond

Attracting cedar waxwings is best accomplished by planting the trees and shrubs they prefer—serviceberry, hawthorn, firethorn, dogwood, chokecherry, viburnums, native honeysuckles, blueberries, cedars, and others with small fruits. They may also visit birdbaths, especially those with moving water. Worldwide, there are only two other species of waxwing: the Bohemian and Japanese waxwings. Waxwings are related to silky flycatchers, a largely tropical family.

Magnolia Warbler

Dendroica magnolia

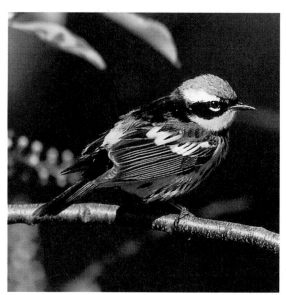

A small and active bird, the magnolia warbler (or "maggie" as some bird watchers call it) is a frequently seen spring migrant because it forages low in shrubby vegetation. The striking magnolia warbler has no particular association with magnolias—it was named in 1810 by early American ornithologist Alexander Wilson when he saw them for the first time in a stand of magnolias in Mississippi.

All About

Magnolia warblers could be the poster bird for bird identification because they have one of everything: a dark mask, white eyeline, gray cap, white wing bars, a black necklace on a contrasting yellow breast, a yellow rump, and white tail panels. As they move about, magnolias almost seem to be trying to show you all of their markings. Adult males in fall plumage are a grayer version of their spring selves, but they retain the yellow breast and white tail panels. Male magnolias sing a highly variable song that sounds like *weeta, weeta, WEETA!* and is more recognizable for its soft delivery than for its rhythmic pattern.

Habitat & Range

During the breeding season, magnolias are found at high elevations or in the far North in young scrubby pine, spruce, fir, and hemlock forests. In migration, magnolias can turn up almost anywhere, but they are most frequently seen in brushy areas with young deciduous trees. Because they are nocturnal migrants, magnolias are frequently seen first thing in the morning,

actively feeding to refuel themselves after a night of travel.

Feeding

Magnolias glean insects, spider eggs, aphids, and beetles from trees and vegetation. As they hop through a sapling, they check the branches, bark, and undersides of leaves for food items. They will also catch insects in midair and will hover briefly to nab an otherwise hard-to-get insect from beneath a hanging leaf.

Nesting

In May and June, magnolia warblers are getting busy with breeding. Both sexes work to build the nest on the male's territory, and the site chosen is usually low and well concealed in a hemlock, spruce, or fir. The female lays three to five eggs and handles the 13-day incubation chores. Young magnolias leave the nest about 10 days after hatching, but the parents will continue to feed them for nearly a month after fledging.

Backyard & Beyond

Magnolias are one of our most common warblers, perhaps due to their preference for habitats with young trees. Finding a maggie in spring is as easy as getting out during the peak spring migration period in late March, April, May, and June. Once the breeding season starts, you'll either need to visit high elevation coniferous forests or head north to the heart of the breeding range.

Yellow-rumped Warbler

Dendroica coronata

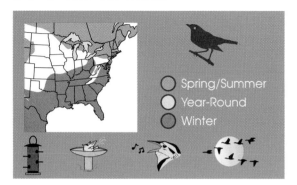

○ Spring/Summer
● Year-Round
○ Winter

One of the best-known warblers in the United States—and easily the most widespread and numerous in winter—the yellow-rumped warbler is a paradox: Its plumage and its habitats are very variable; yet, it is relatively easy to identify whenever you find it. Eastern birds of this species used to be called "myrtle" warblers, while their western counterparts were known as "Audubon's" warblers. They are now all yellow-rumped warblers, despite differences in plumage and habitat. Trendy birders stick to their own favorite name: "butterbutt."

All About

The yellow-rumped warbler is 5 to 6 inches long, with a sharp thin bill and slightly notched tail. In breeding plumage, the eastern male is blue-gray with a white throat and belly, black streaking on the back, a black face patch, two white wing bars, black bib, and yellow spots on the crown, shoulders, and rump. Spring females are browner and duller than their mates. Immatures and fall adults are brown above, with brown-streaked underparts and little or no yellow visible. The one constant in all plumages is the bright yellow rump. That, along with a frequent and distinctive *check!* note, will quickly identify these birds.

Habitat & Range

Breeding in the far North, the eastern race of the yellow-rumped warbler is known in most of the country only as a migrant or winter resident. Migrants can be found in woodlands, hedgerows, thickets, and even along beaches as they stream through in large flocks. Winter birds congregate wherever they can find berries, their principal cold-weather food.

Feeding

In Florida, yellow-rumps are known to drink the juice of broken or fallen oranges, and throughout their winter range they will consume weed seeds large and small. Some yellow-rumps come to backyard feeders where they eat a variety of fare.

Nesting

For nesting, the yellow-rumped warbler selects conifer forests, generally spruce, pine, or cedar. The female builds the nest on a horizontal branch, anywhere from 5 to 50 feet high in the tree, using bark, twigs, weeds, and roots to create an open cup that is then lined with hair and feathers. The female incubates the four or five eggs for 12 to 13 days. When the chicks hatch, both parents feed them for 10 to 12 days until fledging, and then the male feeds them for a time afterward. There are usually two broods per year.

Backyard & Beyond

In winter, yellow-rumped warblers may visit feeders to eat suet, hummingbird nectar, orange halves, or grape jelly. It is possible to lure them with sprigs of bayberry or other wild fruits. Away from home, look for them where natural foods are plentiful, such as in bayberry thickets or stands of wax myrtle.

American Redstart

Setophaga ruticilla

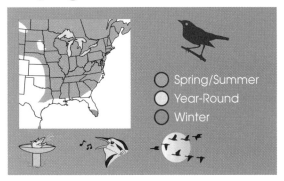

○ Spring/Summer
◐ Year-Round
○ Winter

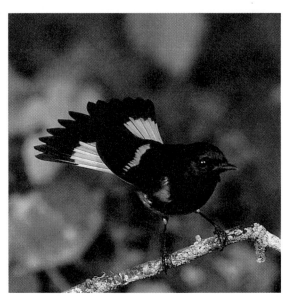

I**f you make** spishing *or* pishing *noises around a mixed flock of migrating warblers, one of the first birds to pop up for a closer look may be this flashy little bird. The American redstart is a wood warbler that was named after a European member of the thrush family. But the American redstart is a true American original, even if its name derives from elsewhere.*

All About

Like Europe's redstarts, the American flashes not red but orange in its tail, as well as on its wings and the sides of its breast. Otherwise, this warbler is black with a white belly. Birders call females and immatures "yellowstarts" because of similarly distinctive flashes of yellow (or in first-spring males yellow-orange) on the tail, wings, and the sides of the breast. Even seasoned birders can be thrown by the redstart's high-pitched, variable song, although some versions are easily recognized, such as *sweet-sweet-sweet-sweet-WHERE*.

Habitat & Range

Within its extensive breeding range across eastern and northern North America, American redstarts nest in a variety of wooded habitats (deciduous or mixed) with an understory of young trees. In mountainous areas, they are common nesters in regrowing forests or at the forest edge. During migration, American redstarts are among the most visible migrating warblers. They primarily winter from Mexico south to northern South America and in the Caribbean, although small numbers winter in Florida and more rarely in Texas and Louisiana.

Feeding

Spiders, caterpillars, and a wide variety of other small invertebrates wind up between the thin mandibles of the flittering redstart. The birds mostly seek insect prey, which they pick off leaves or capture in midair sallies, but redstarts also sometimes eat berries and seeds.

Nesting

The female redstart twines together grasses and other plant materials and spider webs to make its cup nest, which is placed in young trees, often no higher than 15 feet above the ground. The female usually lays four eggs, which she incubates for about 12 days. Both parents feed their young. Before they are 10 days old, the young leave the nest but are attended by either parent.

Backyard & Beyond

Among the most common migrant warblers, American redstarts frequently turn up in backyard trees during spring and fall. You can increase your odds of finding them at home by planting small native trees or shrubs where these insectivorous birds can seek insects. Shallow birdbaths or pools attract redstarts and other warblers; take care to situate water sources near shady cover that will still allow birds to see approaching cats.

Ovenbird
Seiurus aurocapilla

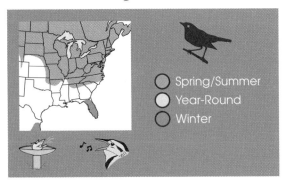

- ◯ Spring/Summer
- ◯ Year-Round
- ◯ Winter

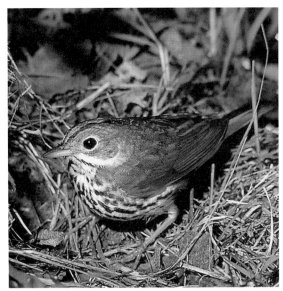

The ovenbird is a warbler that looks like a small speckled thrush. This deep forest bird only thrives where forests remain in large blocks, probably because if clearings are nearby, there are more nest predators and parasitic brown-headed cowbirds. Although spotting the forest-dwelling ovenbird takes patience, the bird's *TEAcher-TEAcher-TEAcher-TEAcher song* is distinctive and rings through the woods in spring and summer.

All About
A good look at the ovenbird's head will help you differentiate it from larger thrushes and same-sized waterthrushes. The wide, white eye ring is the first clue. The waterthrushes lack this, having instead a white stripe (*supercilium*) running from above the eye to the back of the head. Several species of brown-backed thrushes have eye rings that are not as pronounced. These birds are also much larger and have heavier bills than the ovenbird. Thrushes hop and feed, at one moment still, then dashing; the ovenbird walks methodically. The ovenbird has neat "stripes" of spots running down its breast, while the thrushes are more randomly speckled underneath. While not always visible, the ovenbird's black-bordered, orange crown patch is a diagnostic field mark.

Habitat & Range
Ovenbirds nest in mature deciduous or mixed deciduous and pine forests, but they can appear in any habitat during spring and fall migration. Most winter in Mexico, Central America, and on Caribbean islands. Forests that host nesting ovenbirds have a thick layer of dry leaf litter beneath them, providing the birds with feeding and nesting opportunities.

Feeding
The ovenbird quietly chugs along the leafy forest floor, walking and looking for insects, spiders, and other invertebrates (such as earthworms and snails) among the leaves littering the ground.

Nesting
This bird is named for its domed nest, which usually sits on the ground and is so well camouflaged with dead leaves that you can easily walk past without noticing it. Although leaves help conceal the nest, the female ovenbird constructs this structure using grasses, bark, and other materials. There is a side entrance for stealthy exit and entry. Inside, the female lays four or five eggs and incubates them for up to two weeks. Both parents feed the young. They leave the nest after about a week, but they are still fed by the adults for about two weeks afterward.

Backyard & Beyond
If you have a well-treed backyard with ample leaf litter, you may spot a foraging ovenbird walking in your woods during migration. If you hear the ovenbird's loud song, watch for it on a low- to mid-height perch or foraging on the ground.

Common Yellowthroat

Geothlypis trichas

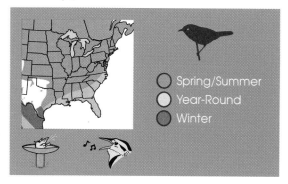

- ○ Spring/Summer
- ○ Year-Round
- ○ Winter

This charming bird may be the most popular warbler in North America. It is certainly one of the most widespread and well known. Its repetitive song, written as *witchety-witchety-witch* actually does sound like that, and beginners trying to learn bird songs find that the yellowthroat's is one of the easiest to master.

All About

Averaging about 5 inches in length, the common yellowthroat packs a lot of personality into a very small frame. Males are olive on top with a lemon-yellow throat and upper breast, white belly, yellow patch under the tail, and a bold black mask across the eyes, thinly bordered in white on top. The female is similar, but lacks the black mask. These are very active little birds and seem to be less timid than most warblers, possibly because they are nearly always low to the ground and therefore relatively easy to view. Their distinctive song continues well into the heat of summer.

Habitat & Range

Only in the dry southwestern states is the common yellowthroat hard to find during the breeding season. Everywhere else this little bird has no trouble locating the moist, shrubby, brushy conditions it needs for nesting. Even a relatively small patch of suitable habitat will do for a single pair, while large areas may host many nests. In winter and on migration, yellowthroats extend their interests to include shrubby backyards, dry woodland edges, and similar sites.

Feeding

Yellowthroats are almost exclusively insect-eaters, though they will add a few small seeds to their diet from time to time. Some favored insects are moths, aphids, leafhoppers, small caterpillars, mayflies, grasshoppers, and grubs. Foraging is done low to the ground, in dense cover.

Nesting

Female yellowthroats build a bulky cup nest quite low to the ground in thick weeds, using grasses, sedges, and other materials taken from the surrounding area. After lining it with fine grasses and hair, she lays three to five eggs and incubates them for 12 days. Her mate will bring her food during this time, and will then help her feed the nestlings for up to 10 days until fledging. The family stays together longer than most warblers, as the adults continue to feed the dependent young. Common yellowthroats are frequent victims of cowbird nest parasitism and do not seem to have an adequate defense against it.

Backyard & Beyond

In breeding season, thickets, hedgerows, marsh edges, and abandoned and overgrown farm fields are good places to look for common yellowthroats. Listen for their *witchety* song from spring through fall. They may be hard to find, but their loud, scolding *chuck* notes will often give them away.

Black-throated Green Warbler

Dendroica virens

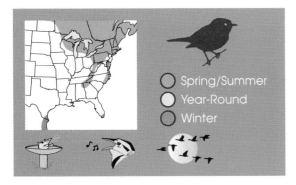

- ○ Spring/Summer
- ○ Year-Round
- ○ Winter

Easy to identify both by sight and by voice, the black-throated green warbler brings spring, summer, and fall cheer to many birders. Listen for its wheezy zoo-zee zoo zoo zee *or* zee zee zee zoo zee *song. Both male and female black-throated greens are colorful and easy to identify.*

All About

This bird often appears in trees high above your head, but even a quick side or belly view reveals important identification clues, such as the bright yellow head framed from below by sharply contrasting black on the breast (and throat in male) and from above by an olive crown. The sides are streaked in black and the birds sport two white wing bars. They also have a yellow bar that runs across their white under-tails, or vents.

Habitat & Range

The black-throated green warbler breeds primarily in coniferous and mixed forests from as far west as British Columbia, east through the Northeast, and down into the Appalachians. A few winter in southern Florida and southern Texas, but most black-throated green warblers migrate to Mexico and Central America for winter. During migration, black-throated green warblers are among the most conspicuous migrant warblers, actively foraging along woodland edges.

Feeding

While nesting, black-throated green warblers eat insects, particularly caterpillars. They capture prey by snatching it from leaves but also by hovering at the tips of branches to locate and grab insects. During migration, poison ivy berries are among the fruits eaten. While on tropical wintering grounds, black-throated greens have been observed feeding on secretions that hang in globules from a commonplace tree called the cecropia.

Nesting

Male and female black-throated green warblers share nest-building duties, making a cup of grassy stems and twigs, spider webs, and bark, which they line with softer materials such as feathers. This construction may take up to eight days and the female seems to choose the nest site, which is frequently between three to nine feet off the ground in a conifer, where two or more branches meet the trunk. Only the female incubates the four (sometimes three or five) eggs, usually for 12 days. The eggs are grayish or whitish drizzled with reddish brown markings. Females feed the young initially, joined after a number of days by the male. Young leave the nest after about 11 days, following one of the parents for about a month.

Backyard & Beyond

This common migrant warbler retains most of its key field marks in its non-breeding plumage. During migration, scour chickadee and titmouse flocks and you may find black-throated green and other warblers in the treetops with these active feeders.

Yellow Warbler

Dendroica petechia

Spring/Summer
Year-Round
Winter

One of North America's most familiar and wide-spread wood warblers, the yellow warbler's sweet-sweet-I'm-so-sweet song can be heard across the continent, from Alaska down to Mexico. In all, there are about forty different subspecies of the yellow warbler. Unlike many other wood warblers, population of the yellow warbler does not seem to be declining.

All About

To many beginning birders, the yellow warbler is the "ambassador of warblers" because it is often one of the first to be identified, thanks to its colorful plumage, easy field marks, and wide breeding range. Males are bright yellow all over, their underparts streaked with rays of orange. Females are also yellow overall, including their undertails and underwings, but they lack bold streaking. The yellow warbler's song varies somewhat and is not always easily distinguished from that of chestnut-sided warblers.

Habitat & Range

Yellow warblers are often found nesting in small trees or shrubs that grow at the edges of marshes, swamps, streams, lakes, and rivers. They sometimes set up housekeeping in drier deciduous forests, orchards, and thickets as well. On tropical wintering grounds, yellow warblers do not favor dense forest, but prefer partially open landscapes. In North America, the breeding range extends from Alaska through Canada, across the northern half of the U. S., as well as along the southern California coast and parts of Arizona down into western Mexico. North American birds winter from Mexico into northern South America.

Feeding

Yellow warblers pick prey off leaves and grab flying insects in midair. Midges, caterpillars, spiders, mayflies, moths, and beetles are among the small invertebrates they capture. They also will eat an occasional berry or two.

Nesting

A female yellow warbler usually builds an open cup nest in the fork of a young tree or shrub. The nest is fashioned from weed stalks, grasses, and bark shreds, but lined with finer materials such as plant fluff and hair. She usually lays between four and five greenish, dark-spotted or speckled eggs, which hatch after 12 days of incubation. After hatching, young are fed by both parents before they fly off when they are between 9 to 12 days old. Brown-headed cowbirds often lay their eggs in yellow warbler nests; to thwart this, the yellow warbler sometimes builds a new level onto the nest to cover the cowbird eggs, then lays a new clutch of eggs.

Backyard & Beyond

Large properties backing up to water may host nesting yellow warblers, as long as waterside thickets are preserved. Yellow warblers also appear in backyard gardens during migration. They seem to show a particular preference for foraging in willow trees, so watch and listen for them there.

Rose-breasted Grosbeak

Pheucticus ludovicianus

Spring/Summer
Year-Round
Winter

With its triangular scarlet breast patch and somewhat penguinlike pied plumage coloration, the male rose-breasted grosbeak is a North American beauty. This gorgeous songbird remains plentiful in a variety of habitats. The male's robinlike song is breezier and punctuated by a *chip* sound like a squeaky sneaker that, once learned, gives the bird away every time.

All About

It is hard to mistake a male rose-breasted grosbeak. No other bird has a black head and back, a triangular rose-red breast patch, and clear white belly. Equally striking in flight, the male flashes rose-red under his wings with a wide, rectangular white wing patch. The female has a dramatically difference appearance. Looking like an overgrown brown and white finch, she is streaked below and has a broad white line both above her eye and below her dark ear patch. In fall, immature males look similar but have an orangey wash across the underparts. Especially near the western edge of the breeding range, care should be taken when identifying females and immatures, which strongly resemble those of the closely related black-headed grosbeak, a western species.

Habitat & Range

The rose-breasted grosbeak breeds from far northwestern Canada, throughout the Midwest and Northeast, and at high elevations in the Appalachians. It prefers to nest in open woodlands or at the forest edge. These requirements are often met in neighborhood parks, along wooded roadsides, and sometimes in suburban neighborhoods. At its wintering grounds in the tropics, this bird also tends to occur in semi-open situations, sometimes with just scattered trees.

Feeding

With its versatile, heavy bill, the rose-breasted grosbeak feeds both on vegetable and animal matter. During fall migration, it mostly eats berries and seeds, including sunflower seeds offered at feeders. Insect prey in spring and summer can include beetles (including the Colorado potato beetle), bees, ants, bugs, and caterpillars.

Nesting

A female grosbeak builds her nest in a tree or tall shrub, usually between 5 and 20 feet above the ground. Assisted a bit by the male, she works twigs, weeds, and leaves into the loosely woven open cup nest, then usually lays four eggs. Both parents incubate for about two weeks, then feed their nestlings, which leave the nest between 9 to 12 days after hatching.

Backyard & Beyond

At the feeder, rose-breasted grosbeaks will eat sunflower and safflower seeds and shelled peanuts. Elderberry, juneberry, raspberry, blackberry, and mulberry are among the shrubs and small trees that can be planted to attract migrant rose-breasted grosbeaks, which also feed on a variety of weed seeds.

Scarlet Tanager

Piranga olivacea

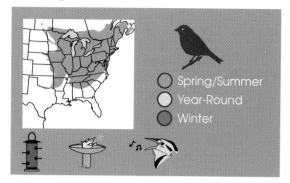

- Spring/Summer
- Year-Round
- Winter

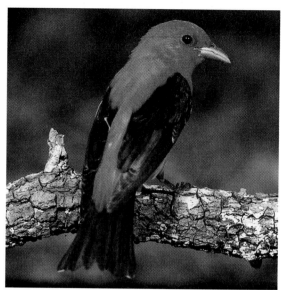

The male scarlet tanager in spring plumage ranks among the most stunningly beautiful birds in North America. One glance at his neon-bright plumage can turn even the most disinterested person into a confirmed bird watcher. Oddly, this dazzling bird's song has been compared to "a robin with a bad cold." A distinctive chick-burr call is often the first clue of a scarlet tanager's presence.

All About

The male scarlet tanager in spring plumage has a solid-red body and jet-black wings and tail, with a black-button eye and bone-gray bill. The female is dull olive above with dark wings and pale yellow underparts. Immatures resemble females, and in late summer the adult males take on the muted olive-yellow plumage. In all plumages, the scarlet tanager's wings are darker than those of the summer tanager. At just 7 inches long, scarlet tanagers are the smallest of the four North American tanager species.

Habitat & Range

Preferring deciduous forests with oaks, maples, and beeches, scarlet tanagers generally inhabit areas farther north (or, in the South, at higher elevations) than summer tanagers. They arrive in April or May and depart by midautumn. Flocks of early migrants are sometimes decimated by sudden late-spring snowfalls or ice storms, which cause them to starve or freeze to death. Sometimes being the early bird is not such a good idea.

Feeding

Basically insectivorous, the scarlet tanager moves quietly about in the upper canopy of deciduous trees in search of prey. Small summer fruits—such as blueberries and mulberries—are also taken, as are fall staples, such as poison ivy berries and sumac fruits. Scarlet tanagers occasionally engage in flycatching, or hovering behavior, to obtain food. Early or late in the season, cold weather may force them to the ground to forage for bugs in sheltered microhabitats.

Nesting

Typically, the scarlet tanager nests in a large, unbroken, wooded tract and high in a deciduous tree—often, but not always—an oak. It will be situated well out from the trunk on a horizontal limb. Made by the female alone, it is shallow and loosely constructed of twigs, rootlets, weeds, and other plant material. Three to five eggs are laid, and the female incubates them for up to two weeks until hatching. Both parents feed the young during the 9- to 14-day nestling period and for two weeks more after fledging occurs.

Backyard & Beyond

Scarlet tanagers are not common at bird feeders, but they do—on occasion—respond to offerings of bread, doughnuts, orange halves, or a peanut butter-cornmeal mixture. They will also eat small fruits and, in fall migration, may be a regular sight along tangled hedgerows overrun by poison ivy or multiflora rose.

Northern Cardinal

Cardinalis cardinalis

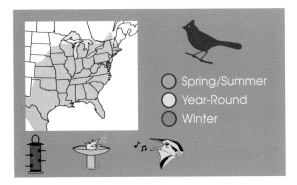

○ Spring/Summer
○ Year-Round
○ Winter

Cardinals are the familiar and beloved "redbird" *found all across the eastern United States. This bird's popularity is such that seven U.S. states and countless sports teams have chosen the cardinal as their official emblem. In spring and summer, cardinal pairs can be found together, often with the male perched high above, singing his* what-cheer-cheer-cheer *song. In fall and winter, cardinals can be found in large loose flocks, especially during harsh weather.*

All About

A black face and a long red crest smartly set off the bright red plumage of the male cardinal. Females are a muted, brownish version of the male. Strongly territorial, mated cardinal pairs will vigorously defend their nesting turf from rivals, even going so far as to attack their own reflections in windows, mistaking the image for another cardinal. One of the cardinal's most notable behaviors is the "courtship kiss" in which a male feeds a bit of food to a female he is wooing.

Habitat & Range

Found in a variety of habitats—from deserts to wetlands to manicured backyards, cardinals prefer an *edge habitat*—a place where woodland and open space meet. They are resident (nonmigratory) and thriving throughout their range, which has expanded northward in recent decades—thanks in part to the availability of food at bird feeders.

Feeding

Cardinals forage on or near the ground. During warm weather, insects, berries, buds, and seeds are their primary diet. Gardeners appreciate cardinals for eating grubs, beetles, caterpillars, and other garden pests. In winter, cardinals shift to a greater reliance on seeds, nuts, and wild fruits. At bird feeders cardinals prefer sunflower seeds, but will also eat mixed seeds, suet, fruits, and peanuts.

Nesting

Female cardinals choose thick cover—vine or rose tangles or shrubs—in which to weave their shallow, cup-shaped nests out of grasses, rootlets, twigs, and bark strips. Into this nest, the female will lay three to five eggs and incubate them for nearly two weeks before they hatch. Both parents feed the youngsters for about 10 days before they fledge. In summer, young cardinals can often be seen following a parent around, begging to be fed. Males will take on this duty while the female starts a second brood.

Backyard & Beyond

You can enjoy cardinals all year long in your backyard by offering them the four things they need to survive: food, water, a place to roost, and a place to nest. A few bird feeders, a chemical-free lawn and garden, and some thick brushy cover will suit their requirements nicely. Watch for cardinals early and late—they are often the first birds active at dawn and the last ones to "turn in" at dusk.

Indigo Bunting

Passerina cyanea

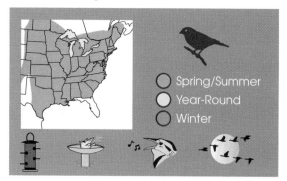

- ○ Spring/Summer
- ◐ Year-Round
- ○ Winter

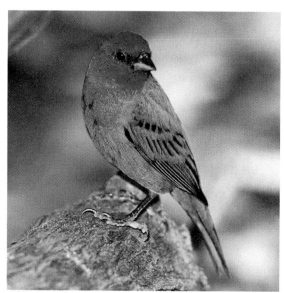

Appearing all black against the light, a male indigo bunting properly lit is an unforgettable sight. A persistent late-season singer, he sings a jingly song comprised of paired notes that are often described as: Fire! Fire! Where? Where? Here! Here! Put it out! Put it out! *Much of what we know about celestial navigation in songbirds derives from work with captive indigo buntings at the Cornell Lab of Ornithology.*

All About

The breathtaking, all-blue male indigo bunting, with his silvery conical bill, is unmistakable. Females and immatures are a warm cocoa-brown overall. This bunting has a habit of twitching its tail to the side, and its *spit!* note is characteristic. Males change their blue feathers for brown in autumn, which makes for some interestingly mottled specimens. They molt again on the wintering grounds and return in spring, blue once more.

Habitat & Range

This species is common on roadsides and disturbed areas where "trashy" vegetation flourishes. Power line cuts, old fields, landfills, railroads, and hedgerows ring with the songs of indigo buntings, especially as summer reaches its fullest. Indigo buntings are strongly migratory, wintering in Central and northern South America.

Feeding

The indigo bunting takes insects when they are available, especially to feed its nestlings. Weed seeds are its mainstay, supplemented by berries and small fruits. It forages on or near the ground, as well as in low shrubs and trees. Watch for them in autumn, bending grass stems and flicking their tails side to side as they forage in weedy patches.

Nesting

Indigo buntings have a rather loose definition of monogamy, with extra-pair copulations being quite frequent. Males visit females in neighboring territories, and females visit males. Males vary in their tendency to feed young; some are attentive parents, whereas others leave most of the chick rearing to their mates. The nest is bulky but compact, cup-shaped, and constructed of bark strips, grass and weed stems, and skeletonized leaves, all bound with spider webs. It's often low in blackberry, sumac, or other brushy vegetation. These birds nest quite late in the season, reflecting their dependence on late-maturing weed seeds. Three to four eggs are incubated by the female for about 12 days, and the young leave the nest from 8 to 14 days later.

Backyard & Beyond

Lucky is the one who hosts indigo buntings! Spring arrivals are most often first seen feasting on dandelion seeds. Later, black-oil sunflower seeds and millet mixes prove attractive. The growing popularity of "meadows in a can" make for rich feeding grounds for indigo buntings, which flock to coneflower, Mexican hat, cosmos, coreopsis, and especially foxtail grasses.

Eastern Towhee

Pipilo erythrophthalmus

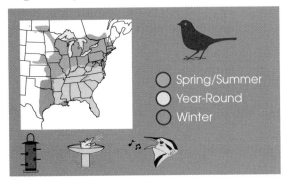

○ Spring/Summer
● Year-Round
○ Winter

Drink your TEA! *sings the towhee throughout the brushy woodlands of the eastern United States. Formerly called the rufous-sided towhee (a much more descriptive name), this large (8¹/₂ inches long) sparrow is boldly patterned and spends nearly all its time on the ground scratching among the leaf litter, looking for food. The name towhee comes from the bird's call, which has also been transcribed as* chewink. *Many people know this bird as the chewink instead of towhee.*

All About

Clean, flashy colors have given the towhee the nickname "Hollywood robin." In flight, the bird's white wing and tail spots are noticeable. Female eastern towhees replace the male's black plumage areas with chocolate brown. Towhees' preference for thick cover and brushy habitat make them harder to see than other common species. The loud scratching of a foraging towhee sounds like a large animal walking through dry leaves; this is often your first clue to a towhee's presence.

Habitat & Range

Widespread across the eastern half of the United States and southern Canada, towhees in the northern part of the range are migratory, but those in the southern half are resident (nonmigratory). During mild winters, towhees may linger until harsh weather forces them to migrate or to seek the cover of wooded valleys and hollows. Brushy woodland thickets and edge habitats are preferred, but towhees are also found in older woodlands and suburban backyards.

Feeding

Towhees eat just about anything found on the woodland floor, including insects, seeds, fruits, and even snails, spiders, and millipedes. They prefer to scratch the ground under feeding stations for mixed seeds, cracked corn, and sunflower seeds (which they crack with their powerful bill).

Nesting

Towhees nest on or near the ground in a well-concealed spot. The female weaves a cup-shaped nest out of rootlets, bark strips, and grass. She also handles all the incubation duty, which typically lasts about 12 days. Normal clutch size is three to four eggs; young towhees fledge in about 10 days. Both towhee parents feed the youngsters, which allows the female to start a second—and sometimes a third—brood.

Backyard & Beyond

Spring is the best time to find an eastern towhee. Male towhees are especially vocal during the breeding season and will leave deep cover to sing from a high perch within their territory. Make your feeders much more attractive to towhees by adding a brush pile nearby to help these shy birds feel more at home. In summer, recently fledged towhees can be confusing and hard to identify with their streaky, gray-brown coloring. Their white tail spots and ground-scratching habits will give them away.

Field Sparrow

Spizella pusilla

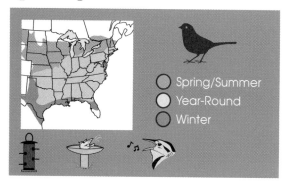

○ Spring/Summer
○ Year-Round
○ Winter

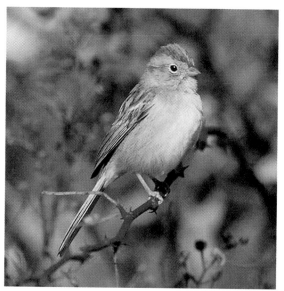

The field sparrow's clear whistled notes on a single tone is an easy bird song to learn and remember. Listen throughout the day, even in summer, for this persistent singer. Its rhythmic pattern resembles a ping-pong ball being dropped onto a table. A subtly beautiful sparrow of farm pastures and shrubby old meadows, the field sparrow is familiar to bird watchers in rural habitats.

All About
The field sparrow is a small bird (5³/4 inches long) with a biggish bill and long tail, but the first field marks most birders notice are the pink bill, plain face, and white ring surrounding the dark eye. Telling the field sparrow apart from chipping or tree sparrows is a matter of noting the field's unmarked buffy-gray breast and indistinct head stripes of brown and gray.

Habitat & Range
As its name suggests, the field sparrow is found in fields, but it prefers brushy, older fields that have the beginnings of reforestation—saplings, small shrubs, and large thick clumps of grass. Field sparrows are found all across the eastern United States, but—unlike many of our migrant songbirds—they may only migrate a few hundred miles to spend the winter. In spring and summer, males do their singing from an exposed perch within their territories.

Feeding
Throughout the year, the field sparrow's diet is grass seeds and other small plant seeds; in spring and summer the diet shifts to insects. Moths, grasshoppers, flies, and other grassland insects make up half of their summer diet, with most of the insects being found on or near the ground. In winter, as flocks of field sparrows forage together, a single bird will perch on top of a tall grass stem, letting its weight bend the stalk to the ground where the seeds can more easily be eaten.

Nesting
In early spring (April to May) field sparrow nests are built on the ground, near a grass clump or small shrub. Later nests (June to July) may be in taller shrubs or vegetation, but the construction is the same—a loosely woven outer cup of grass lined with fine, soft grasses, all built by the female. Three to six eggs are laid and incubated by the female for about 12 days. Like other ground nesters, young field sparrows develop quickly and may leave the nest within a week. Flight is attained in two weeks and independence from the parents two weeks later.

Backyard & Beyond
Within the breeding range, any older farm field should host field sparrows. Look for males perched on top of saplings or fenceposts. Field sparrows will come to cracked corn, mixed seeds, and eggshell bits scattered on the ground beneath bird feeders.

Chipping Sparrow

Spizella passerina

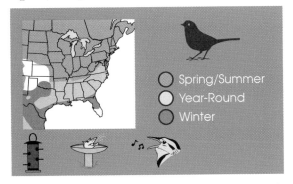

- ○ Spring/Summer
- ○ Year-Round
- ○ Winter

A *close look at this natty little bird reveals much to admire in its quiet and confiding ways. As common as it is around dooryards and gardens, we know surprisingly little about the chipping sparrow's mating systems. One Ontario study showed males not to be monogamous, as assumed, but to mate freely.*

All About

A rusty beret and bold, white eyeline are the best field marks of this slender little sparrow. Plain gray underparts, a streaked brown back, and a small, all-black bill set off its striking head markings. It is an under-appreciated bird, perhaps because it is so small and unobtrusive. Rather dry, monotonous trills, as well as its signature chipping notes, are the ambient sounds of a chipping sparrow's territory.

Habitat & Range

Before the massive expansion of suburbs, the chipping sparrow was limited to open, grassy coniferous forests and parklike woodlands with shrubby understories. Our suburban habitats have just the right mix of short grass, shrubbery, and conifers that chipping sparrows need, so we enjoy their company on doorsteps and sidewalks. Although northern populations are strongly migratory, southern birds flock up but tend to stay near their breeding grounds.

Feeding

Chipping sparrows forage primarily on or near the ground, feasting on weed and grass seeds and some smaller fruits. They feed insects to the young, however, sometimes flycatching on the wing. Winter flocks of up to 50 birds perch in trees, descending *en masse* to the ground to peck for seeds, then adjourning to treetops before the next feeding bout. At feeding stations, they'll peck on the ground or perch on hopper feeders.

Nesting

Female chipping sparrows weave lovely little nests of thin twigs and weed stems, with a center composed of animal hair. These are often concealed in low trees and shrubs, but are easily located by the shrilling of older nestlings. Females incubate the four eggs for around 12 days, and the young leave the nest about 9 to 12 days later. Streaky, brown, and nondescript, they're fed by their parents for three more weeks before forming juvenile flocks.

Backyard & Beyond

Chipping sparrows eagerly accept mixed seeds and suet dough mixtures offered on or near the ground. They're fond of rolled oats, and live mealworms will be taken straight to the young. They greatly appreciate baked and crushed eggshells strewn on a sidewalk. But it's most fun to offer them human or pet hair clippings. A trip to any salon can net a season's worth, and you may have the pleasure of finding a used nest lined with your own hair—the ultimate vanity piece for the discerning gardener.

131

White-throated Sparrow

Zonotrichia albicollis

Spring/Summer
Year-Round
Winter

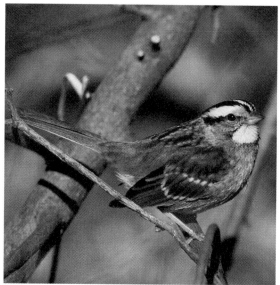

Old Sam Peabody, Peabody, Peabody *is the sweet whistled song of the white-throated sparrow. In Canada, where this species spends the breeding season, the song is transcribed as* Oh sweet Canada, Canada, Canada—*but there's no arguing that the white-throated sparrow's song is easy to recognize. From September to March these northern breeders are with us, in loose flocks with other sparrows, brightening winter days with their cheery sounds.*

All About

The first field mark most bird watchers notice on the white-throated sparrow is not the white throat, but the black-and-white striped head pattern with a yellow spot between the eyes and bill. Even at a distance this striking pattern is obvious. Some white-throated sparrows have tan-striped heads and a tannish throat. These belong to the tan-striped variety of the species, though many ornithologists formerly thought these were young birds not yet in adult plumage. This medium-sized (6³/4 inches long) sparrow has a gray breast and a brown, lightly patterned back.

Habitat & Range

Spending most of the summer in the boreal coniferous forests of the far North and New England, the white-throated sparrow spends fall and winter to the south, where it is a regular at bird feeders and in brushy edge habitat. It prefers a habitat with thick underbrush and is found near the edge of the woods, along hedgerows, and in brushy thickets in parks and backyards.

Feeding

White-throated sparrows prefer to feed on the ground. In spring and summer, the white-throated sparrow's diet is focused on insects—ants, grubs, and spiders—that it uncovers as it scratches through the leaf litter, much like a towhee does. In fall the diet shifts to include berries; in winter it includes mostly seeds from grasses. At bird feeders they are attracted to mixed seed, cracked corn, and sunflower or peanut bits offered on the ground or on a platform feeder.

Nesting

White-throated sparrows nest on or near the ground in a well-concealed spot. The cup-shaped nest is built by the female from grass, pine needles, and twigs and lined with soft material, such as rootlets or fur. The female incubates the four to five eggs for about two weeks; the male assists her in feeding the nestlings for the nine days prior to fledging. The young birds rely on the parents for food for about another two weeks.

Backyard & Beyond

Look for white-throated sparrows on the ground beneath your feeders from late fall through early spring. If your feeders are some distance from cover, consider moving them closer to the woods' edge, or add a brush pile nearby to make woodland birds (such as white-throated sparrows) feel more at home.

White-crowned Sparrow

Zonotrichia leucophrys

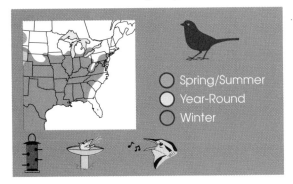

○ Spring/Summer
○ Year-Round
○ Winter

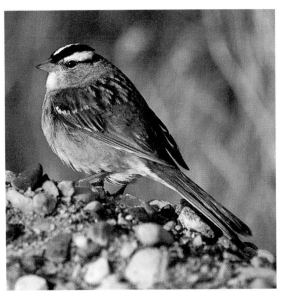

The striking black-and-white stripes on the head of the adult white-crowned sparrow are a field mark that is hard to ignore. Flocks of white-crowned sparrows are fairly common in winter across the Midwest and during spring and fall migrations as the birds travel to and from their breeding range in the far North.

All About

A large sparrow with a badger-striped head, the white-crowned sparrow has a pale gray breast, brown flanks and rump, and two white wing bars on the brown wings. Bill color varies by population from yellow to orange-pink. The white-crowned sparrow's song is a beautiful mix of clear whistled introductory notes, followed by a series of buzzy trills. It can be heard singing on sunny days during winter and prior to spring migration.

Habitat & Range

The white-crowned sparrow breeds in the boreal forest edges, brushy thickets, and scrub of the far North but is also a year-round resident in many parts of the mountainous West. It winters across the southern two-thirds of the U.S. along woodland edges, in brushy fields, hedgerows, and in suburban parks and backyards. In the non-breeding season (September through April) it can often be found in feeding flocks with other sparrow species.

Feeding

The diet of the white-crowned sparrow is composed mainly of plant seeds, which it finds as it forages on the ground. In spring, its diet includes tree buds, fruits, and some insects, especially during breeding season. White crowneds will visit feeding stations, especially if brushy thickets are nearby, preferring to scratch for seed bits on the ground below the feeders.

Nesting

White-crowned sparrows nest on or near the ground, with the females weaving the cup-shaped nest out of grasses, rootlets, twigs, and strips of bark. A grass or animal hair lining holds the four or five eggs as they are laid and helps insulate them during the nearly two-week incubation by the female. Both parents care for the young, which leave the nest within two weeks. In areas where the white-crowned is a year-round resident there may be as many as four broods per year.

Backyard & Beyond

White-crowned sparrow and the closely related white-throated sparrow are common backyard birds in fall and winter across the Midwest. Listen for their high, sweet, whistled songs and their sharp *pink!* call at dawn and dusk from thick brushy habitat. Scatter some mixed seed under your feeders and beneath your shrubs and brush pile to offer these ground feeders something to eat.

Song Sparrow

Melospiza melodia

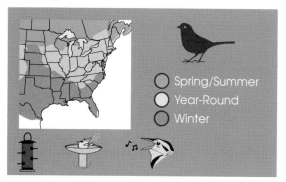

○ Spring/Summer
○ Year-Round
○ Winter

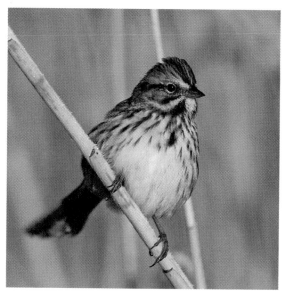

Persistent singing, often year-round, makes this a well-named species. If there's a resident song sparrow in your yard, you'll probably hear its cheery notes at first light—as reliable as, but more pleasant than, a rooster's. One of the best-studied birds in North America, the song sparrow was the subject of Margaret Morse Nice's groundbreaking behavioral study in the 1930s. Much of what we understand about songbird territoriality began with this study.

All About

The classic "little brown job," the song sparrow has a heavily streaked white breast marked with a messy central spot. A grayish, striped face and crown and warm-brown upperparts complete the description. Flight is low and jerky, with the tail twisting distinctively. Three introductory notes leading to a variable jumble of trills and chips distinguish its song. Males and females look similar.

Habitat & Range

Though song sparrows occupy a wide range of habitats, they are most often found in shrubbery near water, from small streams to beach habitats. Song sparrows tend to be migratory in northern climes and year-round residents in the southern United States; this varies by population. The song sparrow is one of the most variable songbirds known. Populations in the Pacific Northwest, for example, are larger, darker, heavier-billed, and virtually unrecognizable compared to southeastern coastal populations.

Feeding

The song sparrow's diet varies seasonally, with insects being its primary prey in spring and summer and with seeds and fruits dominating in fall and winter. Most of the song sparrow's foraging takes place on the ground, where it will scratch and kick about in leaf litter and grasses for weed seeds and insects.

Nesting

The persistent singing of song sparrows is linked to strong territorial behavior; where they are resident year-round, they tend to defend territories year-round. Territory boundaries are quite stable from year to year. Both sexes defend their territory, and they tend to stay with one mate. Females construct a bulky nest of bark strips and weed and grass stems, well hidden deep in a dense shrub. Small, ornamental evergreens are irresistible to song sparrows. The female incubates three to five eggs for about 13 days. Young leave the nest at only 10 days and may be fed by the parents for the next 20 days before they are fully independent.

Backyard & Beyond

Song sparrows readily visit feeders for sunflower seeds, cracked corn, and mixed seeds, preferring to feed on the ground. Peanut butter-based suet mixes are a favorite food, and song sparrows will appear to beg at windows for such fare. They are fond of water and will often nest near a water garden or backyard pond.

Dark-eyed Junco

Junco hyemalis

Spring/Summer
Year-Round
Winter

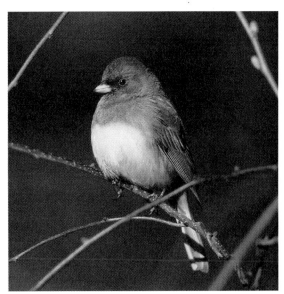

The dark-eyed junco is often called the "snowbird," because it seems to show up at our feeders and in our backyards at the same time as the first snows begin falling over much of the country. But even in the Deep South, this member of the sparrow family is a familiar winter visitor to backyards, gardens, parks, pastures, and feeding stations.

All About

Juncos are medium-sized (6¼ inches long) sparrows, but unlike most sparrows, their plumage lacks streaking. Dark-gray above and white below (or "gray skies above, snow below"), the junco has a conical, pinkish bill and flashes its white outer tail feathers in flight. Male juncos in the East are a darker gray than the brownish-overall females. Western junco forms show a variety of plumage colors, and many of these color forms were considered separate species until recently. Now they are all lumped into a single species: dark-eyed junco. Juncos make a variety of sounds, all of them high-pitched tinkling trills, especially when flushed from cover.

Habitat & Range

Few bird species' ranges cover North America more thoroughly than that of the dark-eyed junco. In winter it can be found in every state. Spring migration begins as early as March and continues through early June. During breeding season, juncos retreat to the far north woods and to coniferous and mixed woodlands at high elevations. Fall migration begins in mid-August through October. Their winter habitat preferences run to brushy edge habitat along woods, fields, and suburban backyards and parks.

Feeding

Juncos find their food on the ground. They are often seen scratching through the leaf litter, grass, or snow when foraging. In spring and summer the junco eats mostly insects, including spiders, caterpillars, ants, grasshoppers, and weevils, but it will also eat berries. In fall and winter the diet shifts to grass and weed seeds, along with birdseed gleaned from the ground beneath feeders.

Nesting

The junco's nest is a simple, open cup of grasses and leaves, loosely woven and lined with finer grasses, fur, or feathers. Nests are normally located on the ground in a concealed spot and built by the female. She incubates her three to five eggs for almost two weeks; the male helps with feeding chores once the young hatch. Within two weeks the young birds leave the nest, and the parents are free to start another brood if the season permits.

Backyard & Beyond

Where there is one junco, there is almost surely a flock. Seek them along the edges of woodlots, old pastures, and in areas with a thick growth of underbrush. Watch for the flashing white in the tail and listen for the juncos' trilling calls.

Eastern Meadowlark

Sturnella magna

Our two meadowlark species (the second being western meadowlark, Sturnella neglecta) are indistinguishable visually, but their songs are different. The eastern meadowlark's sweet whistled song—spring of THE year!—and the western meadowlark's low, descending, whistled and gurgled Swing low sweet chariot! are both signs of spring's arrival.

All About

Familiar birds of rural farm fields, meadows, and grasslands, the eastern and western meadowlarks are known by their distinctive field mark: a bright yellow breast with a "V" of black. Meadowlarks will sing from the ground and in flight, but they often use an elevated perch, such as a fencepost, tree, or power line. In flight, the meadowlark looks chunky and shows white outer tail feathers. A series of shallow, stuttering wingbeats followed by a short glide (sometimes accompanied by a song or chatter) is the typical flight pattern.

Habitat & Range

Eastern meadowlarks prefer grassy meadows, prairies, and pastures with good grass cover. Westerns seem to favor shorter, drier grasslands. Both can also be found along golf courses, in hayfields, and in the grassy margins of airports. As their names suggest, the eastern meadowlark is primarily an eastern bird and the western primarily a western bird, but their ranges overlap significantly in the Midwest. These birds can apparently tell they are different species, because they almost never interbreed.

Feeding

The meadowlark is a ground feeder that searches vegetation in spring and summer for insects, such as crickets, grasshoppers, grubs, and caterpillars. In winter, the diet shifts to seeds, grains, and some fruits. In fall and winter, both meadowlarks often form large single-species flocks, with dozens of birds foraging together in the same field.

Nesting

Meadowlarks nest on the ground in thick grass. The nest is well concealed in a depression on the ground and is woven out of dried grasses. Two to six eggs are laid and incubated for about 14 days. Youngsters fledge about 10 days later. Both parents feed the young. For nesting, meadowlarks seem to prefer grasslands that are cut only once every three to five years. Even so, many meadowlark nests are lost to agricultural activity, predation, and pesticides.

Backyard & Beyond

To find a meadowlark you must locate a suitable habitat, which usually means locating a rural spot with hayfields and pastures. During spring and summer, meadowlarks sing throughout the day, but do so most actively early in the morning. Listen for the slurring whistled song and the sputtering blackbird-like calls. Scan the wires, treetops, and fenceposts for the singing adult bird. Its handsome lemon-yellow-and-black breast should catch your eye.

Brown-headed Cowbird

Molothrus ater

The cowbird's habit of laying its eggs in the nests of other, smaller songbirds makes the brown-headed cowbird a nest parasite. Cowbirds learned this behavior over centuries of following roaming herds of buffalo. The buffalo stirred up insects, the cowbird's main food. But all the movement made it impossible to stop, build a nest, and wait for the young to grow. So the cowbirds did the most convenient thing—laid their eggs in any nest they could find along the way.

All About

The cowbird is a small (7$1/2$ inches long) blackbird. Males have a glossy black body and a dark brown head, while females are a dull gray-brown overall. The short, conical bill and pointed wings help to distinguish the brown-headed cowbird from larger blackbirds. The cowbird's song is a series of liquid gurgles followed by a high, thin whistle.

Habitat & Range

Cowbirds are found in a variety of habitats, but they prefer woodland edges, brushy fields, and old pastures, though they are equally at home in city parks and suburban backyards. Forest fragmentation has allowed the cowbird to parasitize the nests of woodland species, such as thrushes and vireos. In winter cowbirds often join flocks of other blackbirds—red-winged blackbirds, grackles, and European starlings—foraging in fields and grasslands and roosting *en masse* in large woodlots.

Feeding

The diet of the cowbird consists of weed and grass seeds, along with insects, especially grasshoppers and beetles. Nearly all food is taken from the ground.

Nesting

Male cowbirds court females with a variety of songs, bows, and sky-pointing displays. When she is ready to lay an egg, she finds a nest that often already contains the eggs of the nest's owner. This "host" nest is most frequently that of a smaller songbird—yellow warblers, song sparrows, red-eyed vireos, and chipping sparrows seem to be frequent victims—and the female cowbird may even remove one of the host's eggs before depositing her own. Hatchling cowbirds are almost always larger than their nestmates, and are able to out-compete them for food, enhancing the cowbird's chances of survival. Some bird species have evolved to recognize cowbird eggs and will build a new nest on top of the old one or will remove the cowbird egg.

Backyard & Beyond

Finding cowbirds is almost never a problem, but limiting their impact on our songbirds can be problematic. One way to discourage cowbirds is to stop offering mixed seed and cracked corn during spring when they show up at bird feeders before many migratory songbirds return. If you see a songbird feeding a fledgling that is larger than itself, the fledgling is likely a cowbird.

Red-winged Blackbird

Agelaius phoeniceus

The red-winged blackbird's name succinctly describes the male's handsome plumage; yet, the females of this ubiquitous species have baffled many a bird watcher. Their streaky brown plumage is confusingly sparrowlike. Studies have shown that one dominant male red-winged blackbird may have many adult females nesting on his territory.

All About

The *conk-a-ree* call of the male red-winged blackbird fills the air over marshes and fields all across North America. As he gives this call, announcing himself loudly to rivals and potential mates alike, he spreads his shoulders just so, showing bright red and yellow epaulets against his black wings. Redwings are medium-sized (8¾ inches long) blackbirds with an all-black body, an orange-red and yellow patch on the shoulder, and a nearly conical black bill. Females are streaky brown overall, but their longer bill helps separate them from the sparrows (which have stouter bills).

Habitat & Range

Wet meadows, cattail marshes, upland grasslands, and pastures are all breeding habitat for red-winged blackbirds. In fall and winter, they may join with other blackbird species to form huge flocks. Northern-nesting redwings migrate (starting in September and October) to the southern U.S., while southern-nesting birds are nonmigratory. Fall blackbird flocks move during the day in oblong, loose clouds of birds. These flocks forage by day in agricultural fields and are often perse-

cuted as a nuisance species for the crop damage they inflict. Spring migration begins in mid-February and continues through mid-May.

Feeding

The red-winged blackbird's diet is mostly plant matter—weed seeds, grain, sunflower seeds, and tree seeds—along with some insects, all of which are gleaned from the ground. They will also visit feeding stations for sunflower seeds, cracked corn, peanuts, and suet. Surprisingly, they are able to use a variety of feeder types.

Nesting

Nesting starts early for the red-winged blackbird, with males singing from an exposed perch on their territories as early as February in the South, later in the North. Females choose a nest site on a male's territory and build cup-shaped grass nests that are suspended from vertical supporting vegetation. Mud forms the foundation of the nest and soft grasses are the inner lining. Clutch size is three to four eggs, and the female alone incubates them for 10 to 13 days. Both parents care for the nestlings for about two weeks, until they are ready to leave the nest.

Backyard & Beyond

Red-winged blackbirds are present continent-wide for most of the year. Wet meadows, swamps, and salt marshes are common habitats for these birds, especially in spring and summer. Listen for the male's loud *conk-a-ree* song.

Common Grackle

Quiscalus quiscula

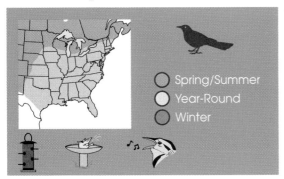

- ○ Spring/Summer
- ● Year-Round
- ○ Winter

Grackles are large, conspicuous, and noisy birds that are equally at home in a town or country setting. This species benefited greatly from the European settlement of North America as forests were turned into farm fields and new feeding and nesting opportunities emerged for the common grackle. Residential areas and farmland are particularly attractive to grackles.

All About

Nearly half of the common grackle's 12¹/₂-inch length is its tail. The grackle's black plumage is glossy and can show bright purple, bronze, or green highlights, especially on the head. Adult common grackles show a pale yellow eye, contrasting sharply with the dark head. The powerful bill is long and sharply pointed. In flight, grackles hold their long tails in a "V", much like the keel of a boat. Males and females are very similar in appearance. Grackles utter a variety of harsh, metallic tones.

Habitat & Range

Common grackles are found in almost every habitat in eastern North America; though, in winter the population is more concentrated in the eastern and southern United States. Grackles prefer edge habitat and open areas with scattered trees or shrubs. From late summer to early spring, grackles gather in large roosts with other blackbirds. These roosts can contain as many as half a million birds, and are notable both for their noise and their droppings.

Spring migrants may reach breeding territories as early as mid-February. Fall migration begins in September and peaks in October.

Feeding

During breeding season, grackles eat mostly insects, but they are opportunists and will take nestling birds or eggs, small fish, mice, and frogs. In winter the diet shifts to seeds and grain. The impact of foraging winter flocks on crops has earned the common grackle a reputation as an agricultural pest. Most of the grackle's foraging is done on the ground, where the birds toss aside leaves and rubbish to uncover their food.

Nesting

Grackles prefer to nest in dense conifers, close to rich foraging habitat. The large, open-cup nest is built by the female from grass, twigs, and mud and is lined with soft grass. She incubates the four to five eggs for about two weeks. The male joins her in feeding the nestlings an all-insect diet until fledging time arrives about 20 days later.

Backyard & Beyond

Look for long dark lines of migrating common grackles during the day, especially in fall. Migrating flocks can contain thousands of birds and may stretch from horizon to horizon. At feeders grackles relish cracked corn and sunflower seeds most of all. Grackles are also known to take hard, stale pieces of bread and dunk them in a birdbath to soften them up.

Baltimore Oriole

Icterus galbula

Spring/Summer
Year-Round
Winter

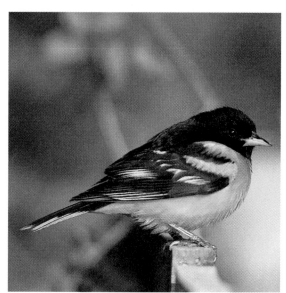

The colorful Baltimore oriole, like many long-distance migrants, leads three flamboyant lives: backyard, park, and forest nester in North America; winter nectar, fruit, and insect-eater in the tropics; and long-distance wanderer while transiting between its two homes. Named for the colonial family that settled Maryland—the family crest of which sported the bird's striking orange and black colors—the Baltimore oriole is one of only two widespread eastern orioles.

All About

At rest and in flight, the male Baltimore oriole is a fireball of citrus orange blazed with black. The bird's head, back, and much of its wings and tail are black. In flight, a bright orange shoulder and white wing bars flash, as do its orange tail corners. The female Baltimore oriole is also colorful, lacking the entirely black head of the male but having vibrant orange-yellow underparts. The Baltimore oriole's unusually rich song and two-note whistle often reveal its presence.

Habitat & Range

The Baltimore oriole breeds in open parklike woodlands, at forest edges—including along waterways—as well as in suburbs and city parks. This bird favors tall, mature deciduous trees, often in very open, widely scattered stands. During migration and on its wintering grounds, it is similarly adaptable, inhabiting forests, hedges, gardens, shade coffee and cacao plantations, and even pastures with scattered trees. Baltimore orioles nest from central Canada, across the

southeast of the country, then south through much of the eastern U.S. north of Texas and the southeastern coastal plain. Most of the population winters from Mexico south to northwestern South America and in the northern Lesser Antilles, including Cuba. Some winter in Florida. Each winter, individuals pop up along many other parts of the East Coast and even in southern California.

Feeding

During warm months, Baltimore orioles feed on a wide variety of insects, including caterpillars—at times tearing open tent caterpillar nests. Fruits are also eaten, including some cultivated varieties. In winter, Baltimore orioles eat berries, insects, and nectar, which they extract from flowers with their bristly tongues.

Nesting

A female Baltimore oriole constructs a pendulous nest, sometimes with the help of her mate. Woven of plant fibers, string, and other materials, the nest hangs near the end of a large branch, usually between 20 and 30 feet off the ground. Within the enclosed nest, the female lays four or five bluish or grayish eggs, which are marked with brown and black. She incubates the eggs about two weeks, then both parents feed the nestlings, which leave the nest about two weeks after hatching.

Backyard & Beyond

Halved oranges and sugar water in special feeders often entice Baltimore orioles to visit yards.

House Finch

Carpodacus mexicanus

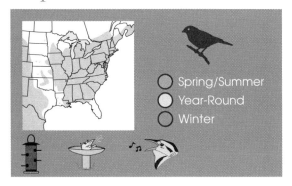

○ Spring/Summer
○ Year-Round
○ Winter

Bird watchers who rely on an eastern field guide that is more than thirty years old may be forgiven for some confusion. This bird won't be in it! The house finch, native to the West, is a well-established, but recently arrived resident of the eastern United States. Released upon the passage of protective legislation forbidding trade in native wild birds, a small population of the so-called "Hollywood linnets" began breeding on Long Island in 1940, and they have now blanketed the eastern United States with their progeny.

All About

People who feed birds are familiar with the house finches that sometimes cover feeders with fluttering, tweeting flocks. It's easy to see why they were kept as cage birds; the male's cheery, rich song, marked by a few harsh notes, tumbles brightly down the scale. Females are streaky, pale brown birds with white undersides; males have a rich pinkish-red rump, head, and upper breast. By comparison, male purple finches have an overall "dipped in wine" look, with a reddish suffusion to their back and wings, while female purple finches are much more boldly streaked with brown and white than are female house finches.

Habitat & Range

As its name suggests, the house finch prefers nesting and feeding near homes. It's a thoroughly suburban bird in the East, but in its native West, it is found in undisturbed desert habitats as well. This species appears to be developing migratory behavior in the East, with a general movement toward the South in winter.

Feeding

Most of the house finch's diet is vegetarian, and it spends a great deal of time feeding on the ground. Weed seeds, buds, and fruits are its mainstays away from feeding stations.

Nesting

House finch nests are shallow twig platforms with a finely woven inner cup composed of rootlets, grass, feathers, and string. They are tucked into dense ornamental evergreens, hanging baskets, ledges, ivy-covered walls, and other nooks where there is an overhanging structure. Two to five eggs are incubated by the female, while the male feeds her. Young are fed regurgitated seeds and fledge from 12 to 16 days later.

Backyard & Beyond

For most feeding station proprietors, the question is not how to attract house finches, but how to discourage them. Even attractive birds with pleasant songs wear out their welcome when they descend in dozens, monopolizing feeders. Black-oil sunflower seeds are a favorite, closely followed by Niger and mixed seeds. Some people resort to removing perches from tube feeders, thus discouraging house finches, which are poor clingers.

141

Purple Finch

Carpodacus purpureus

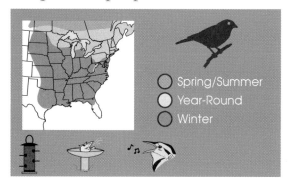

- Spring/Summer
- Year-Round
- Winter

The male purple finch is a rich raspberry-red (not purple) color and is often confused with the much more common male house finch (which is orange- or brick-red). Purple finches travel in flocks during the non-breeding seasons, and may descend on feeding stations for a few hours or weeks as they roam in search of a winter food source.

All About

"Like it was dipped headfirst in raspberry wine" is how many bird watchers describe the color of the male purple finch, and it's an apt description, because the raspberry color completely encircles the bird's upper body. On the similar male house finch, the red covers only the head, face, and breast. The house finch's back and wings are brown and streaky. Large-headed with a stout bill, the purple finch is hard to miss, often announcing its arrival with a loud *pik!* call. Their song, which is sung beginning in late winter, is a loud, rich warble delivered from a treetop perch. Females are brown-backed with dark brown and white face patterns and dark cheek patches. Their white breasts are boldly streaked with brown.

Habitat & Range

Purple finches breed in a variety of woodland habitats from cool coniferous woods to deciduous forests, orchards, and edge habitat. During migration and in winter, they can be found almost anywhere in the eastern United States from woodland edges to weedy fields and backyard feeding stations. They go wherever food is available and purple finch "invasions" in winter are often caused by shortages of natural food supplies in the North.

Feeding

Seeds, blossoms, buds, and fruits comprise the purple finch's diet, with some insects also being consumed. Favorite food trees include elms, tulip poplars, maples, sweet gums, sycamores, and ashes. Typical foraging involves a flock of purple finches ranging amid the upper branches, grabbing and eating young buds. Sunflower seed is their preferred food at feeders.

Nesting

Female purple finches do most of the nest building after the pair chooses a site in the outer branches of a large conifer tree. She weaves together bark strips, rootlets, and twigs into a cup and lines it with animal hair and fine grass. Three to seven eggs are deposited and incubated by the female for about two weeks. Both parents feed hatchlings until fledging time, about two weeks later.

Backyard & Beyond

You may have both purple finches and house finches at your feeders, which means you have a great opportunity to learn to tell them apart. Once you see the differences in plumage (on males check the distribution of the red, on females check the facial pattern) you'll find that it's not that hard after all.

Pine Siskin

Carduelis pinus

Spring/Summer
Year-Round
Winter

This slender, streaky little finch is often over-looked—mistaken for a female house finch or a winter-plumaged goldfinch. But a closer look reveals a slender-billed, finely streaked finch adorned with yellow in its wings and tail.

All About

Your first clue to a pine siskin's presence may be its loud, descending *Tzeeeew!* call as a flock drops into your backyard trees. Siskins also give a rising *Zweeeeet!* sound and sing a jumbled twitter of notes similar to a goldfinch's song. Fine brown streaks cover the pine siskin's body, but as the bird moves its yellow wing stripes and tail spots flash—a surprise bit of color on this otherwise drab bird.

Habitat & Range

Across the Midwest and eastern U.S. the pine siskin is a winter visitor. It nests in the coniferous forests of the far North and throughout the West, but makes nearly annual appearances throughout eastern North America. During spring and summer, pine siskins are never far from conifers, alders, and the mixed woodlands in which they breed and forage. In winter, siskins often move southward—sometimes in great numbers—in search of food. They forage in weedy fields, hedgerows, pine woods, and at backyard feeding stations.

Feeding

Siskins eat grass and weed seeds, especially wild thistle seeds, plus tree buds, pine seeds, berries, and some insects. Expert clingers, siskins will hang upside down on a catkin clump, pinecone, or weed stem and pry seeds loose with their finely pointed bills. Caterpillars, insect larvae, and spiders are also consumed. At feeders, siskins relish sunflower bits (they are unable to crack open the whole seeds themselves) and thistle (Niger) seed.

Nesting

Male siskins begin courting females in late winter, before reaching their breeding grounds, as the winter feeding flocks are dispersing. Siskins are known to nest in loose colonies in conifer or mixed conifer-deciduous forests. The female builds the cup-shaped nest out of weed stems, grasses, bark strips, vines, and rootlets and lines it with soft material such as animal fur, feathers, thistledown, or moss. She lays three to five eggs and incubates them for about two weeks, during which time the male may bring her food. Both parents feed the nestlings, which leave the nest about 15 days after hatching.

Backyard & Beyond

Add a thistle feeder and seed to your backyard offerings and you'll increase your chances of attracting siskins. Sunflower bits are another attractant, as is a source of open, moving water. Listen for the sharp, zippy calls of siskin flocks as they fly over. And be sure to look carefully at your flocks of drab winter goldfinches—a siskin may be accompanying them.

American Goldfinch

Carduelis tristis

Spring/Summer
Year-Round
Winter

The bright canary-yellow and black plumage of the breeding male American goldfinch has earned this species the nickname "wild canary." It is a familiar visitor to bird feeders at all seasons, especially in winter. The goldfinch's undulating flight is accompanied by a twittering call of perchickoree or potato chip!

All About

American goldfinches appear very different in summer and winter. The male's brilliant yellow body and black cap in summer give way to a drab, olive-brown plumage in winter. Female goldfinches, though never bright yellow, also lose most of their color. Both sexes retain their black wings and tail year-round. The sweet, high-pitched, warbling song of the male is often given in early spring, just as these small (5 inches long) birds are beginning to show their first bright yellow feathers.

Habitat & Range

Weedy fields, brushy woodland edges, and open habitats with scattered shrubs are the American goldfinch's normal habitats. In the breeding season, they prefer weedy fields with thistles and other seed-producing plants. In winter, goldfinches roam in noisy flocks, seeking food in fields, gardens, and at feeding stations.

Feeding

Goldfinches are seedeaters in all seasons, consuming a huge variety of weed, grass, and plant seeds as well as tree buds. In goldfinch nests par-asitized by brown-headed cowbirds, young cowbirds are unable to survive the all-seed diet fed to nestling goldfinches. Goldfinches are agile birds, able to exploit seed sources that other finches cannot, by hanging upside down from seedheads, plant stalks, and bird feeders.

Nesting

Goldfinches' nesting season begins late, a timing adaptation so that nesting occurs when there is the greatest natural abundance of seeds, as well as the soft thistle down that goldfinches use to line their nests. Late June is the earliest nesting time, but peak nesting season is late July, though some nesting occurs as late as September. The nest site is in a shaded spot in a sapling or shrub and is selected by the pair. The female builds the open-cup nest from twigs (attached with spider web), rootlets, and plant stems, and she lines it with soft thistle down or a similarly soft material. Four to six eggs are incubated by the female for about two weeks, with the male bringing food to her on the nest. Both parents tend the nestlings for 12 to 17 days before they fledge.

Backyard & Beyond

The twittering calls of goldfinches will alert you to the presence of these energetic songbirds. At bird feeders, goldfinches especially like thistle seeds (sometimes called Niger seeds), sunflower seeds and bits, and peanut bits. Goldfinches love to drink and bathe in shallow birdbaths and are especially attracted to moving water.

House Sparrow

Passer domesticus

Introduced to North America in the early 1850s from England to help control wireworms, the house sparrow population spread across the continent in just 50 years. The house sparrow enjoys a close association with humans, almost always nesting and living in proximity to our settlements. It is one of the world's most successful and widespread species.

All About

The chunky little house sparrow is known for its constant *cha-deep*, *cha-deep* calls and for the male's black bib in breeding plumage. Breeding males have a black bill and a contrasting black, gray, and brown head and face pattern. Winter males are a muted version of the breeding plumage. Females are drab gray-brown overall and lack the bib. House sparrows are constantly chirping and are aggressive competitors at feeders and nest sites.

Habitat & Range

House sparrows are year-round residents. It's easier to describe where you *won't* find house sparrows because they are utterly ubiquitous. Pristine natural habitats—forest, grassland, or desert—that are lacking human development will also lack house sparrows. Historically, the house sparrow associated with horses (and the seeds and insects in their droppings) and other livestock. Today, house sparrows are found in the most urban of habitats, living on food scraps and nesting in building crevices—though they are still a common inhabitant of horse barns, farmyards, and feedlots.

Feeding

Seeds and grains will be on the house sparrow's normal menu throughout the year. In spring and summer, they take advantage of bountiful insect populations. At any time, house sparrows are quick to take food at bird feeders or scraps of food offered directly or indirectly by humans in parks, picnic areas, fast food restaurants, and strip malls. Cracked corn, sunflower seeds, peanut bits, and bread products are favorite foods.

Nesting

Males choose a cavity and sing by it to attract the female. Both build the messy nest of grass, weed stems, feathers, paper, and string. House sparrows will appropriate nest boxes from bluebirds, swallows, and purple martins (forcing many nest box landlords to use controls and special housing to discourage house sparrows), and they may even kill nest box competitors. The female lays between three and six eggs, which are incubated by both parents for 10 or more days. The parents share feeding duties until the nestlings are ready to fledge at about two weeks.

Backyard & Beyond

House sparrows are feeding station regulars, especially in towns and cities. To discourage house sparrows from dominating nest boxes, use boxes with interiors less than 5 inches deep, remove their nesting material regularly, and place nest boxes far from buildings and thick shrubbery.

Lack of Birds

■ During spring and summer, the diet of many of our seed-eating feeder visitors shifts to a greater reliance on insects, fruits, and other natural, abundant food sources. Even during the traditional fall and winter bird-feeding seasons, birds may not immediately find a feeding station. Once the first chickadee, goldfinch, or titmouse "tunes in" to your feeders, the word will spread quickly and other birds will show up. Temporary loss of birds at a feeder can be caused by the presence of a hawk, a cat, or by stale birdseed.

Discouraging Squirrels

■ It is a battle that has been going on for nearly a century: humans trying to keep squirrels from getting to bird feeders. There are many squirrel-proof feeders available, but squirrels figure out many of these after a time. Placing your feeders on baffled poles far from any tree, deck railing, or other potential launching pad that a squirrel could use seems to be the most successful strategy. Alternatively, offer the furry menaces some cracked corn (or ears of field corn) far away from your feeders. Keep squirrels happy elsewhere, and you may keep them off your feeders.

Blackbirds, Pigeons, Jays, and Sparrows

■ Certain birds can hog all the space and food at your feeders to the exclusion of the smaller, less aggressive species. You can limit the impact of these "feeder hogs" by removing their preferred food from the menu. For blackbirds, pigeons, and doves, limit the cracked corn and mixed seed; for jays and crows, limit the suet, peanuts, cracked corn, and table scraps; for sparrows, limit the cracked corn and do not feed bread. Larger birds (such as grackles, rock pigeons, and blue jays) can also be discouraged through the use of small tube feeders with short perches—small birds can use 'em, but big birds can't.

Hawk at Feeders

■ Cooper's hawks and sharp-shinned hawks are songbird specialists that can be attracted to the bird activity at your feeders. Their tactic is a quick surprise attack, scattering the feeder visitors and perhaps catching a slow, sick, or unwary individual. As unpleasant as it may seem, it is perfectly natural and is an important aspect of nature's balance.

Cat at Feeders

■ Place your feeders a short distance away from thick cover where hunting cats might lurk. Mount your feeders high enough (above 4 feet) that a leaping cat cannot reach feeding birds. A circle of short (1-foot-high) wire fencing can make it more difficult for charging cats to catch birds.

Night Marauders

■ If your feeders empty out overnight, you probably have a mammal making nocturnal visits to your feeder. This furry critter could be a raccoon, an opossum, a flying squirrel, deer, or even a bear! Feed only as much seed as can be eaten by your birds during a single day, and you'll discourage these late-night diners.

Sick Bird at Feeders

■ Sick birds often show up at feeders, desperate for an easy meal, and they usually succumb to their illness within a short while. Although most bird illnesses are not transferable to humans, it pays to be cautious. Contact your local wildlife officials about any sick birds you see at your feeders—they often monitor wildlife health trends. If you find a dead bird, avoid making direct contact with it (wear gloves or use a plastic bag to pick it up), and bury it or discard it in the trash. Clean your feeders thoroughly and consider halting your feeding for a few days to allow the healthy birds to disperse temporarily.

Food and Feeder Chart

Species	Food
Quail, pheasants	Cracked corn, millet, wheat, milo
Pigeons, doves	Millet, cracked corn, wheat, milo, Niger (thistle seed), buckwheat, sunflower, baked goods
Hummingbirds	Plant nectar, small insects, sugar solution
Woodpeckers	Suet, meat scraps, sunflower hearts/seed, cracked corn, peanuts, fruits, sugar solution, mealworms
Jays	Peanuts, sunflower, suet, meat scraps, cracked corn, baked goods
Crows	Meat scraps, suet, cracked corn, peanuts, baked goods, leftovers, dog food
Titmice, chickadees	Peanut kernels, sunflower, suet, peanut butter, mealworms
Nuthatches	Suet, suet mixes, sunflower hearts and seed, peanut kernels, peanut butter, mealworms
Wrens, creepers	Suet, suet mixes, peanut butter, peanut kernels, bread, fruit, millet (wrens), mealworms
Mockingbirds, thrashers, catbirds	Halved apples, chopped fruit, mealworms, suet, nutmeats, millet (thrashers), soaked raisins, currants, sunflower hearts
Robins, bluebirds, other thrushes	Suet, suet mixes, mealworms, berries, baked goods, chopped fruit, soaked raisins, currants, nutmeats, sunflower hearts
Kinglets	Suet, suet mixes, baked goods, mealworms
Waxwings	Berries, chopped fruit, canned peas, currants, dry raisins
Warblers	Suet, suet mixes, fruit, baked goods, sugar solution, chopped nutmeats
Tanagers	Suet, fruit, sugar solution, mealworms, baked goods
Cardinals, grosbeaks	Sunflower, safflower, cracked corn, millet, fruit
Towhees, juncos	Millet, sunflower, cracked corn, peanuts, baked goods, nutmeats, mealworms
Sparrows, buntings	Millet, sunflower hearts, black-oil sunflower, cracked corn, baked goods
Blackbirds, starlings	Cracked corn, milo, wheat, table scraps, baked goods, suet
Orioles	Halved oranges, apples, berries, sugar solution, grape jelly, suet mixes, soaked raisins, dry mealworms, currants
Finches, siskins	Thistle (Niger), sunflower hearts, black-oil sunflower seed, millet, canary seed, fruit, peanut kernels, suet mixes

Nest Box Chart

Species	Interior Floor Size of Box (inches)	Interior Height of Box (inches)	Entrance Hole Diameter (inches)	Box Mounting Height (feet)	Habitat for Box Placement
Chickadees	4x4	9–12	$1^1/_8 - 1^1/_2$	5–15	Open woods and edges
Prothonotary Warbler	4x4	12	$1^1/_4$	5–12	Wooded areas, swamps and streams
Titmice	4x4	12	$1^1/_2$	5–12	Wooded areas and edge habitat
White-breasted Nuthatch	4x4	12	$1^1/_2$	5–12	Wooded areas and edge habitat
Carolina Wren	4x4	9–12	$1-1^1/_2$	5–10	Old fields and thickets
Eastern Bluebird	4x4	12	$1^1/_2$	5–6	Open land with scattered trees
Tree Swallow	5x5	10–12	$1^1/_2$	5–10	Open land near pond or lake
Purple Martin	6x6	6	$2^1/_8$	15–25	Open country near water
Great-crested Flycatcher	6x6	12	$1^3/_4 - 2$	6–20	Open woods and edges
House Finch	5x5	10	$1^1/_2$	5–10	Backyards and porches
Downy Woodpecker	4x4	12	$1^1/_2$	5–20	Forest openings and edges
Hairy Woodpecker	6x6	14	$1^1/_2$	8–20	Forest openings and edges
Red-bellied Woodpecker	6x6	14	2	8–20	Forest openings and edges

Nest Box Chart

Species	Interior Floor Size of Box (inches)	Interior Height of Box (inches)	Entrance Hole Diameter (inches)	Box Mounting Height (feet)	Habitat for Box Placement
Red-headed Woodpecker	6 x 6	14	2	8–20	Forest openings and edges
Northern Flicker	7 x 7	16–24	2$\frac{1}{2}$	10–20	Farmland, open country
Pileated Woodpecker	12 x 12	24	4	15–25	Mature forest
Bufflehead	7 x 7	17	3	5–15	Wooded lakeshores, swamps
Wood Duck	12 x 12	24	3 x 4 oval	5–20	Wooded swamps, bottomland
Hooded Merganser	12 x 12	24	3 x 4 oval	5–30	Wooded swamps, bottomland
Goldeneyes	12 x 12	24	3$\frac{1}{4}$ x 4$\frac{1}{4}$ oval	15–20	Wooded lakeshores, swamps
Common Merganser	12 x 12	24	5 x 6 oval	8–20	Wooded lakeshores, swamps
Saw-whet Owl	7 x 7	12	2$\frac{1}{2}$	8–20	Forest clearings and edges
Eastern Screech-owl	8 x 8	18	3	8–30	Farmland, orchards, woods
Barred Owl	14 x 14	28	8	15–30	Mature bottom-land forest
Barn Owl	12 x 36	16	6 x 7 oval	15–30	Open farmland, marshes
American Kestrel	9 x 9	16–18	3	12–30	Farmland

A Glossary of Common Bird Terms

- **Avifauna:** The community of birds found in a given region or habitat type.

- **Cavity nester:** A bird that nests inside an enclosed area such as a hollow tree, an old woodpecker hole, or a bird house.

- **Crown:** The top of a bird's head.

- **Diurnal:** Active during daylight hours.

- **Edge habitat:** A place where two or more habitats come together, such as where woodland meets an old meadow. Edge habitat typically offers a rich diversity of birds.

- **Endemic:** A breeding species that is unique to a given geographical region.

- **Extinct:** A bird that no longer exists in the wild. The Carolina parakeet is an example of an extinct species.

- **Extirpated:** A bird that once was present in a given area but no longer is. It does exist in other areas, however. For example, the red-cockaded woodpecker has been extirpated from much of its original range throughout the South, but remains in small pockets of its former range.

- **Eyeline:** Refers to a line of contrasting colored feathers over or through a bird's eye, often used as a field mark for identification.

- **Field mark:** An obvious visual clue to a bird's identification. Field guides are based on describing field marks of birds.

- **Fledgling:** A bird that has left the nest, but may still be receiving care and feeding from a parent.

- **Hotspot:** A location or habitat that is particularly good for bird watching on a regular basis.

- **Juvenile/Juvenal:** *Juvenile* (noun) refers to a bird that has not yet reached breeding age. *Juvenal* is an adjective, referring to the plumage that a juvenile bird wears.

- **Life bird:** A bird seen by a bird watcher for the first time is a life bird. Life birds are usually recorded on a birder's life list, a record of all the birds he or she has seen at least once.

- **Lores:** The area between a bird's bill and its eyes.

- **Migrant:** A bird that travels from one region to another in response to changes of season, breeding cycles, food availability, or extreme weather. Many of our warbler species that spend the spring and summer in North America *migrate* to Central or South America for the winter.

- **Mimic:** A term used to describe birds that imitate other sounds and songs. Three common bird species are mimics: the northern mockingbird, gray catbird, and brown thrasher.

- **Nape:** The back of a bird's neck, often referred to in reference to a field mark for identification.

- **Neotropical migrant:** Refers to migratory birds of the New World, primarily those that travel seasonally between North, Central, and South America.

- **Nestling:** A bird that is still being cared for in the nest.

A Glossary of Common Bird Terms

- **Peeps:** A generic term for groups of confusingly similar small sandpipers.

- **Pishing (or spishing):** A sound made by bird watchers to attract curious birds into the open. Most often made by repeating the sounds *spshhh* or *pshhh* through clenched teeth.

- **Plumage:** Collective reference to a bird's feathers, which can change both color and shape through the process of seasonal molt. During a molt, a bird loses some or most of its old worn-out feathers and grows new healthy feathers to replace them. Breeding plumage is worn by birds during the breeding season and this is often when a bird is at its most colorful. Non-breeding or winter plumage is worn during fall and winter, generally, and is often less colorful than breeding plumage.

- **Primary feathers (primaries):** The long flight feathers originating from the "hand," or end, of a bird's wing.

- **Raptor:** A term used to refer to a bird of prey, including hawks, owls, osprey, and vultures.

- **Resident:** A non-migratory species—one that is present in the same region all year.

- **Spotting scope:** A single tube optical device mounted on a tripod and used to look at distant birds. Most birding scopes are between 15x and 60x in magnification power.

- **Suet:** The large chunks of hard, white fat that form around the kidneys of beef cattle. Suet is used by bird watchers as a high-energy winter food for birds.

- **Tail spot:** Spots, usually white, on a bird's tail, often used as a field mark for identification.

- **Underparts:** A term referring to the lower half of a bird (breast, belly, undertail), often used in relation to a field mark.

- **Upperparts:** A term referring to the upper half of a bird (crown, back, top of tail), often used in relation to a field mark.

- **Vagrant:** A bird that wanders far from its normal range.

- **Wing bars:** Obvious areas of contrasting color, usually whitish, across the outer surface of a bird's wings.

General

Q. There is a bird in my backyard that not only sings throughout the day, but also *all night long!* This particular bird has many, many songs. Do you have any idea what kind of bird this is?

A. Your bird is most likely a northern mockingbird. Don't worry, male mockingbirds only perform this nocturnal singing in the spring and summer, during the time of the full moon. Try running an electric fan (to create a buffer of sound) or using your earplugs on those nights when the male mockingbird is singing. Having a mocker around is a good thing—some would even consider you lucky!

Q. A female robin recently built a nest in a tree on my patio. On May 10, she started laying her eggs—four in total. How long before they hatch, and how long after that do they still need the nest?

A. Robins incubate their eggs for 12 to 14 days. Once hatched, the nestlings remain in the nest for another 14 to 16 days before fledging. Two weeks is normally the incubation period for most songbirds. Another two weeks is an average time before the young leave the nest.

Q. Many times I have seen hawks being mobbed by American crows. Is this a common phenomenon, and why does it occur?

A. Mobbing behavior by crows is common. The crows are reacting to the potential threat that the hawk poses as a predator to the adult crows and their offspring. The mobbing often serves to harass the hawk into leaving the area. Occasionally, a mobbed hawk will turn the tables and attack and kill a crow.

Q. A woodpecker is pecking holes in my house siding. Is there anything I can do to get it to stop?

A. A woodpecker drilling on your wooden house is only doing what comes naturally—drilling into wood in search of shelter or food. Most house-wrecking woodpeckers do their damage in fall, which is when they begin making their winter roost holes. Try mounting a nest box with an appropriately sized hole over the drilled area. Fill the house with wood chips, and you may divert the bird's attention and gain a tenant.

Woodpeckers also use wood and sometimes metal parts of houses as drumming sites. They drill their bills against the surface in a rapid staccato beat. This drumming noise is a territorial announcement and a method for attracting a mate. Drumming happens most regularly in spring. There are several things you can try; one of them may work.

1. Place some sheet metal or heavy aluminum foil over the area the bird is using.

2. Hang some aluminum pie plates around the affected area. Make sure they move in the wind (to scare the bird away).

3. Place a rubber snake near the drilling area (to scare the bird away).

4. Repeatedly frighten the bird by yelling or clapping when it lands on your house.

5. If nothing else works, call your local wildlife official to see if someone can come to your house to remove the offending bird.

Q. Is seeing a robin a true sign of spring's arrival? Where do they go in winter?

A. American robins are surprisingly hardy as long as they have access to their winter food sources: fruits. They switch over in winter from their mostly insect-based summer diet. As such, robins are *facultative migrants*. This means that they will migrate only as far south as they need to or are forced to by bad weather or food shortages. During ice storms, when fruits are covered in a thick coating of ice, many robins flock together and move south. In the same way, if a robin spends the winter in your region, it's probably because there's enough food to see it through.

The idea that robins are the first true sign of spring is somewhat mythical. In much of northern North America, a few robins overwinter, but they stick to woods and thickets where they can find fruit. Most backyard bird watchers do notice the robins' return when these birds appear on lawns with the onset of warm weather, seeking their warm-weather food: earthworms, grubs, caterpillars, and other insects.

Q. Do all birds mate for life?

A. No. Some species have unusually strong pair bonds between mated birds. These species include some eagles, cranes, swans, geese, and ravens. Being mated "for life" means, really, for as long as both birds are alive. When one of the pair dies, the other will take a new mate. Most North American bird species pair up primarily to reproduce, and then go their separate ways soon after they have nested. In some species, the pair bond is brief. In the case of ruby-throated hummingbirds, the pair bond lasts only as long as courtship and copulation. The male has nothing to do with the incubation or raising of the young birds.

Q. Do all birds migrate?

A. Not all bird species migrate, but most do. Migration in North America is defined as the seasonal movement of birds, northward in spring from the wintering grounds, and southward in fall from the breeding grounds. Among the birds that are *resident*, or that do not migrate, are many grouse, ptarmigan, and quail species; many owl species; pileated, red-bellied, downy, and hairy woodpeckers along with white-breasted nuthatch, Carolina wren, northern cardinal, wrentit, ring-necked pheasant, Townsend's solitaire, common raven, gray jay, and northern mockingbird.

Bird Care

Q. Is it true that if you find a baby bird out of the nest, you should not touch it because the parent birds will detect your scent and abandon the nest?

A. No, most birds do not have a well-developed sense of smell. However, most mammalian predators (skunks, foxes, raccoons, weasels, and so forth) do have a good sense of smell and may follow your scent trail to a bird's nest. If you are going to handle a baby bird be sure to place it out of harm's way, back in the nest or in an open-topped cardboard box propped in a tree. Many bird species are equipped to survive outside the nest at a very young age. These species include many shorebirds, gamebirds, and birds such as robins and wrens.

Q. If I find a baby bird that has fallen from a nest, what should I do?

A. Try to place the nestling back in its nest if at all possible. This will be the baby bird's best chance at a normal life. If you can't find the nest or a place to put the nestling out of harm's way, you will need to get the bird to a licensed rehabilitator as soon as possible.

Baby birds are unable to *thermoregulate* (regulate their body temperature), and so must be kept in a protected area with a heat source. A soft nest made of tissues inside a small cardboard box, placed on a heating pad set on LOW temperature, is a good example of a temporary home. A moist sponge placed in the box will add a touch of desired humidity. This will warm the bird.

Try to contact a wildlife rehabilitator as soon as possible. Your state fish and wildlife officers are responsible for licensing and regulating the activities of rehabilitators and have listings for those in your region. Make sure anyone else giving you advice is familiar and current with the specialized needs of wildlife.

Q. I found an injured bird. What should I do with it?

A. A person must have special permits from the federal, state, or provincial government to handle injured or dead non-game bird species. While your first instinct may be to call your local veterinarian, many vets are unwilling to care for "wildlife cases." In many situations, the best thing to do is to let nature take its course. Birds and other creatures are part of nature's natural cycle of life and death. An injured or dead bird may be a meal for another animal. If you feel you *must* do something to help an injured bird, call your local wildlife office, department of the environment, fish and game, or extension office. Your local vet may take rehabilitation cases—or may know of a licensed rehabilitator in your area.

Window Strikes

Q. A bird is flying from window to window, butting its head against the glass while looking into the house. Can you explain this behavior?

A. Your bird is fighting its reflection in the windows, thinking that the reflection is a rival bird. The behavior will last through the breeding season. One solution is to place screens over the outside of the window. Plastic wrap stuck to the outside will also work—anything that will break up the reflection will do. You may also offer your bluebirds places to perch, such as snags and posts, far from windows. Bluebirds love a perch in the middle of a lawn or field. This has worked to distract the birds from windows.

Q. How can I keep birds from flying into my windows?

A. Silhouettes of flying hawks or falcons do work, but they perform best when applied on the outside of the glass. Hanging ornaments such as wind chimes, wind socks, and potted plants also helps. Misting the outside of the window with a very weak detergent or soda solution will eliminate the reflection, but will also impair visibility for you. Awnings, eave extensions, and window screens will eliminate reflection and stop the collision problem. Plastic cling wrap applied to the outside of the window can also be effective. One of the most effective solutions we have found is FeatherGuard, a series of bright-colored feathers strung on fishing line and hung over the outside surface of the glass.

Bird Feeding

Q. What is the best seed to offer birds?

A. Black-oil sunflower seed is the most universally eaten seed at bird feeders. But there are many other seeds and foods to offer birds. What is most popular with your birds depends on where you live and what birds are present.

Q. What is the best feeder for bird feeding?

A. There is no single best feeder for bird feeding. A well-rounded feeding operation will include a platform feeder, a tube feeder, a hopper feeder, a suet feeder, and a peanut feeder. And don't forget the birdbath!

Q. I recently purchased a bird feeder, but have yet to see any birds. What am I doing wrong?

A. You're not doing anything wrong. It takes time for birds to locate a new feeding source. A spell of bad weather always drives birds to concentrate at feeders. Try putting your feeder in a new location far from your house and the portion of your yard where you are active. Put the feeder in or near a tree that the birds regularly use.

Q. Do birds that eat at feeders lose their ability to find food naturally? If I stop feeding them, will they starve?

A. No. Birds are not totally reliant on the food offered at your feeding station. Birds are programmed by instinct to forage for food, and they have evolved over millions of years to be very mobile in their food-finding habits. Because they can fly, birds are efficient at going to where the food is. Though feeding stations have been linked to slightly improved survival rates for birds in harsh weather conditions, overall bird feeding does not drastically affect the birds' survival. Also, when warmer weather comes, many of the seed-eating birds that frequented your feeders during winter switch to an insect-based diet in spring.

Q. How do I keep squirrels away from my bird feeders?

A. Baffling your feeders (preventing squirrels from gaining access to the feeders) is the best way. Feeders can be strung from a thin wire, far from any object from which the squirrels can leap. String the wire with empty 35mm film canisters (with the lids on) or short lengths of 1-inch PVC pipe, which will spin and dump the squirrels off. There are many squirrel-proof feeders on the market. These may give the squirrels a small electric shock, may prevent them from reaching the seed, or may rotate or bounce to dump the squirrels off. But be forewarned: Squirrels have been known to outsmart the most ingenious of the squirrel-proof inventions.

And if you can't beat 'em, join 'em! Feed squirrels ears of dried corn, but place the corn away from your bird feeders. Given the choice, squirrels will always go for the easiest food, and they *love* corn.

Q. What can I do to protect the birds in my yard from cats?

A. Hang feeders at least 5 feet above the ground. For ground-feeding birds, arrange ornamental border fencing in two or three concentric circles about 16 inches to 2 feet apart, to disrupt a cat's ability to leap at feeders or to spring on birds. Harass offending cats with a spray of water to train them to avoid your yard. If all else fails, use a live trap to catch the cats and take them to the local animal shelter. If the cats belong to your neighbors, ask them to restrain their pets from accessing your yard.

Hummingbirds

Q. What is the best ratio of water to sugar to use for feeding hummingbirds?

A. Four parts water to one part sugar (a 4:1 ratio) has been shown to be the closest to the sucrose content of natural flower nectar. Concentrations stronger than this (such as a 3:1 ratio or stronger) are readily consumed by hummers, but no scientific evidence exists regarding the potential helpful or harmful effects on hummingbirds.

Q. Can I use molasses or honey instead of sugar to make my hummingbird nectar?

A. No. White table sugar is the only human-made sweetener that, when mixed with the right amount of water, closely resembles natural flower nectar. Resist the urge to use other sweeteners, which spoil quickly and may not be good for hummingbirds to consume.

Q. Is the red dye found in premixed solutions bad for hummingbirds?

A. Though no conclusive scientific evidence exists showing harmful effects of red food dye on hummingbirds, this chemical additive is certainly not a necessary ingredient in hummingbird solution.

Many commercially available brands of hummingbird solution contain red food coloring that is meant to be attractive both to hummingbirds and to shopping bird watchers. Brightly colored flowers are nature's way of attracting the eye of a foraging hummingbird, so the red solution in feeders is aimed at attracting hummingbirds. Bright red feeder parts (which most hummer feeders have) or a bright red ribbon hung near the feeder can be just as attractive as red-dyed solution. Red dye or food coloring may or may not be harmful to hummingbirds, but it is completely unnecessary.

Q. How do I foil a "bully" hummer?

A. Many hummingbird species defend feeding territories, and assemblages at feeders usually develop hierarchies. The behavior exemplifies natural selection at work, and you should do nothing except enjoy it.

If you're worried about hungry hummers, put up several more feeders near your original one. The bully will be overwhelmed by the sheer numbers of other birds and will quit being so territorial.

Q. Do hummingbirds migrate on the backs of Canada geese?

A. No. This is either a Native American myth or just an old wives' tale. Hummingbirds are excellent, strong-flying migrants. A healthy ruby-throated hummingbird can easily handle the 500-mile flight across the Gulf of Mexico.

Q. Is it true that hummingbirds at my feeder will not migrate if I leave my feeder up in the fall?

A. No. This is another in a long line of bird myths. Birds are genetically programmed to migrate when their internal "clocks" tell them to do so. They will depart when the time is right—whether your feeders are up or not. However, leaving your feeders up in fall, and getting them up early in spring may help early or late migrants that are passing through your area.

How to Build a Simple Birdhouse

These plans are designed to help you build a simple birdhouse—one that is easy to put together and will attract a number of species. The 1½-inch entrance hole will allow birds as large as bluebirds to enter the house, but even tiny house wrens and chickadees will find this house appealing.

Before you begin the building process, read through this entire plan. This will make the building go more smoothly and should prevent costly, frustrating errors. Study the instructions and drawings together. The letters in the instructions refer to the drawing that illustrates a particular section of directions.

Now, let's look at materials. Cedar will last, but it can be expensive. Pound for pound, cedar is the most durable, weather resistant, and provides the best insulation—so if your budget permits it, cedar is the best wood to use for birdhouses. After years of weather, nails in cedar can become loose, so I suggest using screws in place of nails for cedar construction. Pine is easy to nail and does not split easily, but it will decay unless preservatives are used (on the outside of the box only).

An excellent alternative material is ⅝-inch thick exterior plywood. It is tough, weathers well, and will not split along the edge if you use nails of the proper size, usually four-penny galvanized box nails. Called T 1-11, this wood has vertical grooves to resemble boards and is often used for exterior siding on homes. Most lumber yards and home centers sell T 1-11 in large 4-x-8-foot sheets. When assembling a birdhouse using exterior plywood, always remember to keep the weather surface of the wood on the outside of the birdhouse. It is an obvious point, but one that is easily forgotten in the midst of the building process.

Unless otherwise instructed, use four-penny galvanized box nails for nailing house parts

together. Remember to use screws when using cedar or pine or when you feel extra strong binding is necessary.

It's impossible to predict which bird species is most apt to settle in your new birdhouse. Half a dozen cavity-nesting birds prefer a box with a single slant roof and a 1½-inch-diameter entrance. Depending on your location, it could be tree swallows, hairy or downy woodpeckers, or perhaps titmice, chickadees, Carolina or house wrens, or even bluebirds.

Good luck with your building—and with being a landlord to the birds!

Materials:

western red cedar, exterior plywood, or T 1-11 siding scraps (⅝ inch thick, 31 × 14 inches), which will be cut into the following pieces:

bottom: 5 × 5 inches
sides (cut 2): each 10 × 9 × 5 inches
back: 12 × 6¼ inches
front: 9½ × 6¼ inches
roof: 8¼ × 8¼ inches
four-penny galvanized box nails
right-angle screw hook, about 1½ inches long
caulking compound
sixteen-penny galvanized framing nails
2 galvanized siding nails (or wood screws), 1¾ inches long

Tools:

square	2 C clamps (optional)
ruler	rasp
pencil	hammer
saw	wood blocks of
plane	various sizes
drill or brace,	drill, with assorted
with 1½-inch	small bits
expansion bit	
and ½-inch	
diameter bit	

Instructions:

A

1. On the weather surface of the plywood, measure and mark with a pencil the exact outlines of each piece. Be sure the grain of the wood runs vertically on the two side pieces, the back, and the front. The T 1-11 siding has a vertical groove running down it. This won't hurt anything—but when laying out the parts, keep the groove away from the edge of each piece to avoid problems with nailing later on.

2. Lay out the two side pieces with a common line along the 9-inch dimension so that the tops angle toward the center line, making a shallow V. In this way, when you assemble the house, the weather surface will end up on the outside.

3. After checking the measurements once more, carefully saw or cut out all the parts. Trim the rough edges with a plane to knock off splinters. You won't need to sand anything—this is going to be rustic!

4. Lay the parts on the workbench and mark them, just to keep track. There are six parts—two sides, a roof, a bottom, a front, and a back.

5. To accommodate the roof slant, you will need to bevel the top edges of the front and back panels with a plane. Set the two pieces in front of you, just as they will be when assembled. On the weather surface of the front panel and on the inside surface of the back, draw a horizontal line 1/8 inch down from the top. Then bevel off 1/8 inch from each piece individually.

6. On the front panel, center a vertical line running 3 inches down from the top. Put a cross

A Simple Birdhouse

Note: Dimensions are in inches

mark on the line, 1³/4 inches from the top. Open the expansion bit to precisely 1¹/2 inches, then test it on a scrap board and measure the hole. Now, to ensure a clean cut, clamp the panel tightly to a board. Center the bit on the cross mark and drill the hole. (If you have no C clamps, lay the panel on a board and drill halfway. Turn it over and drill through the other side.) Round off the sharp edges with a rasp.

7. On the bottom piece, measure ³/8 inch in on each side of each corner and mark. Place a ruler diagonally across each corner and connect the two marks. Saw off the four corners at these points. The resultant openings in the finished house will allow adequate drainage and air circulation for the birds.

8. On the back panel, with the weather side up, center a vertical line—2 inches long—down from the top. At the bottom of the line, drill a $1/2$-inch hole.

9. Mark a line across the weather surface of both side panels, 1 inch up from the bottom. On the right panel, extend the bottom line across the edges. Mark a line across the face of the front panel, 1 inch up from the bottom. It, too, should extend across the edges.

10. Now, mark a line across the weather surface on the back panel, $2^1/2$ inches up from the bottom, and extend it across the edges.

B

1. You are now ready to start putting things together. Lay the right-hand side panel (the one on the right when the entrance of the completed birdhouse faces you), weather surface up, on the bench. Start two nails, each $1^1/2$ inches in from the edge and $1/4$ inch below the bottom line. Drive them in until they barely peek through the other side. Be sure they are straight.

2. Place the bottom panel (weather side toward you) on edge and at a right angle to the bench, against a flat wall or solid surface. (When the corners are cut off, it is easier to get the side and bottom flush when both are pressed against a flat wall.) Lay the right side panel (weather side out) across the upper edge of the bottom piece, matching the line on the side panel with the interior surface of the bottom. (Place a block under the other end of the right panel.) Drive the nails in part way—just enough to hold.

C

1. Turn the assembled pieces over so the right side faces you. Place two nails in the weather surface of the back panel, $1/4$ inch below the line you marked earlier and $1^1/2$ inches from the ends of the bottom panel. Drive them in until they begin to show on the other side.

2. Put the back piece on the two pieces that you assembled. Make sure that the lines marked on the bottom match, and that the edges are flush with the outside of the side panel.

B.

C.

159

D.

2. Put the front in place, matching the lines marked at the bottom with the interior surface of the bottom panel. There should be about a $1/2$-inch gap at the top of the right side when the roof is on.

3. Drive the nail into the bottom, nearest the enclosed side, until the nail holds. Then start a nail 2 inches down from the top of the front panel and $1/4$ inch in from the edge. Make sure that the front panel edge and the side are flush. Drive the nail in part way. Spring the bottom corner into alignment, and drive the nail near the open edge part way into the bottom. Start another, 2 inches up from the bottom, and drive it in part way. If everything looks good, pound in all the nails.

3. Drive the nail into the bottom, nearest the side panel, enough to hold. Start another nail along the edge of the back panel, 2 inches down from the top and about $1/4$ inch from the edge. Check to see that the back panel edge and the side are flush. Drive the nail in part way.

4. Now check the bottom. Its outer corner may be sprung slightly. Press it into alignment with the back panel marks, hold, and drive the other bottom nail in part way. Check it over to see if the bottom is lined up. If so, place one more nail along the edge, 4 inches up from the bottom of the back panel, and drive in all the nails.

E.

D

1. Turn the unit on its back. Lay out the front panel, weather side up—racing stripe dazzling your eyes—and start two nails $1/4$ inch below the bottom line and $1 1/2$ inches in from each edge. Be sure the points have just come through the other side.

E

1. Fit the left-hand side panel into position. If it is tight, plane down the edge for a looser fit. You want this "door" to open easily even when the wood swells in wet weather, so you can inspect the nest and clean out the house at the season's end.

2. Check for about a 1/2-inch gap at the top. Drive two nails—one into the bottom and one into the front, halfway up—part way in to hold temporarily. (They will be removed later.)

3. On the left edge of the front panel, make a mark 1 inch from the top. Using a square, draw a horizontal line across the left side panel on the mark. At one end of this line, drive a nail through the front panel into the edge of the left panel. At the other end of the line, drive a nail through the back panel into the edge of the left panel. These nail hinges will allow the "door" to be opened.

4. Put a mark on the front panel 2 inches up from the bottom and centered over the edge of the door. Drill a small hole, about 2 inches deep, at the mark. Use a right-angle screw hook twisted into place as a lock nail. It is not likely to fall out of the hole, as a nail might, when the box is tipped forward. Remove the temporary nails and test the door.

F

1. On the roof, start two nails, each 1/4 inch in from the back or top edge of the roof, and about 2 inches in from the left and right sides. Remember that the roof slants, and you want the nail angled so it goes straight into the edge of the back panel. Stand the box upright with a block under the front. Run a strip of caulking compound along the top edge of the back panel. Place the top on, with the wood grain running down the slant, not across it.

2. Adjust the roof for equal overhang on each side. It should be flush with the back. Drive the nail in part way.

3. Sight along the front and drive two more nails—gingerly—into the top edge of the front panel until they hold. If it looks right, hammer them in.

G

1. Now for hanging the birdhouse. If there are predators in your area, resist the temptation to hang your house on a tree or fencepost. If your area is predator-free (and not many areas are in North America), trees or fenceposts may be acceptable. To be safe, I suggest baffling all of your bird houses.

F.

Hanger hole — Roof — Wall — Nail hinge — Back — Left side (door) — Lock — Block — Workbench

G.

Hooked on nail at back — 2 nails

Bird-Friendly Plants for Your Yard

TREES

Common Name	Latin Name	Good For/Other Notes
Apples	*Malus* spp.	Fruit, insects, cavities
Ashes	*Fraxinus* spp.	Seeds, insects, cover
Aspens	*Populus* spp.	Seeds, insects, cover, cavities
Birches	*Betula* spp.	Seeds, insects, cover
Cedars	*Juniperus* spp.	Fruit, year-round cover
Cherries	*Prunus* spp.	Fruit
Chokecherry, common	*Prunus virginiana*	Fruit
Cottonwoods	*Populus* spp.	Cavities, shelter
Crabapples	*Malus* spp.	Fruit, insects
Dogwoods	*Cornus* spp.	Fruit
Firs	*Abies* spp.	Year-round cover
Hackberries	*Celtis* spp.	Fruit, cover
Hawthorns	*Crataegus* spp.	Fruit, cover, nesting
Hemlocks	*Tsuga* spp.	Seeds, insects, shelter
Hollies	*Ilex* spp.	Fruit, year-round cover
Junipers	*Juniperus* spp.	Year-round cover
Larches	*Larix* spp.	Seeds
Madrones	*Arbutus* spp.	Fruit
Maples	*Acer* spp.	Seeds, cover
Mesquites	*Prosopis* spp.	Shelter
Mountain ashes	*Sorbus* spp.	Fruit
Mulberry, red	*Morus rubra*	Fruit
Oaks	*Quercus* spp.	Acorns, cover, insects
Pines	*Pinus* spp.	Year-round cover, insects
Poplars	*Populus* spp.	Cavities, shelter
Sassafras	*Sassafras albidum*	Fruit, cover, cavities
Shadbush, or serviceberry	*Amelanchier laevis*	Fruit, flowers
Spruces	*Picea* spp.	Year-round cover
Sycamores	*Platanus* spp.	Cavities, shelter, insects
Willows	*Salix* spp.	Cavities, shelter, insects

Bird-Friendly Plants for Your Yard

SHRUBS

Common Name	Latin Name	Good For/Other Notes
Arrowwood viburnum/ Viburnums	Viburnum dentatum/ Viburnum spp.	Fall fruit. Tolerates shade
Bayberry, northern	Myrica pensylvanica	Fruit. Male & female plants needed for fruit
Blackberry, American	Rubus allegheniensis	Fruit, dense cover, nesting
Blueberry, highbush	Vaccinium corymbosum	Fruit, flowers, cover. Needs acid soil
Chokeberry, red	Aronia arbutifolia	Fruit. Moist soil preferred
Cranberry, highbush	Viburnum trilobum	Fruit. Shade tolerant
Dogwoods	Cornus spp.	Fall fruit, dense cover
Elderberry, American	Sambucus canadensis	Fruit, dense cover
Hercules' club	Aralia spinosa	Fruit
Hobblebush	Viburnum alnifolium	Fruit. Shade tolerant
Hollies, deciduous	Ilex decidua, Ilex spp.	Winter fruit. Male & female plants needed for fruit
Huckleberry, black	Gaylussacia baccata	Fruit. Sandy soil preferred
Inkberry	Ilex glabra	Fruit. Thicket-forming. Needs acid soil
Mahonia	Mahonia aquifolium	Fruit, year-round cover
Manzanitas	Arctostaphylos spp.	Early fruit, thick cover
Nannyberry	Viburnum lentago	Fruit. Shade-tolerant
Pokeweed	Phytolacca americana	Fall fruit.
Roses	Rosa spp.	Winter fruit. Summer flowers
Shadbushes	Amelanchier spp.	Early fruit
Spicebush	Lindera benzoin	Fruit. Needs moist soil
Sumacs	Rhus spp.	Fruit available all winter
Winterberry, common	Ilex verticillata	Fruit. Male & female plants needed for fruit
Yews	Taxus spp.	Year-round cover. Some fruit

VINES

Common Name	Latin Name	Good For/Other Notes
Ampelopsis, heartleaf	Ampelopsis cordata	Fruit. Resembles a grape vine
Bittersweet, American	Celastrus scandens	Fruit. Avoid Asian species.
Grapes, wild	Vitis spp.	Fruit attracts 100 species, cover

Bird-Friendly Plants for Your Yard

VINES

Common Name	Latin Name	Good For/Other Notes
Greenbriars	*Smilax* spp.	Fruit, thick cover
Trumpet honeysuckle	*Lonicera sempervirens*	Nectar, fruit, cover. Avoid Asian species
Trumpet vine	*Campsis radicans*	Nectar, summer cover
Virginia creeper	*Parthenocissus quinquefolia*	Fruit attracts 40 species

FLOWERS

Common Name	Latin Name	Good For/Other Notes
Asters	*Aster* spp.	Flowers attract butterlies, seed
Bachelor's button	*Centaurea cyanus*	Seed
Black-eyed Susan	*Rudbeckia serotina*	Seed
Blazing star	*Liatris* spp.	Seed, flowers attract butterflies
California poppy	*Eschscholzia californica*	Seed
Coneflower, purple	*Echinacea purpurea*	Seed, flowers attract butterflies
Coreopsis	*Coreopsis* spp.	Seed, flowers attract butterflies
Cornflower	*Centaurea cyanus*	Seed
Cosmos	*Cosmos* spp.	Seed
Daisy, gloriosa	*Rudbeckia* cv.	Seed
Goldenrods	*Solidago* spp.	Flowers for butterflies, winter cover
Joe-Pye weeds	*Eupaorium* spp.	Flowers for butterflies, winter cover
Marigolds	*Tagetes* spp.	Seed
Penstemons	*Penstemon* spp.	Nectar, seed
Poppies	*Papaver* spp.	Flowers attract butterflies, seed
Primroses	*Oenothera* spp.	Seed
Sedums	*Sedum* spp.	Flowers attract butterflies, seed
Sunflowers	*Helianthus* spp.	Seed
Thistles, globe	*Echinops* spp.	Flowers, seed, nesting material
Zinnias	*Zinnnia elegans*	Seed, flowers attract butterflies

Bibliography

American Bird Conservancy. 2003. *Guide to the 500 Most Important Bird Areas in the United States.* New York: Random House.

American Ornithologists' Union. 1998. *Check-List of North American Birds.* 7th edition. Washington, DC: American Ornithologists' Union.

Choate, E. A. 1985. *The Dictionary of American Bird Names, Revised Edition.* Boston: Harvard Common Press.

Ehrlich, P. R.; Dobkin, D. S.; and Wheye, D. 1988. *The Birder's Handbook.* New York: Fireside Books.

Kaufman, K. 1996. *Lives of North American Birds.* Boston: Houghton Mifflin Co.

Kaufman, K. 2000. *Birds of North America, A Kaufman Focus Guide.* Boston: Houghton Mifflin Co.

National Geographic Society. 1999. *Field Guide to the Birds of North America.* 3rd edition. Washington, D.C.: National Geographic Society.

Peterson, R. T. 1996. *A Field Guide to the Birds* (Eastern). Boston: Houghton Mifflin Co.

Poole, A., and Gill, F., eds. 1992–2002. *The Birds of North America.* Philadelphia, PA: American Ornithologists' Union/Birds of North American, Inc.,

Sibley, D. A. 2000. *The Sibley Guide to the Birds.* New York: Alfred A. Knopf, Inc.

Stokes, D., and Stokes, L. 1996. *Stokes Field Guide to Birds: Eastern Region.* Boston: Little, Brown and Co.

Terres, J. K. 1995. *The Audubon Encyclopedia of North American Birds.* New York: Wings Books.

Thompson III, B. 1995. *An Identification Guide to Common Backyard Birds.* Marietta, OH: Bird Watcher's Digest Press.

Thompson III, B. 1997. *Bird Watching For Dummies.* New York: John Wiley & Sons.

Thompson III, B. 2003. *The Backyard Bird Watcher's Answer Guide.* Marietta, OH: Bird Watcher's Digest Press.

Zickefoose, J. 1995. *Enjoying Bird Feeding More.* Marietta, OH: Bird Watcher's Digest Press.

Zickefoose, J. 2001. *Natural Gardening for Birds.* Emmaus, PA: Rodale Organic Living Books.

National Organizations for Bird Watchers

National Organizations

American Bird Conservancy
P.O. Box 249
The Plains, VA 20198
(540) 253-5780
www.abcbirds.org

American Birding Association
P.O. Box 6599
Colorado Springs, CO 80934-6599
800-850-2473
www.americanbirding.org

Cornell Laboratory of Ornithology
Attn: Communications
159 Sapsucker Woods Road
Ithaca, NY 14850
800-843-2473
www.birds.cornell.edu

National Audubon Society
700 Broadway
New York, NY 10003
(212) 979-3000
www.audubon.org

National Wildlife Federation
11100 Wildlife Center Drive
Reston, VA 20190-5362
800-822-9919
www.nwf.org

The Nature Conservancy
4245 North Fairfax Drive, Suite 100
Arlington, VA 22203-1606
800-628-6860
www.tnc.org

Field Guides to Birds

Griggs, J. L. 1997. *All the Birds of North America.* New York: Harper Collins.

Kaufman, K. 2001. *Birds of North America* (Kaufman Focus Guides). Boston: Houghton Mifflin Co.

National Geographic Society. 1999. *National Geographic Field Guide to the Birds of North America, 3rd edition.* Washington, D.C.: National Geographic Society.

Peterson, R. T. 2002. *A Field Guide to the Birds of Eastern and Central North America (Peterson Series).* 5th ed. Boston: Houghton Mifflin Co.

Robbins, C. S., et al. 1983. *Birds of North America: A Guide to Field Identification (Golden Field Guide Series).* Revised edition. New York: Golden Press.

Sibley, D. A. 2000. *The Sibley Guide to the Birds. New York:* Alfred A. Knopf, Inc.

Stokes, D., and Stokes, L. 1996. *Field Guide to the Birds of North America.* Boston: Little, Brown and Co.

Audio Guides to Birds

Elliott, L. 2004. *Know Your Bird Sounds, volumes 1 and 2.* Mechanicsburg, PA: Stackpole Books.

Elliott, L.; Stokes, D.; and Stokes, L. 1997. *Stokes Field Guide to Bird Songs: Eastern Region (Stokes Field Guide to Bird Songs).* New York: Time Warner Audio Books.

Peterson, R. T. 2002. *A Field Guide to Bird Songs of Eastern and Central North America. Revised edition.* Boston: Houghton Mifflin Co.

Walton, R. K., and Lawson, R. W. 1989. *Birding By Ear, Eastern and Central North America (Peterson Field Guide Series).* Boston: Houghton Mifflin Co.

Walton, R. K., and Lawson, R. W. 1994. *More Birding By Ear (Peterson Field Guide Series).* Boston, MA: Houghton Mifflin Co.

Periodicals for Bird Watchers

The Backyard Bird Newsletter
P. O. Box 110
Marietta, OH 45750
800-879-2473
www.birdwatchersdigest.com

Bird Watcher's Digest
P. O. Box 110
Marietta, OH 45750
800-879-2473
www.birdwatchersdigest.com

Living Bird
Cornell Laboratory of Ornithology
159 Sapsucker Woods Road
Ithaca, NY 14850
800-843-2473
www.birds.cornell.edu

Photography Credits

Arthur Morris/Birds as Art: Pages 35, 46, 47, 48, 49, 50, 51, 52, 53, 54, 55, 56, 59, 61, 63, 64, 65, 66, 67, 68, 69, 70, 73, 74, 75, 76, 77, 79, 82, 85, 87, 88, 89, 91, 93, 95, 96, 98, 99, 101, 102, 103, 104, 106, 107, 109, 111, 112, 113, 114, 115, 116, 117, 119, 122, 125, 127, 129, 131, 132, 133, 134, 135, 136, 137, 138, 139, 140, 141, 144, 145

Bird Watcher's Digest: Pages 34, 37, 38 (both photos), 39 (both photos), 40, 41

Tom Vezo: Pages 60, 72, 80, 81, 92, 108, 118, 130

Maslowski Photography: Pages 78, 84, 86, 142, 143

Robert McCaw: Pages 71, 90, 100, 105, 123

Cliff Beittel: Pages 57, 62, 124

Brian Henry: Pages 94, 110, 121

Barth Schorre: Pages 120, 126

Julie Zickefoose: Pages 43, 176

Ron Austing: Page 83

Bill Bevington: Page 128

Randall Ennis: Page 33

Charles Melton: Page 42

Gary Meszaros: Pages 58

Marie Read: Page 97

Index

Sighting Notes

Date	Species/Description	Location

Sighting Notes

Date	Species/Description	Location